Workshop on Coreference Resolution Beyond OntoNotes 2016 (CORBON 2016)

Held at the 2016 Conference of the North American Chapter of the Association for Computational Linguistics: Human Language Technologies (NAACL HLT 2016)

San Diego, California, USA
16 June 2016

ISBN: 978-1-5108-2523-9

CORBON 2016

Coreference Resolution beyond OntoNotes

Proceedings of the Workshop

NAACL-HLT 2016 Workshop
June 16, 2016
San Diego, California, USA

Introduction

Many NLP researchers, especially those not working in the area of discourse processing, tend to equate coreference resolution with the sort of coreference that people did in MUC, ACE, and OntoNotes, having the impression that coreference is a well-worn task owing in part to the large number of papers reporting results on the MUC/ACE/OntoNotes corpora. This is an unfortunate misconception: the previous SemEval 2010 and CoNLL 2012 shared tasks on coreference resolution have largely focused on entity coreference, which constitutes only one of the many kinds of coreference relations that were discussed in theoretical and computational linguistics in the past few decades. In fact, by focusing on entity coreference resolution, NLP researchers have only scratched the surface of the wealth of interesting problems in coreference resolution.

The decision to focus on entity coreference resolution was initially made by information extraction (IE) researchers when coreference was selected as one of the tasks in the MUC-6 coreference in 1995. Many interesting kinds of coreference relations, such as bridging and reference to abstract entities, were left out not because they were not important, but because "it was felt that the menu was simply too ambitious". It turned out that this decision had an important consequence: the progress made in coreference research in the past two decades was largely driven by the availability of coreference-annotated corpora such as MUC, ACE, and OntoNotes, where entity coreference was the focus.

Given the plethora of work on entity coreference and aware of other fora gathering coreference-related papers (such as LAW, DiscoMT or EVENTS), we believed that time was ripe for a new workshop on the single topic of coreference resolution that would bring together researchers who were interested in under-investigated coreference phenomena, willing to contribute both theoretical and applied computational work on coreference resolution, especially for languages other than English, less-researched forms of coreference and new applications of coreference resolution.

Our call attracted 20 submissions out of which we have selected 4 long and 2 short papers for oral presentation and 7 papers for poster presentation based on reviewers' recommendations.

We would like to thank the Program Committee members who reviewed the submissions and the workshop participants for joining in!

— Maciej Ogrodniczuk and Vincent Ng

Organizing Committee and Proceedings Editors:

Maciej Ogrodniczuk, Institute of Computer Science, Polish Academy of Sciences
Vincent Ng, University of Texas at Dallas

Program Committee:

Anders Björkelund, University of Stuttgart
Antonio Branco, University of Lisbon
Dan Cristea, A. I. Cuza University of Iaşi
Sobha Lalitha Devi, AU-KBC Research Center, Anna University of Chennai
Lars Hellan, Norwegian University of Science and Technology
Veronique Hoste, Ghent University
Yufang Hou, Heidelberg University
Sandra Kübler, Indiana University
Sebastian Martschat, Heidelberg University
Ruslan Mitkov, University of Wolverhampton
Costanza Navaretta, University of Copenhagen
Anna Nedoluzhko, Charles University in Prague
Vincent Ng, University of Texas at Dallas
Michal Novak, Charles University in Prague
Maciej Ogrodniczuk, Institute of Computer Science, Polish Academy of Sciences
Constantin Orasan, University of Wolverhampton
Simone Paolo Ponzetto, University of Mannheim
Massimo Poesio, University of Essex
Sameer Pradhan, Boulder Language Technologies
Marta Recasens, Google Inc.
Agata Savary, François Rabelais University Tours
Olga Uryupina, University of Trento
Yannick Versley, Heidelberg University
Desislava Zhekova, Ludwig Maximilian University of Munich
Heike Zinsmeister, Universität Hamburg

Invited Speakers:

Andrew Kehler, University of California, San Diego
Michael Strube, Heidelberg Institute for Theoretical Studies GmbH

Table of Contents

Workshop Program: June 16, 2016

Session 1

09:00–09:10   *Introduction*

09:10–10:10   *Invited talk*

The (Non)Utility of Semantics for Coreference Resolution (CORBON Remix)
Michael Strube

10:10–10:30   *Sense Anaphoric Pronouns: Am I One?*
Marta Recasens, Zhichao Hu and Olivia Rhinehart

Coffee break

Session 2

11:00–11:30   *Experiments on Bridging Across Languages and Genres*
Yulia Grishina

11:30–12:00   *Bridging Relations in Polish: Adaptation of Existing Typologies*
Maciej Ogrodniczuk and Magdalena Zawisławska

12:00–12:30   *Beyond Identity Coreference: Contrasting Indicators of Textual Coherence in English and German*
Kerstin Kunz, Ekaterina Lapshinova-Koltunski and José Manuel Martínez

Lunch break

Session 3

14:00–15:00   *Invited talk*

A Bayesian Model of Pronoun Production and Interpretation
Andrew Kehler

15:00–15:30   *Exploring the Steps of Verb Phrase Ellipsis*
Zhengzhong Liu, Edgar Gonzàlez Pellicer and Daniel Gillick

Coffee break

Sense Anaphoric Pronouns: Am I *One*?

Marta Recasens
Google Research
1600 Amphitheatre Parkway
Mountain View, CA 94043
recasens@google.com

Zhichao Hu
Department of Computer Science
University of California, Santa Cruz
Santa Cruz, CA 95064
zhu@soe.ucsc.edu

Olivia Rhinehart
Google Research
1600 Amphitheatre Parkway
Mountain View, CA 94043
orhinehart@google.com

Abstract

This paper focuses on identity-of-sense anaphoric relations, in which the sense is shared but not the referent. We are not restricted to the pronoun *one*, the focus of the small body of previous NLP work on this phenomenon, but look at a wider range of pronouns (*that*, *some*, *another*, etc.). We develop annotation guidelines, enrich a third of English OntoNotes with sense anaphora annotations, and shed light onto this phenomenon from a corpus-based perspective. We release the annotated data as part of the SAnaNotes corpus. We also use this corpus to develop a learning-based classifier to identify sense anaphoric uses, showing both the power and limitations of local features.

1 Introduction

Anaphora and coreference are two linguistic phenomena that often occur together and as a result are sometimes regarded to be the same, but one can happen without the other. Compare (1) and (2)[1]: in the former *them* is anaphoric since its interpretation depends upon another expression in the context (*multiple loans*) with which it also corefers; in the latter example, in contrast, *ones* anaphorically depends on *loans* but they do not corefer since the demanded and existing loans are different discourse entities.

(1)   If you have *multiple loans*, you can consolidate **them** into a single loan.

(2)   Consumers and companies demand fewer *loans* and struggle to pay back existing **ones**.

---

[1] Anaphors are shown in bold, and antecedents in italics.

In this paper we focus on (2)-like anaphoric relations, which have been called *identity-of-sense anaphora* (Grinder and Postal, 1971; Hirst, 1981)— we use the term *sense anaphora* for short. Sense anaphoric pronouns inherit the sense from their antecedent but do not denote the same referent. The meaning of these anaphoric forms remains empty if they are not identified and resolved, thus the importance for most natural language understanding tasks.

While a good deal of previous work in linguistics (Grinder and Postal, 1971; Bresnan, 1971) has discussed the underlying syntactic representation of this phenomenon (syntactic deletion, interpretive rules, etc.) and closely related ones like noun ellipsis (Sag, 1976; Dalrymple et al., 1991), there have been few computational studies on sense anaphora and these have focused on the pronoun *one* (Gardiner, 2003; Ng et al., 2005).

We target a wider set of sense anaphoric pronouns, not only *one* but also *that*, *many*, *some* and others. We annotate a third of English OntoNotes (Weischedel et al., 2011) with sense anaphoric pronouns together with their antecedent, going beyond the existing coreference annotations. To our knowledge, this is the first annotation effort of this phenomenon on a large corpus, and it uncovers distributional statistics and real-world usage patterns.

Our second contribution is using the annotated data to train a learning-based system that identifies anaphoric uses (2) from non-anaphoric uses of the target pronouns such as generics (3), when their meaning is equivalent to 'some people'.

(3)   While **some** think that the estimate may be inflated, the consensus is that drier seasons are on the horizon.

1

Proceedings of the Workshop on Coreference Resolution Beyond OntoNotes (CORBON 2016), co-located with NAACL 2016, pages 1–6,
San Diego, California, June 16, 2016. ©2016 Association for Computational Linguistics

By using only local lexical and syntactic features, the system reaches 79.01% F1 on *one*, and 67.34% F1 on an extended list of sense anaphors.

2 Sense Anaphora

The majority of studies on identity-of-sense anaphora (Grinder and Postal, 1971; Bresnan, 1971) focus on verb rather than noun phrases. We focus on the latter, considering not only *one*, but also other expressions that can similarly borrow their sense from a contextual expression (4), (6), (8). We target single-token anaphors in the following categories:

- ONE (*one, ones*)
- Quantifiers
    - INDEFINITES (*all, any, few, many, more, most, much, some*)
    - NUMERALS (*two, three, ..., hundred, etc.*)
    - MEASURE NOUNS (*bit(s), bunch, couple, dozen(s), lot(s), pair, plenty, ton(s)*)
- DEMONSTRATIVES (*that, those*)
- POSSESSIVES (*mine, yours, his, hers, ours, theirs*)
- OTHER (*other(s), another*)

Previous studies (Dahl, 1985; Luperfoy, 1991; Gardiner, 2003; Payne et al., 2013) have classified *one* in terms of its uses—determiner, count noun, pronoun, etc.—and antecedent types—a kind, a set, an individual. Drawing on these previous classifications, we extend them to all types of sense anaphora and consider that every (sense) anaphor–antecedent pairing falls into one of two broad classes:

Partitive Denotes a subset relationship between the anaphor and antecedent (the set), where the anaphor not only shares the sense with the antecedent but also the specified characteristics. For this reason, the whole noun phrase is considered the antecedent (4). Non-anaphoric partitives, those followed by *of* plus the set (5), are excluded, following Gardiner (2003).[2]

(4) The blast kills *two cameramen*, **one** from Spanish TV, **another** from Reuters.

(5) That's **one** of the problems that they are facing so far.

---

[2]Note that Gardiner (2003) uses the term *partitive* exclusively for non-anaphoric partitive uses of *one*, i.e., *one of*.

The partitive class is similar to bridging anaphors of the set-membership or subset types (Clark, 1975; Poesio et al., 1999; Markert et al., 2012), but we focus on the pronoun-like sense anaphors listed above (which can be seen as headless noun phrases), whereas bridging anaphors usually target full noun phrases, e.g., *a group of students ... three boys*.

Instantiator The anaphor is a new instance created from the same sense as the antecedent (6), (7).

(6) In both quantity and quality, the *English teaching materials* of today leave **those** of before in the dust.

(7) High-tech *industries* need to be constantly innovative, while traditional **ones** have to undergo transformation.

The newly created instance may inherit only the core sense or include some of the specifics of the antecedent, so antecedent spans only include the inherited modifiers: all of them in the case of (6), or none in the case of (7), where inheriting the modifier *high-tech* would contradict the anaphor's modifier, *traditional*. The category of *other*-anaphora or comparative anaphora (Markert and Nissim, 2005) falls into the instantiator class, but similarly to set-membership bridging, the study of *other*-anaphora has focused on full noun phrases rather than headless ones.

The line between the partitive and instantiator classes can be blurry, especially when the antecedent is a kind rather than a set (8), but we find the distinction helpful to conceptualize sense anaphora.

(8) He has done research on *traditional Chinese poetry*, and has included **some** in his Portuguese-language writings.

3 SAnaNotes

3.1 Annotation

Annotators identified sense anaphors and their antecedent phrases using a custom GUI. Strings from the target anaphor categories were automatically highlighted in the text; annotators first determined if the highlighted tokens were anaphors and, if so, they identified their corresponding antecedent. Considering whether the pairing belonged to the partitive or instantiator class helped them determine what the boundaries of the antecedent were, but the partitive/instantiator distinction was not annotated.

When the antecedent is part of a coreference chain, annotators chose the phrase that directly preceded the anaphor, unless it was a relative pronoun. In (9), *it* is chosen as the antecedent instead of *debate* because it is the closest mention in the antecedent's coreference chain. The tool allowed for two anaphors to share the same antecedent (10).

(9) That debate, *it*'s a hard **one** when Hardball returns.

(10) Added to this is the perennial problem of class sizes being too large, and not enough *English classes* scheduled – only **one** or **two** a week.

There was also a 'no explicit antecedent' option for cases in which an anaphor borrows its sense from an antecedent that is not available in the text. In (11), both anaphors *ones* inherit a sort-of-*issue* sense, but this antecedent is not explicit but built up in the context of the passage.

(11) It must be advanced with a plan, the easy **ones** first and the tough **ones** last.

Four human annotators participated in the annotation. After an initial pilot training period, they completed single-annotation on 1 138 documents. In a final stage of annotation, the annotators completed four-way annotation on a set of 25 documents to measure inter-annotator agreement. We used Fleiss' (1971) kappa to measure agreement on anaphor identification: $\kappa = .67$, which indicates substantial agreement according to Landis and Koch (1977). For the commonly identified anaphors, pairwise agreement on their antecedent spans was 63%. The most common annotation errors are anaphor omissions: given the small percentage of anaphoric uses for some of the categories (see Table 1), sense anaphors are easy to be missed.

3.2 Data

The source data for annotation was a third of the English documents from OntoNotes (Weischedel et al., 2011), a 1.6-million-word corpus covering a variety of domains (newswire, broadcast conversation, weblogs, magazine, New Testament, etc.), sampled so as to keep the proportion of OntoNotes domains. We annotated 1 163 documents in total. We release this annotated corpus as SAnaNotes, available from `https://github.com/dmorr-google/sense-anaphora`.

Token	TRAIN			TEST		
	Freq.	Ana.	%	Freq.	Ana.	%
one	1 099	148	13.5	268	33	12.3
ones	49	29	59.2	8	3	37.5
all	720	13	1.8	185	0	0.0
another	41	28	68.3	13	8	61.5
few	142	11	7.7	45	3	6.7
many	448	18	4.0	121	3	2.5
more	846	13	1.5	231	0	0.0
most	336	6	1.8	103	1	1.0
much	369	1	0.3	90	1	1.1
other	597	21	3.5	141	5	3.5
others	139	43	30.9	32	11	34.4
some	214	26	12.1	49	5	10.2
that	940	25	2.7	248	13	5.2
those	296	27	9.1	65	13	20.0
NUM	6 046	120	2.0	1 880	16	0.9
TOTAL	12 282	529	4.3	3 479	115	3.3

Table 1: Distribution of sense anaphors in SAnaNotes (*Ana.* stands for 'anaphoric'). TRAIN subsumes the development data. The Freq. column excludes determiner uses.

The average number of sense anaphors per document is 0.6. Of the target categories, the OntoNotes data contain a small number of POSSESSIVES (*hers, yours*, etc.) and MEASURE NOUNS (*bunch, ton*, etc.), of which anaphoric examples represent an even smaller number. Table 1 shows the distribution of anaphors belonging to categories for which there are at least 10 anaphoric examples, that is, keeping ONE, INDEFINITES, NUMERALS, DEMONSTRATIVES, and OTHER; and excluding POSSESSIVES and MEASURE NOUNS. While the ONE and OTHER classes show a large proportion of anaphoric uses, and DEMONSTRATIVES to a smaller extent, only a small number of INDEFINITES and NUMERALS are anaphoric.

4 Anaphoric Classification

Using the SAnaNotes corpus, we built a classifier to distinguish sense anaphors (example 2) from other uses like determiners, numerals, generics (example 3), deictics, etc. Given the composition of SAnaNotes, we target all anaphors listed in Table 1.

4.1 Previous Work

To our knowledge the only computational approaches to resolving sense anaphoric pronouns have focused on *one* anaphora, namely the studies by Gardiner (2003) and Ng et al. (2005). Both split the problem into two steps: identification of anaphoric uses and resolution to an antecedent. We overview the first step since it is our current focus.

Gardiner (2003) developed a rule-based system based on five heuristics to distinguish non-anaphoric uses—numeric (*one* is a quantifier or numeric adjective), partitive (*one*'s immediate post-modifier is *of* introducing a plural noun phrase), generic (*one* is a subject of a modal or animate verb)—from anaphoric ones (the rest). She extracted from the British National Corpus a test set of 773 sentences containing *one*, but highly biased towards anaphoric examples (71.5%) and far from reality (compare with 12.3% in Table 1). On this test set her system obtained 85.4% precision and 86.9% recall.

Ng et al. (2005) developed a learning-based system by turning Gardiner's (2003) heuristics into seven learning features. They trained a C4.5 decision tree classifier using 10-fold cross validation on a set of 1 577 *one* expressions, also from the British National Corpus, but this time randomly selected, thus mirroring the natural distribution of anaphoric *one* (15.2% in their data set). They obtained 68.3% precision and 80.0% recall, and noted that discriminating between the anaphoric and generic classes offered the most complexity out of all six classes.

4.2 System

In contrast to previous work, our goal is to address a wider variety of sense anaphors and to use simple lexical and syntactic features that could identify the constructions characteristic of sense anaphoric uses, e.g., anaphoric *that* is usually followed by an *of*-phrase, generic *one* is often the subject of specific animate verbs, etc.

We generate a training instance for every token matching one of those in Table 1 and every token with NUM category, and exclude determiners (tokens with 'det' label). Filtering 'num' or 'amod' labels gave poorer results on the development set and so we kept them, leaving it to the classifier to learn when to filter them out. Given the multiple senses of *that*, we exclude its uses as a relative pronoun (tag: 'WDT') or conjunction (tag: 'IN').

We train an SVM classifier–LIBLINEAR implementation (Fan et al., 2008)–to distinguish between the anaphoric class and the rest using 31 lexical and

syntactic feature types:

- Lowercased word, POS tag, dependency label and word cluster from Brown et al. (1992) for:
  - Anaphor candidate
  - Two previous tokens
  - Two following tokens
  - Candidate's syntactic head (e.g., *says* is the head of *another* in *another says . . .*)
  - Candidate's syntactic leftmost child (e.g., *the* is the leftmost dependent of *one* in *the second one he has missed*)
- Conjoined features with these pairs:
  - Lowercased candidate and POS tag of the previous token (and vice versa)
  - Lowercased candidate and POS tag of the following token (and vice versa)
  - Lowercased candidate and leftmost child

We also try adding the finer-grained features used by Ng et al. (2005), but they do not help, presumably because they are already covered.

4.3 Evaluation

We split the SAnaNotes corpus into train, development, and test partitions. Once development was over, we merged that partition with the train set. The anaphoric class usually represents a small percentage of all occurrences of every candidate token (Table 1). For the feature generation, we annotated the data with a dependency parser similar to MaltParser (Nivre et al., 2007).

We use precision (P) and recall (R) to measure the number of correct anaphoric predictions made by our system, and the proportion of gold anaphors identified by our system.

For comparison, we reimplemented the two previous systems that focused on *one*: (1) the rule-based system by Gardiner (2003), and (2) an unpruned J48 decision tree classifier trained with Ng et al.'s (2005) features in Weka 3.6.12 (Hall et al., 2009), using the same train/test SAnaNotes split.[3]

4.4 Results and Discussion

Table 2 compares the results of our system on *one* and *ones* with those obtained by the two previous

---

[3]The scores for a pruned decision tree were all 0.

System	P	R	F1
Gardiner (2003)	40.00	94.44	56.20
Ng et al. (2005)	62.50	55.60	58.80
Our system	74.42	88.89	79.01

Table 2: Comparison of our *one*-anaphor classifier (including *one* and *ones*) with previous work on the test set of SAnaNotes.

Anaphor class	P	R	F1
ONE	71.11	88.89	79.01
INDEFINITES	38.46	38.46	38.46
NUMERALS	27.78	31.25	29.41
DEMONSTRATIVES	87.50	53.85	66.67
OTHER	61.54	66.67	64.00
ALL	61.02	62.61	61.80
ALL excl. NUMERALS	67.00	67.68	67.34

Table 3: Evaluation of our anaphor classifier on the test set of SAnaNotes.

systems on the same test set from SAnaNotes. Gardiner's precision is especially low, which did not show in her original test set highly biased towards anaphoric instances. Our features, though less targeted to the ones used by Ng et al. (2005), turn out to perform better. In addition, they generalize to the additional sense anaphors not tackled before. Ng et al.'s features are very specific and fail to learn to discriminate between some anaphoric patterns that our more general system learns (12).

(12) The hottest gift this Christmas could be *Sony's new PlayStation 2*, but good luck finding **one**.

Table 3 breaks down the performance of our anaphor classification results by anaphor category. Classification of anaphors other than *one* and *ones* is considerably harder, especially for numerals, followed by indefinites. The small number of positive training instances (Table 1) probably accounts for the poor performance. Given the limited number of sense anaphors per document, a larger corpus is likely to make a significant difference. Our feature set generalizes better than Ng et al.'s (2005), which only obtains 38.60% F1 on all anaphors excluding numerals (vs. 67.34% F1 by our system) and 31.30% F1 when including numerals (vs. 61.80% F1 by our system).

The classification errors illustrate the complexity of the task: (13) is a precision error given that *few* refers to the number itself, but it is arguably a bor-

derline case; (14) is a recall error that shows the limitation of surface features in a small context window because *some* would be interpreted generically if there was no previous context.

(13) They were able to whittle it down the number of missing aircraft uh to a **few**.

(14) *Today's Tanshui residents* are living their own stories [...] **Some** are active in the morning, **some** late at night.

5 Conclusion

We tackled a tail phenomenon in natural language understanding, that of sense anaphora, going beyond the pronoun *one* and generalizing to other similar identity-of-sense expressions. While not very common in the OntoNotes domains, we suspect they are more common in conversational language, for example voice queries, thus being especially important for the next generation of voice assistants.

Apart from annotating and releasing SAnaNotes, we experimented with the anaphoric classification task, achieving 61.80% F1 with a set of local features. As future work, we would like to approach the antecedent resolution task jointly with anaphor identification, as the hardest cases of the anaphoric/generic distinction require knowing whether an antecedent is available in the context. This would also make it possible to explore features that look at a wider context, for example to capture parallel structures between antecedent and anaphor (e.g., *high-tech industries* and *traditional ones*) as well as features that take discourse structure into account, e.g., discourse relations such as comparison and conjunction between the discourse units containing the antecedent and anaphor.

Acknowledgments

This work was done when the second author was an intern at Google. We would like to thank all the annotators who worked on SAnaNotes (Melanie Bolla, Katy DiNatale, Grace Gaspardo, Patrick Hegarty) as well as Amanda Morris and Edgar Gonzàlez for their support and productive discussions, and Dave Orr for making the data release possible. Many thanks also to the nNLP team, especially Qiwei Wang and David Huynh, for customizing the annotation tool for this task. Finally, we would like to thank our anonymous reviewers for their helpful comments.

References

Joan Bresnan. 1971. A note on the notion "identity of sense anaphora". *Linguistic Inquiry*, 2:589–597.

Peter F. Brown, Peter V. deSouza, Robert L. Mercer, Vincent J. Della Pietra, and Jenifer C. Lai. 1992. Class-based *n*-gram models of natural language. *Computational Linguistics*, 18(4):467–479.

Herbert H. Clark. 1975. Bridging. In R. C. Schank and B. L. Nash-Webber, editors, *Theoretical Issues in Natural Language Processing*, pages 169–174.

Deborah Anna Dahl. 1985. *The structure and function of one-anaphora in English*. Ph.D. thesis, University of Minnesota.

Mary Dalrymple, Stuart M. Shieber, and Fernando C.N. Pereira. 1991. Ellipsis and higher order unification. *Linguistics and Philosophy*, 14:399–452.

Rong-En Fan, Kai-Wei Chang, Cho-Jui Hsieh, Xiang-Rui Wang, and Chih-Jen Lin. 2008. LIBLINEAR: A library for large linear classification. *Journal of Machine Learning Research*, 9:1871–1874.

Joseph L. Fleiss. 1971. Measuring nominal scale agreement among many raters. *Psychological Bulletin*, 76(5):378–382.

Mary Gardiner. 2003. Identifying and resolving *one*-anaphora. B.S. Thesis, Department of Computing, Macquarie University.

John Grinder and Paul M. Postal. 1971. Missing antecedents. *Linguistic Inquiry*, 2:589–597.

Mark Hall, Eibe Frank, Geoffrey Holmes, Bernhard Pfahringer, Peter Reutemann, and Ian H. Witten. 2009. The WEKA data mining software: An update. *SIGKDD Explorations*, 11:10–18.

Grame Hirst. 1981. *Anaphora in natural language understanding: a survey*. Lecture Notes in Computer Science. Springer-Verlag, Berlin, New York.

J. Richard Landis and Gary G. Koch. 1977. The measurement of observer agreement for categorical data. *Biometrics*, 33(1):159–174.

Susann Luperfoy. 1991. *Discourse Pegs: A Computational Analysis of Context-Dependent Referring Expressions*. Ph.D. thesis, University of Texas at Austin.

Katja Markert and Malvina Nissim. 2005. Comparing knowledge sources for nominal anaphora resolution. *Computational Linguistics*, 31:367–401.

Katja Markert, Yufang Hou, and Michael Strube. 2012. Collective classification for fine-grained information status. In *Proceedings of ACL*, pages 795–804.

Hwee Tou Ng, Yu Zhou, Robert Dale, and Mary Gardiner. 2005. A machine learning approach to identification and resolution of *one*-anaphora. In *Proceedings of IJCAI*, pages 1105–1110.

Joakim Nivre, Johan Hall, Jens Nilsson, Atanas Chanev, Gülşen Eryiğit, Sandra Kübler, Svetoslav Marinov, and Erwin Marsi. 2007. MaltParser: A language-independent system for data-driven dependency parsing. *Natural Language Engineering*, 13:95–135.

John Payne, Geoffrey K. Pullum, Barbara C. Scholz, and Eva Berlage. 2013. Anaphoric *one* and its implications. *Language*, 89(4):794–829.

Massimo Poesio, Florence Bruneseaux, and Laurent Romary. 1999. The MATE meta-scheme for coreference in dialogues in multiple languages. In *Proceedings of the ACL Workshop Towards Standards and Tools for Discourse Tagging*, pages 65–74.

Ivan A. Sag. 1976. *Deletion and logical form*. Ph.D. thesis, Massachusetts Institute of Technology.

Ralph Weischedel, Eduard Hovy, Mitchell Marcus, Martha Palmer, Robert Belvin, Sameer Pradhan, Lance Ramshaw, and Nianwen Xue. 2011. OntoNotes: A large training corpus for enhanced processing. In Joseph Olive, Caitlin Christianson, and John McCary, editors, *Handbook of Natural Language Processing and Machine Translation: DARPA Global Autonomous Language Exploitation*, pages 54–63. Springer.

Experiments on bridging across languages and genres

Yulia Grishina
Applied Computational Linguistics
FSP Cognitive Science
University of Potsdam
`grishina@uni-potsdam.de`

Abstract

In this paper, we introduce a typology of bridging relations applicable to multiple languages and genres. After discussing our annotation guidelines, we describe annotation experiments on the German part of our parallel coreference corpus and show that our inter-annotator agreement results are reliable, considering both antecedent selection and relation assignment. In order to validate our theoretical model on other languages, we manually transfer German annotations to the English and Russian sides of the corpus and briefly discuss first results that suggest the promise of our approach. Furthermore, for the complete exploration of extended coreference relations, we exploit an existing near-identity scheme to augment our annotations with near-identity links, and we report on the results.

1 Introduction

High-quality coreference resolution is necessary to establish coherence in discourse. In comparison to recent large-scale annotation efforts for identity coreference such as OntoNotes (Hovy et al., 2006), it is now becoming more interesting to investigate understudied coreference relations other than identity – namely, near-identity and bridging.

Bridging relations are indirect relations that can only be inferred based on the knowledge shared by the speaker and the listener. They encompass a wide range of relations between anaphor and antecedent, such as part-whole, or set membership. Additional complexity arises when two expressions refer to "almost" the same thing, but are neither identical nor

non-identical. In this case, we speak of near-identity, which can be seen as a 'middle ground' between identity and non-identity coreference (Recasens et al., 2010).

The goals of the paper are: (i) to introduce a typology of extended coreference relations based on the related work and experimental annotation rounds; (ii) to validate our theoretical model by applying it to a multilingual and multi-genre corpus; and (iii) to explore the existing near-identity scheme using the same dataset. Our primary interest lies in developing a domain-independent typology that would serve as a basis for subsequent creation of larger annotated resources for different languages and domains.

The paper is organized as follows: Section 2 summarizes previous efforts of classifying bridging and near-identity relations. Section 3 presents our corpus annotation in detail. Section 4 discusses the results, and Section 5 concludes.

2 Previous annotation efforts

Bridging. The concept of bridging was initially introduced by Clark (1975) who postulated that a definite description can be implicitly related to some previously mentioned entity. Clark makes a distinction between direct reference and indirect reference. Direct reference is what we usually understand by identity coreference, when two NPs share the same referent in the real world.[1] What we are interested in (and what is called 'bridging' in the coreference literature, as opposed to the identity relation) is indi-

---

[1] It is worth pointing out that reference to one or more members of a set to the whole set is also seen by Clark as direct reference.

Proceedings of the Workshop on Coreference Resolution Beyond OntoNotes (CORBON 2016), co-located with NAACL 2016, pages 7–15,
San Diego, California, June 16, 2016. ©2016 Association for Computational Linguistics

rect reference. Clark names 3 classes of indirect reference: (i) indirect reference by association, (ii) indirect reference by characterization, and (iii) a separate group encompassing reasons, causes, consequences and concurrences.

Since we only deal with noun phrase coreference for the time being, we can not make use of the last group, as the antecedent in that case is often an event, not an object. The first two groups have much in common: they are subdivided into necessary and optional parts and roles respectively, e.g.:

(1) (a) During [the terrorist attack in Mumbai] [the attackers] did not hide their faces.
     (b) Daisy walked into [the office] and saw a bunch of flowers on [the windowsill].

The difference between the two examples is that in (1a) *the attackers* is an absolutely necessary role of the mentioned event, while from (1b) we can infer that *the office* has one *windowsill* (which is not necessarily true for all the offices). Necessary and optional components of entities or events vary in their predictability by the listener from absolutely necessary to quite unnecessary (Clark lists three levels of 'necessity' of this continuum).

The recent approaches to the annotation of bridging derive from two different annotation frameworks. First, bridging can be annotated as a part of the information structure (IS) of texts, along with other information status categories. Second, bridging can be seen as a separate category of textual coreference, besides identity and near-identity coreference. We will deal with bridging on the coreference level, but we consider both approaches in the review of the related work.

Bridging at the IS level. Bridging is an individual subcategory among other categories of information status, as introduced in the work of Nissim et al. (2004), subsequently enhanced and applied by Gardent et al. (2003), Ritz et al. (2008), Riester et al. (2010) and Markert et al. (2012). Usually the results are reported on the entire scheme and are somewhat lower for the single categories. To our knowledge, the highest agreement for the bridging anaphor recognition in particular ($\kappa = 0.6$-0.7) was reported by Markert et al. (2012), whose interpretation of bridging is to some extent different from the others (they do not restrict the annotation scope

to definite noun phrases, allowing indefinite NPs to participate in bridging relations as well). However, all these approaches treat the bridging category as a whole, not making any distinctions between individual subcategories. For our purposes here, this is a more challenging task and the one we are primarily interested in.

Bridging at the coreference level. Recent related literature distinguishes between the following most common types of bridging relations: part-whole, set membership and generalized possession (Poesio et al., 2004), (Poesio and Artstein, 2008), (Hinrichs et al., 2005). In addition to these, in the Prague Dependency Treebank, contrast was annotated as a bridging relation as well (Nedoluzhko et al., 2009). Baumann and Riester (2012) additionally annotated cases of bridging-contained NPs, where the bridging anaphor is anchored to an embedded phrase, e.g. *[the ceiling of [the hotel room]]*. However, these relations seem to be underspecified in the sense that part-whole is a very general relation; in contrast, we are interested in a more fine-grained classification of relations that could emerge from part-whole.

More specific relations are proposed in NLP approaches to extract bridging automatically. For example, a more complex and detailed classification of bridging relations was introduced in (Gardent et al., 2003) who distinguished between 5 classes of bridging relations: set-membership, thematic (links an event to an individual via a thematic relation defined by the thematic grid of the event, e.g. *murder - the murderer*), definitional (relation is given by the dictionary definition of either the target or the anchor, e.g. *convalescence - the operation*), co-participants, and non-lexical (relation could be established due to discourse structure or world knowledge).

For developing a rule-based system to resolve bridging, Hou et al. (2014) used 8 relations that were based on related literature and their document set, which comprises 10 documents from the ISNotes Corpus[2], which contains the Wall Street Journal portion of the OntoNotes corpus (Hovy et al., 2006): building - part (*room - the roof*), relative - person (*the husband – she*), geopolitical entity - job title (*Japan – officials*), role - organization, percentage

---

[2]http://www.h-its.org/english/research/nlp/download/isnotes.php

NP (*22% of the firms – 17%*), set - member (*reds and yellows – some of them*), argument taking NP I (different instances of the same predicate in a document likely maintain the same argument fillers; *Marina residents - some residents*), argument taking NP II (an argument-taking NP in the subject position is a good indicator for bridging anaphora, *Poland's first conference - the participants*).

Bridging was shown to be a very complex category that poses difficulties for the annotators. It includes the following subtasks: (a) recognizing bridging anaphors and selecting their antecedents, and (b) assigning appropriate bridging types. In general, inter-annotator agreement for (a) tends to be lower than for standard identity coreference; the scores vary between 22 and 50% F1-score for selecting bridging anaphors and antecedents (Poesio and Vieira, 1998), (Poesio, 2004), (Nedoluzhko et al., 2009). As for types of relations, not much was reported lately. To our knowledge, only Nedoluzhko et al. (2009) reported on the scores for four basic relation types (average $\kappa = 0.9$). However, we are not aware of any other agreement studies for more complex relation sets.

In sum, corpus creation approaches to bridging classification are quite coarse-grained, while applied work (bridging resolution) tends to be very domain-specific. Both paths are rather problematic if we want to create reliable multi-genre annotated resources with a fine-grained classification of bridging relations.

Near-identity. The concept of near-identity has been introduced by Recasens et al. (2010). The near-identity relation is defined as a middle-ground between identity and bridging, and it emerged out of the inter-annotator disagreements while annotating identity coreference. Near-identity holds between two NPs whose referents are almost identical, but differ in one crucial dimension. Recasens et al. (2010) introduce four main categories of near-identity relations:

- name metonymy;

- meronymy;

- class;

- spatio-temporal function.

	# DE
Sentences	598
Tokens	11894
Referring expressions	1395
Identity chains	273
Bridging pairs	432
Near-identity pairs	107

Table 1: Corpus statistics for German

Each of the categories includes several subcategories (not mentioned in the list above). To our knowledge, no large-scale near-identity annotation on different text genres has been done so far. Recasens et al. (2010) reported the results of their stability study only for pre-selected NP pairs. In a follow-up paper, Recasens et al. (2012) showed that explicit near-identity annotation is a very difficult task for the annotators, due to the infrequency of the near-identity links in their corpus of newswire texts, as identified by the annotators. The same annotation scheme was subsequently applied to annotate the Polish Coreference Corpus by Ogrodniczuk et al. (2014), however, the inter-annotator agreement scores were quite low ($\kappa = 0.22$).

3 Corpus annotation

For the annotation, we used the parallel coreference corpus from (Grishina and Stede, 2015) which consists of texts in three languages (English, German, Russian) and of three different genres (newswire, narratives, medicine instruction leaflets). The German part of the corpus, which already contained identity coreference annotations, was given to the annotators to add bridging and near-identity links.

In order to evaluate the applicability of our annotation scheme for other languages and to speed up the annotation process, we transferred the German annotations to the English and Russian sides of the corpus.

Corpus statistics are shown in Table 1. In this section, we present statistics for German, including the number of identity, near-identity and bridging links. Details on the annotation transfer for the two other languages are provided in Section 4.

3.1 Bridging scheme

We base our work on the main principle identified by Clark (1975): We assume that the speaker intends the listener to be able to compute the shortest possible bridge from the previous knowledge to the antecedent which is therefore unique (determinate) in the natural language discourse.

Hence, only definite descriptions can be annotated as bridging anaphors. However, not all the definite descriptions that appear in a text for the first time have a bridging antecedent – some of them are definite due to the common knowledge shared by the speaker and the listener.

In our pilot experiments, we identified several bridging categories, which were common across genres, and applied them to annotate the corpus. Below, we describe these categories and give typical examples from different genres for each of them.

1. **Physical parts - whole**

   One NP represents a physical part of the whole expressed by the other NP.

   - *the militant organisation - the offices in the whole country*
   - *the telephone - the dial pad*
   - *the knee - the bone*

2. **Set-membership**

   Sets can be represented by multiple entities or events. One can refer to a certain subset or to a single definite element of the set and bridge from this subset or element to the whole collection. We do not distinguish between sets and collections, as is done in some of the related work. Sets are homogeneous and imply that their elements are equal.

   A. SET-SUBSET

   - *the European Union - the least developed countries*
   - *the patients - the patients treated with Abraxane*

   B. SET-ELEMENT

   - *these studies - the main study*
   - *Pakistan major cities - the most populous city*

3. **Entity-attribute/function**

   An entity is a person or an object that has certain attributes characterizing it and certain functions it fulfills with respect to some other entity.

   A. ENTITY-ATTRIBUTE

   - *Kosovo - their current policy of rejection*
   - *Mrs. Humphries - the monotonous voice*

   B. ENTITY-FUNCTION

   This relation involves a bridge holding between individuals with one of the related individuals being described by his profession or function with respect to the other (Gardent et al., 2003).

   - *Trends, the shop - Mr. Rangee, the owner*
   - *Kosovo region - the government*

4. **Event-attribute**

   Core semantic frame elements of events are commonly time and place, while optional ones can include duration, participants, explanation, frequency etc. From these frame elements one can bridge to the event itself.

   - *the regional conflict - the trained fighters*
   - *the attack - the security offices*
   - *the surgical intervention - the operating room*

5. **Location-attribute**

   As locations we consider geographical entities that have permanent locations in the world. Such locations exhibit different semantic frames as compared to entities and events.

   - *the Balkans - the instability on the Balkans*
   - *Germany - in the south*
   - *Afghanistan - the population*

6. **Other**

   Other bridging relations (if any), that can not be described using the categories presented above.

Bridging and near-identity relations are generally directed from right to left. Each markable can have only one outgoing relation, but multiple ingoing relations are allowed. Cataphoric bridging and near-identity relations (directed from left to right) are allowed if the cataphoric antecedent is semantically closer to the anaphor than the possible anaphoric antecedent. Following (Baumann and Riester, 2012), we annotated BRIDGING-CONTAINED NPs and marked them as such.

3.2 Near-identity scheme

We used the definitions provided by Recasens et al. (2010) and made an attempt to apply them to our texts. The annotators' goal was to extend existing annotations on top of the identity coreference. We only chose the four top categories mentioned in Section 2, without distinguishing among their subtypes. In order to differentiate between the category of meronymy, which is common for both near-identity and bridging[3], we introduced the principle of primacy, according to which, in case of doubt, identity was preferred over near-identity and near-identity over bridging. However, the annotations of our corpus exhibited a small number of near-identical markables, which was not sufficient to compute inter-annotator agreement. For that reason, we merged the annotations from the first and the second annotator and then analysed their distribution according to the near-identity types across genres in Section 4. It is worth pointing out that our results for a multi-genre corpus conform to the results obtained by Recasens et al. (2012).

3.3 Bridging agreement study

We carried out an agreement study with 2 annotators – students of linguistics, native speakers of German, with prior experience in other types of corpus annotation tasks. All the markables in the texts were manually pre-selected by the author of this paper. The annotation guidelines were developed on 7 training documents, and 4 of them were given to the annotators for training. During the pilot annotation round, the annotators discussed the disagreements, and necessary changes to the guidelines were made. Inter-annotator agreement was measured on 5 doc-

Relation	A1: #	A1: %	A2: #	A2: %
Part-Whole	20	9.09	18	8.57
Set-Membership	2	0.92	19	9.05
Entity-Attr/F	146	66.36	109	51.91
Event-Attr	20	9.09	29	13.81
Location-Attr	29	13.18	33	15.71
Other	3	1.36	2	0.95

Table 2: General distribution of relations for A1 and A2

	%
F1 anaphor recognition	64.0
F1 antecedent selection	79.0
κ Part-Whole	1.0
κ Set-Membership	N/A
κ Entity-Attr/F	0.97
κ Event-Attr	0.96
κ Location-Attr	1.0

Table 3: Agreement between two annotators

uments, with A1 marking 220 and A2 marking 210 pairs as bridging. Table 2 shows the distribution of the types of relations for the first (A1) and the second annotator (A2).

We measured (i) F-1 score for anaphor recognition (the number of common bridging anaphors) and antecedent selection (the number of common anaphor-antecedent pairs based on the commonly recognized markables) and (ii) Cohen's κ for individual categories for those pairs that both annotators agreed upon. Table 3 shows agreement results, which we consider as overall reliable for bridging when compared to related work on extended coreference. We were able to achieve even higher agreement scores on bridging categories (average κ = 0.98), introducing a wider range of relations than Nedoluzhko et al. (2009). We do not give an agreement score for set-membership, the reason for that being data scarcity and the preference of A1 towards other relations: A1 marked only about 0.1% of all bridging pairs as set-membership, and did not agree on antecedent selection with A2 for any of them, therefore it was not possible to measure agreement for this category.[4]

Table 4 shows the distribution of types for those pairs that were labelled differently by both annotators. The most controversial category is entity-attribute/function, which correlates with this cate-

---

[3]According to (Recasens et al., 2010), in near-identity, meronymy can take place between two NPs that could be substituted by one another in the text, while in bridging these NPs should be clearly different and could be linked only via a 'part-of' relation.

[4]One of the possible reasons for the low number of set-membership pairs could be the fact that our scheme for identity coreference includes discontinuous group markables.

Relation	#	%
Part-Whole	32	14.95
Set-Membership	21	9.81
Entity-Attr/F	95	44.39
Event-Attr	30	14.03
Location-Attr	32	14.95
Other	4	1.87

Table 4: Distribution of different pairs for A1 and A2

gory being the most frequent one; the other types are almost equally disagreed upon. Particularly interesting is that only 3% of all the different bridging pairs are marked as near-identity pairs by the other annotator; accordingly, these categories in general do not intersect.

4 Discussion

4.1 Does bridging correlate with coreference chains?

To answer this question, we first looked at the number of bridging anaphors that actually start a new coreference chain further in the text. On average for all the texts, only 17% of all the bridging anaphors are being referred to later on. These chains are on average 3.28 markables long, which is 1 markable shorter than the average length of coreference chains in the corpus (4.05). The most frequent relation that starts a new chain is entity-attribute/function (44%), followed by location-attribute (21%) and event-attribute (18%).

Secondly, we were interested in whether bridging markables correlate with the prominent coreference chains in the text. Our study showed that 56% of all the chains have bridging markables connected to them. We computed the average lengths of a target chain and a non-target chain for bridging, which is 6.1 markables and 2.4 markables, respectively. These numbers show that a target 'bridging' chain is usually longer than an average chain in the text (see above) while a 'non-bridging' chain is shorter. The longest 'bridging' chain can reach up to 22 markables, while the longest 'non-bridging' chain can only reach up to 9 markables.

We computed the correlation between the length of identity chain and the number of bridging markables that are linked to this chain. Using Spearman's rank correlation coefficient, we found that there is a strong correlation between the chain length and

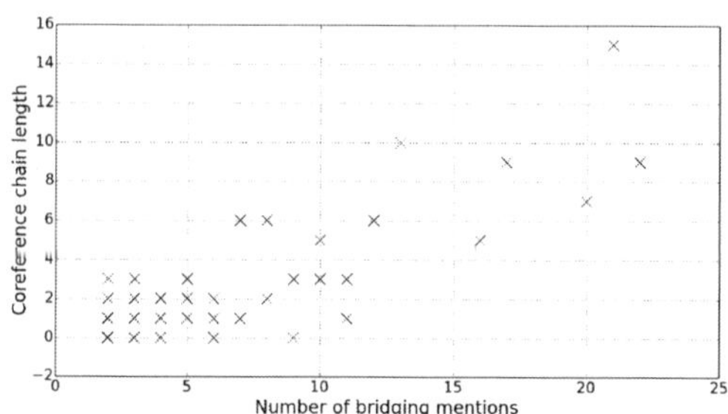

Figure 1: Length of identity chains and number of their bridging markables with Spearman's $\rho = 0.6595$

the number of its bridges: 0.6595, with p-value of 1.35E-008. Figure 1 shows the relation between the chain length and the number of its bridging markables.

4.2 How far can we bridge in the natural text?

Our guidelines do not limit the scope of the study at any point, allowing annotators to bridge back over an unlimited number of sentences if they find the antecedent semantically close to the anaphor. However, we postulated several principles in order to set priorities and help annotators resolve controversial issues, one of them being the principle of SEMANTIC RELATEDNESS: in case of multiple antecedent candidates, pick the one that is more semantically related to the anaphoric (or cataphoric) markable. This principle wins over the principle of PROXIMITY, according to which one has to bridge to the nearest semantically close antecedent in the text. For example:

(2) [The telephone] rang. I came into [the office] and picked up [the receiver].

In this case, we link *the telephone* to *the office* and *the receiver* to *the telephone* (because it is more sematically close), and not to *the office* (that is a closer possible antecedent).

We computed the average bridging distance (anaphora + cataphora), which is 20.55 tokens for all texts,[5] with the average sentence length being 24.87. The average distances for anaphora and cataphora, if computed separately, are 30.96 and -3.6 tokens, respectively. It is worth noticing that the

---

[5] We excluded bridging-contained markables from this computation.

12

Relation	News	Narrative	Med. leaflets
Part-Whole	9.77	37.14	16.66
Set-Membership	3.9	0.0	10.0
Entity-Attr/F	58.3	62.85	72.22
Event-Attr	12.08	0.0	1.12
Location-Attr	14.33	0.0	0.0
Other	1.62	0.0	0.0
Metonymy	15.79	100.0	0.0
Meronymy	76.32	0.0	28.57
Spatio-temporal func.	7.89	0.0	71.43
Other	0.0	0.0	0.0

Table 5: Distribution of bridging and near-identity relations across genres

Relation	DE	EN	RU
Part-Whole	13.27	10.11	12.77
Set-Membership	3.7	5.84	3.72
Entity-Attr/F	62.04	70.74	72.87
Event-Attr	7.41	2.66	3.72
Location-Attr	13.58	10.64	6.92

Table 6: Distribution of bridging relations across languages

furthest bridging antecedent was found 410 tokens away from its anaphor.

Finally, our study has shown that distance does not seem to correlate with prominence: Both longer and shorter chains can have close and long-distance bridging anaphors.

4.3 How transferable is bridging across languages and genres?

One of the main goals of our study was to introduce the classification of relations that could be applied to various languages and domains. In the following, we present the results of (a) analysis of bridging and near-identity distribution across different genres and (b) results of the experiment on manual transfer of German annotations into English and Russian.

Different genres. Table 5 shows the percentage of near-identity and bridging in the German part of the corpus. Interestingly, all of the genres exhibit a big proportion of entity-attribute/function relations. However, in the newswire texts, other relations are almost equally distributed, as opposed to the medicine leaflets and the narratives. In narratives, we encountered a lot more part-whole relations than in the other genres.

As for near-identity, it is worth noticing that the annotations of medical texts exhibited a very high percentage (71.43) of spatio-temporal relations, the reason for that being the specificity of the texts (instruction leaflets). In narratives, we only found metonymic relations, while medical texts did not contain them. In the newswire texts, all types of relations were found, with meronymy being the most common one (76.32).

Different languages. Taking German annotations as a starting point, we annotated the English and Russian sides of our parallel corpus. Table 6 shows the distribution of different types of relations for German, English and Russian.[6] The resulting number of bridging anaphors for the English and Russian sides of the corpus is 188 each, which is about 44% of the total number of German bridging markables.

This 'transfer' of annotations across languages posed additional difficulties in some cases. In particular, it was more difficult to transfer existing German annotations across newswire texts, while for the stories, all of the markables were successfully transferred. The majority of the NPs that could not be transferred is explained by two reasons: (a) due to our restriction on the definiteness status of bridging markables; and (b) because they were already participating in identity chains. Below, we give examples for the first case in English and German:

(3)   (a) Race relations in [the US] have been for decades at the center of political debate, to the point that racial cleavages are as important as income as determinants of political preferences and attitude.
(b) Die Beziehungen zwischen den Rassen standen in [den USA] über Jahrzehnte im Zentrum der politischen Debatte. Das ging so weit, daß Rassentrennung genauso wichtig wie [das Einkommen] wurde, um politische Zuneigungen und Einstellungen zu bestimmen.

In this example, we bridge from *das Einkommen* to *den USA*, however, in the English part *income* is indefinite and thus it is no bridging markable according to our guidelines.

For Russian, the lack of articles impeded the identification of bridging markables and made the deci-

---

[6]We excluded medical texts from this distribution, as they were available only for 2 languages.

13

sion on their definiteness much more complex. We applied the following strategy in doubtful cases in order to identify bridging markables: We used a substitution test, replacing the NP in question with the corresponding genitive NP. If the test succeeded, we considered the markable as a bridging anaphor, otherwise the markable was not annotated. For example:

(4) (a) Daisy was in [the office] when somebody knocked on [the door].
(b) Дейзи была в [офисе], когда кто-то постучал в [дверь].

In this example, *the door* in English is definitely unique, while in Russian we need to apply our test first: дверь офиса (*the door of the office*) is appropriate in this case, hence there is a bridging relation between the two NPs.

The analysis of the resulting annotations has shown that our guidelines are in general applicable to the three languages in our corpus; even though there are some differences across languages and genres that we will investigate in more detail. In particular, the category of entity-attribute/function requires a more careful analysis.

5   Conclusions

The focus of this study was to explore extended coreference relations, namely near-identity and bridging. Our primary goal was to introduce a domain-independent typology of bridging relations, which can be applicable across languages. We subsequently applied our annotation scheme to a multilingual coreference corpus of three genres, and for near-identity relations we use the typology introduced in the related work. Our scheme achieves reliable inter-annotator agreement scores for anaphor and antecedent selection, and on the assignment of bridging relations. The infrequency of near-identity relations in our corpus leaves this part as a step for the future work. We conducted a detailed analysis of the nature of bridging relations in the corpus, focusing on the distance between anaphor and antecedent. Furthermore, we examined the correlation between bridging and identity coreference and presented the distribution of bridging and near-identity relations across three different languages and genres.

In future work, we are interested in refining our typology by introducing a set of possible sub-relations, conducting a more detailed comparative analysis of bridging relations across languages using annotation transfer, and exploring in detail set-membership relation and the category of near-identity on a larger amount of texts. We intend to reconsider the definition of markables in our guidelines (which probably has to vary from language to language), which was one of the main reasons for markables being missed in the annotation transfer. We aim at keeping our approaches applicable to multilingual data and to different genres of text.

Our annotation guidelines and the annotated corpus will be made available via our website `http://angcl.ling.uni-potsdam.de`.

Acknowledgements

I thank Manfred Stede for his insight and expertise, and the annotators Erik Haegert and Mathias Bisping for their help with corpus annotation. I am also grateful to Costanza Navaretta for our fruitful discussions, and to the anonymous reviewers for their suggestions on improving the paper. This work was supported by a scholarship from the Friedrich Wingert foundation.

References

Stefan Baumann and Arndt Riester. 2012. Referential and lexical givenness: Semantic, prosodic and cognitive aspects. *Prosody and meaning*, 25:119–162.

Herbert H Clark. 1975. Bridging. In *Proceedings of the 1975 workshop on Theoretical issues in natural language processing*, pages 169–174. Association for Computational Linguistics.

Claire Gardent, Hélène Manuélian, and Eric Kow. 2003. Which bridges for bridging definite descriptions. In *Proceedings of the EACL 2003 Workshop on Linguistically Interpreted Corpora*, pages 69–76.

Yulia Grishina and Manfred Stede. 2015. Knowledge-lean projection of coreference chains across languages. In *Proceedings of the 8th Workshop on Building and Using Comparable Corpora, Beijing, China*, page 14. Association for Computational Linguistics.

Erhard W Hinrichs, Sandra Kübler, and Karin Naumann. 2005. A unified representation for morphological, syntactic, semantic, and referential annotations. In *Proceedings of the Workshop on Frontiers in Corpus*

Annotations II: Pie in the Sky, pages 13–20. Association for Computational Linguistics.

Yufang Hou, Katja Markert, and Michael Strube. 2014. A rule-based system for unrestricted bridging resolution: Recognizing bridging anaphora and finding links to antecedents. In *EMNLP*, pages 2082–2093.

Eduard Hovy, Mitchell Marcus, Martha Palmer, Lance Ramshaw, and Ralph Weischedel. 2006. OntoNotes: the 90% solution. In *Proceedings of the human language technology conference of the NAACL, Companion Volume: Short Papers*, pages 57–60. Association for Computational Linguistics.

Katja Markert, Yufang Hou, and Michael Strube. 2012. Collective classification for fine-grained information status. In *Proceedings of the 50th Annual Meeting of the Association for Computational Linguistics: Long Papers-Volume 1*, pages 795–804. Association for Computational Linguistics.

Anna Nedoluzhko, Jiří Mírovský, Radek Ocelák, and Jiří Pergler. 2009. Extended coreferential relations and bridging anaphora in the Prague Dependency Treebank. In *Proceedings of the 7th Discourse Anaphora and Anaphor Resolution Colloquium (DAARC 2009), Goa, India*, pages 1–16.

Malvina Nissim, Shipra Dingare, Jean Carletta, and Mark Steedman. 2004. An annotation scheme for information status in dialogue. In *Proceedings of the International Conference on Language Resources and Evaluation (LREC)*.

Maciej Ogrodniczuk, Mateusz Kopec, and Agata Savary. 2014. Polish coreference corpus in numbers. In *Proceedings of the International Conference on Language Resources and Evaluation (LREC)*, pages 3234–3238.

Massimo Poesio and Ron Artstein. 2008. Anaphoric annotation in the ARRAU corpus. In *Proceedings of the International Conference on Language Resources and Evaluation (LREC)*.

Massimo Poesio and Renata Vieira. 1998. A corpus-based investigation of definite description use. *Computational linguistics*, 24(2):183–216.

Massimo Poesio, Rahul Mehta, Axel Maroudas, and Janet Hitzeman. 2004. Learning to resolve bridging references. In *Proceedings of the 42nd Annual Meeting on Association for Computational Linguistics*, page 143. Association for Computational Linguistics.

Massimo Poesio. 2004. The MATE/GNOME proposals for anaphoric annotation, revisited. In *Proceedings of the 5th SIGdial Workshop on Discourse and Dialogue*, pages 154–162.

Marta Recasens, Eduard H Hovy, and Maria Antònia Martí. 2010. A typology of near-identity relations for coreference (NIDENT). In *Proceedings of the International Conference on Language Resources and Evaluation (LREC)*.

Marta Recasens, Maria Antònia Martí, and Constantin Orasan. 2012. Annotating near-identity from coreference disagreements. In *LREC*, pages 165–172.

Arndt Riester, David Lorenz, and Nina Seemann. 2010. A recursive annotation scheme for referential information status. In *Proceedings of the International Conference on Language Resources and Evaluation (LREC)*.

Julia Ritz, Stefanie Dipper, and Michael Götze. 2008. Annotation of information structure: an evaluation across different types of texts. In *Proceedings of the International Conference on Language Resources and Evaluation (LREC)*.

Bridging Relations in Polish: Adaptation of Existing Typologies

Maciej Ogrodniczuk
Institute of Computer Science
Polish Academy of Sciences
Jana Kazimierza 5
01-248 Warsaw, Poland
maciej.ogrodniczuk@ipipan.waw.pl

Magdalena Zawisławska
Institute of Polish Language
Warsaw University
Krakowskie Przedmieście 26/28
00-927 Warsaw, Poland
zawisla@uw.edu.pl

Abstract

The paper attempts at presenting initial verification of existing approaches to annotation of bridging relations by proposing a compiled model based on schemata used in previous annotation projects and testing its validity on a corpus of Polish. The categorization features structural relations, dissimilation, analogy, reference to label, class, entailment and attribution. Multiple categories can be assigned to model situations where several aspects of the relation play a part. The relations are organized hierarchically which allows varied granularity of processing depending on computational needs. The classification is confronted with existing annotation of other-than-identity relations in a portion of Polish Coreference Corpus. Results of manual annotation involving two annotators and adjudicator are presented. Findings from the process are intended to facilitate development of annotation guidelines of a new reference-related project.

1 Introduction

The term *bridging* (bridging anaphora, indirect anaphora, associative anaphora) refers to relations between non-coreferential expressions that influence the text coherence. In most cases these expressions are nominal (and we will limit our analysis to such cases in this paper), although bridging between events can be also distinguished.

Several classifications of bridging relations are available, both in theoretical approaches (Clark, 1975; Prince, 1981; Löbner, 1996; Asher and Lascarides, 1998) and previous annotation projects (Poesio et al., 1997; Poesio, 2000; Gardent et al., 2003; Poesio et al., 2004; Poesio and Artstein, 2008). Another source of inspiration can be found in ontologies such as Cyc (Lenat, 1995) or lexical databases such as WordNet (Fellbaum, 1998) Yet there seem to be no consensus over general classification of such phenomenon.

In the article we attempt to compile the existing taxonomies of bridging relations into a common model, validate it on corpus data and present findings from the process which are planned to help develop annotation guidelines for the new project involving annotation of referential relations in Polish.

2 Related Work

Clark's classic classification of indirect implicature (Clark, 1975) lists *set membership*, *indirect reference by association* (necessary/probable/inducible parts) *indirect reference by characterization* (necessary/optional roles), *reason*, *cause*, *consequence* and *concurrence*.

Poesio, Vieira and Teufel's classification (Poesio et al., 1997) is composed of six classes: *synonymy/hyponymy/meronymy*, *names*, *compound nouns*, *events*, *discourse topic* and *inference*.

Gardent et al. (2003) summarize bridging relations identified in the literature listing 13 cat-

Proceedings of the Workshop on Coreference Resolution Beyond OntoNotes (CORBON 2016), co-located with NAACL 2016, pages 16–22,
San Diego, California, June 16, 2016. ©2016 Association for Computational Linguistics

egories (*set–subset, set–element, event–argument, individual–function, individual–attribute, whole–part, whole–piece, individual–stuff, collection–member, place–area, whole–temp.subpart, location–object* and *time–object*) and propose their own approach applied in annotation of PAROLE corpus, limited to: *set membership* (inclusion relation), *thematic relation* (thematic roles such as agent, patient etc.), *definitional relation* (attribute, meronymy etc.), *co-participant relation* and *non-lexical relation* (defined by discourse structure or world knowledge).

Poesio and Artstein's annotation scheme for AR-RAU (Poesio and Artstein, 2008) allows *part–of*, *set–membership* and *converse* relation, which probably results from successful annotation of such limited number of relations in GNOME (Poesio, 2000) and VENEX corpora (Poesio et al., 2004). The solution is similar to Recasens' annotation in CESS-ECE corpus (Recasens et al., 2007), using 3 basic relations and *rest* type with no further subtype specification.

Irmer's classification (Irmer, 2010) splits indirect references into mereological (*part-of, member-of*) and frame-related (thematic, causal, spatial, temporal) and offers a useful comparison of four other analyzed classifications (Winston et al., 1987; Iris, 1988; Vieu and Aurnague, 2007; Kleiber, 1999) which seem to differ in detail only.

Greek Coreference and Bridging Team's annotation guidelines (GCBT: Greek Coreference & Bridging Team, 2014) use *contrast, possession–owner*, two predicate relations, *entity–property* and *object–function* apart from traditional *set–subset* and *part–whole* relations. Other relations (spatial, temporal, generic–specific, thematic or situational association) are represented as *rest*.

Prague Dependency Treebank (PDT) in its present 3.0 version (Zikánová et al., 2015, chapter 4) uses six bridging relation types: *part–whole, set–subset/element, entity–singular function, contrast* (linking coherence-relevant discourse opposites), *non-coreferential explicit anaphoric relation* and *rest* (further unspecified group with *location–resident*, relations between relatives, *author–work, event–argument* and *object–instrument*).

3 Compilation of Typology of Bridging Relations

The proposed initial classification unifying existing approaches is depicted in Figure 1. Each main branch represents the intended relation type; leaf relations are specified as examples only.

3.1 Metareference

The relation allows to model relations such as *has–model, has–name* or *has–label*. This covers e.g. PDT's meta-linguistic reference, a subtype of non-cospecifying anaphoric relation.

(1)   *Byłem wczoraj w restauracji „Smaczna rybka", ale ich ryby mi w ogóle nie smakowały.*
'I was yesterday in a restaurant called "Delicious Fish" but I didn't like their fish at all.'

3.2 Class

Class-instance relation, for some seen as of privileged nature, is represented similarly to standard *part–whole* or *set–member*, so reference between class and instance can be modelled in a unified manner.

(2)   *Kobiety mają prawo do takiej wolności. Dlatego dobrze, by Ewa przekonała się, że nie wszystko musi być tak, jak było w rodzinnym domu.*
'Women have the right to such freedom. It is all right then for Eve to get convinced that not everything must be as it was in her family home.'

3.3 Temporal Relation

Temporal relation will be used to represent near-identical temporal aspects of the object (e.g. 'pre-war Warsaw' and 'Warsaw of today'). Note that traditional temporal expressions such as anaphoric references to the time when the antecedent situation takes place (e.g. 'this time' and an event; a subtype of PDT's non-cospecifying anaphoric relation) will not be marked as temporal bridging relations (due to nominal intention of the current typology).

(3)   *Warszawa jest pięknym miastem, ale przedwojenna Warszawa była jeszcze*

Figure 1: Bridging relations: compiled version

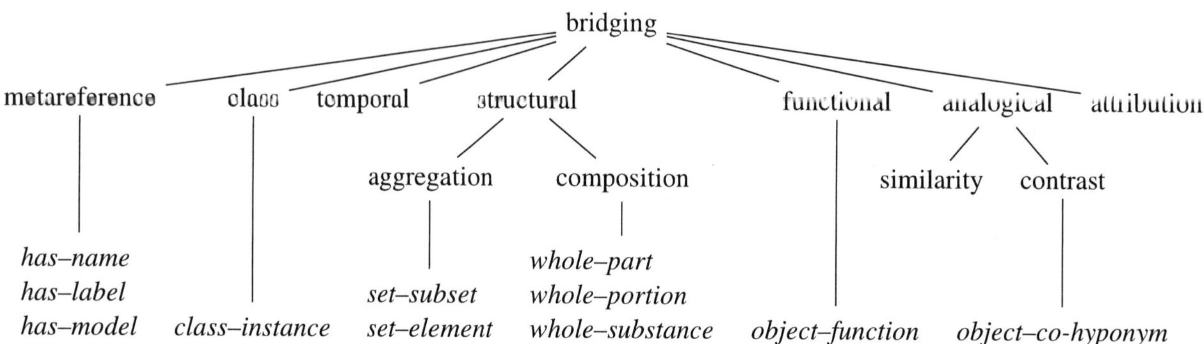

piękniejsza.
'Warsaw is a beautiful city, but <u>pre-war Warsaw</u> was even more beautiful.'

3.4 Structural Relation

Structural or meronymic relations are probably the least controversial part of the taxonomy, starting with Clark's necessary/probable/inducible parts through standard aggregation (*set–subset*, *set–element*) and composition (*whole–part*) to relations introducing inseparability such as *whole–portion* (also called *segment*, e.g. 'cake/slice') or *whole–substance* (e.g. 'cake/flour'). A ready-to-use sub-classification of meronymic relations can be found e.g. in (Winston et al., 1987).

(4)   *Dobrze się czuję jako matka <u>synów</u>. <u>Mój pierwszy syn</u> nazywa się Adam.*
'I am feeling good as a mother of <u>sons</u>. <u>My first son</u> is Adam.'

3.5 Functional Relation

The basic *function–object* relation (as e.g. in PDT), causal relations from literature, Clark's necessary/optional role and Gardent's *thematic relation* can be interpreted as functional relations. Most PDT's 'other' relations such as *location–resident*, *event–argument* or *author–work* are also regarded as functional.

Clark's indirect reference by characterization also falls into this category, though it is mostly used for events and not objects.

The most interesting aspect of the functional relation is its correspondence with Recasens' near-identity (Recasens et al., 2012). In our opinion such weak near-identity cases as *representation* (e.g. between a manuscript and its content printed in a book) should be modelled as functional relations.

(5)   *Intencja <u>konkursu</u> nie jest literacka, ale socjologiczna. Jeśli w <u>wyniku</u> wyłonią się jakieś talenty, będzie bardzo dobrze.*
'Intention of <u>the contest</u> is not literary but sociological. If any talents emerge as <u>a result</u>, we will be very fine.'

3.6 Analogical Relation

Both similarity relations (signaled by *such as* etc.) and contrast relations are intended to be marked as analogical.

(6)   *<u>Jego głowa</u> była ogromna. Jak <u>wielki balon</u>.*
'<u>His head</u> was enormous. Like a <u>big balloon</u>.'

3.7 Attribution

Attribution is a type introduced to represent relations between an object and someone's opinion on the object (i.e., what is believed, doubted etc.) or indicate incomplete certainty about the nature of identity between two mentions.

(7)   *— Jak się nazywa <u>mąż Ani</u>?*
— Chyba <u>Michał</u>.
'— What's the name of <u>Anna's husband</u>?
— <u>Michał</u>, I guess.'

In most projects this relation is annotated as coreference, but in general case (e.g., when several clashing opinions are represented in one discourse) such approach seems to be inappropriate.

		Metareference	Class	Temporal	Aggregation	Composition	Functional	Similarity	Contrast	Attribution	Coreference	Predicate	Other	ALL
1	Metareference	1	2		2								1	6
2	Class	1	15		7					1			1	25
3	Temporal		2	2										4
4	Aggregation	1	15		70	3	1			3	5	3	2	103
	Composition		1			8	1				2	2		14
5	Functional		3		5	1	9	2	1		3		1	25
6	Similarity							4						4
	Contrast				6									6
7	Attribution				2									2
8	Coreference		9		12	2	3	2		6	11	1	2	48
	Predicate				1	1				4		3		9
	Other		1		1	1	1			1			4	9
	ALL	3	48	2	106	16	15	8	1	15	21	9	11	255

Table 1: Results of the annotation experiment.

4 From Quasi-identity To Bridging Relations

The proposed classification was initially validated on the Polish Coreference Corpus (Ogrodniczuk et al., 2015, chapter 8). During its annotation, apart from marking direct identity-of-reference, annotators were asked to identify 'quasi-identity' relations, i.e. relations distorting or distinguishing properties of an object, metaphorical relations between substance and container, set-element relations and other relations not characterized by identity or nonidentity. Over 5100 instances of such relations were marked, making a useful resource for corpus-based investigation of bridging.

4.1 Preliminary Corpus-based Verification

Randomly selected 5%, i.e. 255 relations, were reviewed to provide material for evaluation of the proposed taxonomy. The process was carried out by two annotators previously involved in classification of quasi-identity relations in the Polish Coreference Corpus. Cases incompatible with the current proposal of the typology were marked as 'other' with three subtypes: 1) coreference, for cases where original annotators of the Polish Coreference Corpus set quasi-identity type to a direct coreferential relation by mistake, 2) predicate, where relation was used to link mention with a predicate noun, and 3) error, for cases when no relation could be identified reasonably.

The results of this experiment are presented in Table 1. The annotation agreement was 0.50 (Cohen's $\kappa = 0.36$) which indicates that the typology is not precise enough to be used efficiently in practice.

The prevailing share of structural relations (60%) is compatible with Gardent's findings (Gardent et al., 2003, Figure 5) where 52% of the investigated relations were of meronymic type.

Figure 2: Bridging relations: updated version

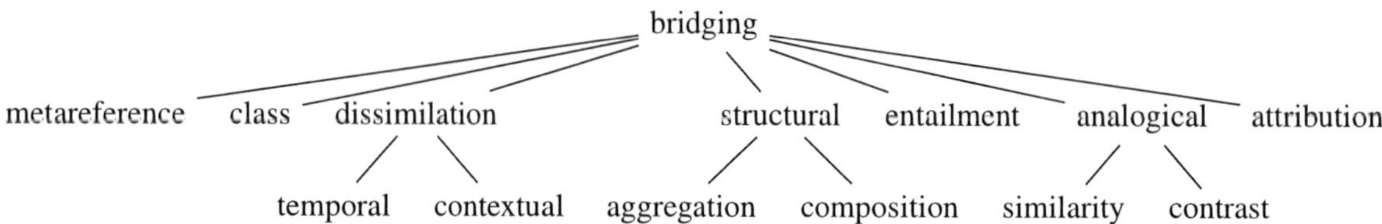

4.2 Error Analysis

The probable causes of divergence in the annotation are: 1) too extensive annotation categories, 2) too vague definition of some categories, 3) too many non-classified phenomena, 4) confusion of the coreference, near-identity and other semantic relations.

Some categories distinguished at the beginning turned out to be too extensive. Almost 44% examples were classified as of the *set* category. On the other hand, this category includes very diverse examples which calls for its division into subcategories in the prospective annotation.

The definitions of the *predicative* and *attribution* classes were not clear enough which led to confusion. Other difficult pairs were: *class* and *set*, *class* and *function*, *class* and *meta*.

In the proposed classification the category *other* was included for all doubtful examples. The annotations had shown that too many examples were classified as *other* and that there are quite distinct categories like: causality, connection of content or dissimilation.

In some cases making the distinction between definiteness and indefiniteness is virtually impossible. For example, when previous part of the text includes information on a merger of companies A and B and then someone comments that the idea of a merger of companies is cost-justified, it depends on interpretation whether it refers to this particular merger (and in such case makes an *composition* relation between *companies* and *A*) or it refers to a general statement which makes *A* an instance of companies referred to in the subsequent statement. Such cases are a frequent cause of disagreement in our annotation.

The data shows numerous coreferential links which are reported as other since only non-coreferential relations should be present in the annotated set. This can be explained with problems related to distinguishing other-than-coreferential re-

lations from different linguistic means of expressing proper coreference, particularly in the initial phase of the annotation. A common observed mistake was treating mentions from indirect speech as non-coreferential with their direct speech equivalents — despite their identical reference targets.

Functional category calls for subclassification; several cases were commented as being best defined by WordNet's entailment relation (e.g. *to sleep* is entailed by *to snore*); a few others were marked as metonymy (e.g. *Ottawa* meaning *Canada*, also confused with a simple *part–whole* relation).

Temporal category needs to be confronted with Recasens' near-identity which defines more aspects of dissimilation.

5 Updated Version of the Typology

5.1 The Revised Model

Figure 2 presents the revised version of the typology of bridging relations based on findings from the annotation process. *Contextual dissimilation* can be used in cases when different realization or representation is being referred to in the process of refocusing (Fauconnier, 1994); *entailment* is mostly *effect* which corresponds to reason–cause relation (war–occupation, manure–smell, competition–result etc.) while function groups general role-casting relations such as place–inhabitant, writer–work etc.

Within the most coarse-grained and abundantly represented aggregation subclass several evident subcategories were identified: *collection*, *group* and *hyponymy–hypernymy*. Collections are ad hoc sets of generally unrelated objects, e.g. shopping items while elements of a group are related, e.g. members of the same organization. Hyponyms are collections of objects related by a common hypernym (e.g. animals vs. monkeys, elephants etc.)

Table 2 presents statistics of different relations observed in the analyzed set (after adjudication and conversion of annotation results to the new typology).

Relation facet	Count
Structural	**122**
Aggregation	105
Collection	7
Group	63
Hyponymy	35
Composition	17
Class	**44**
Entailment	**14**
Effect	8
Function	6
Attribution	**13**
Analogical	**5**
Similarity	3
Contrast	2
Metareference	**3**
Dissimilation	**2**
Temporal	1
Contextual	1
Error	**52**
Coreference	17
Apposition	11
Predicate	9
Other	15

Table 2: Post-adjudication statistics of bridging relations.

5.2 Transitivity of Facets

An important aspect of referential associations which does not seem to be covered by existing approaches is transitivity of basic relations, i.e. ability to maintain a more distant but still decodable relation than just atomic link between a pair of referents. To illustrate the case, Example 8 shows a mixture of aggregation and composition: the link between a set and part of one element in the set is clear to understand yet reasonably complex: my sons → my son → my son's broken leg. Example 9 shows a similar mixture of functional relation and attribution.

(8) *Moi synowie uwielbiają niebezpieczną jazdę na desce. Nawet złamana noga nie zniechęciła ich do startu w kolejnych*

zawodach.
    'My sons love risky skateboarding. Even the broken leg did not discourage them from entering the next competition.'

(9) *Oto Jean. Niektórzy mówią, przyszły prezydent Francji.*
    'This is Jean. Some say, the future president of France.'

6   Conclusions

The presented unified classification of bridging relations intends to be an initial step towards annotation of referential relations on a larger scale. The typology covers only relations available in existing models and preliminarily annotated data but several other aspects of referentiality should be verified against the corpus, e.g. the issue of definiteness, negation or natural ambiguity.

The experiment confirmed that clear identification of types of bridging relations is a difficult task, particularly when fine-grained distinctions are introduced. This leads to conclusion that shallow semantics is probably insufficient to describe such a complex phenomenon as reference. A new annotation guidelines taking into account discourse structure, lexical-semantic models and extra-linguistic knowledge are currently under preparation.

Acknowledgements

The work reported here was carried out within the research project financed by the Polish National Science Centre (contract number 2014/15/B/HS2/03435).

References

Nicholas Asher and Alex Lascarides. 1998. Bridging. *Journal of Semantics*, 15(1):83–113.

Herbert H. Clark. 1975. Bridging. In *Proceedings of the 1975 Workshop on Theoretical Issues in Natural Language Processing*, TINLAP 1975, pages 169–174, Stroudsburg, PA, USA. Association for Computational Linguistics.

Gilles Fauconnier. 1994. *Mental Spaces: Aspects of Meaning Construction in Natural Language*. Cambridge University Press.

Christiane Fellbaum, editor. 1998. *WordNet. An Electronic Lexical Database*. The MIT Press, Cambridge, MA; London, May.

Claire Gardent, Hélène Manuélian, and Eric Kow. 2003. Which bridges for bridging definite descriptions? In *Proceedings of the EACL 2003 Workshop on Linguistically Interpreted Corpora*, pages 69–76.

GCBT: Greek Coreference & Bridging Team. 2014 Coreference & Bridging Annotation Guidelines.

Madelyn Anne Iris. 1988. Problems of the Part-Whole Relation. In Martha Evens, editor, *Relational Models of the Lexicon*, pages 261–288. Cambridge University Press, New York, NY, USA.

Matthias Irmer. 2010. *Bridging Inferences in Discourse Interpretation*. Ph.D. thesis, University of Leipzig.

Georges Kleiber. 1999. Associative anaphora and part-whole relationship: The condition of alienation and the principle of ontological congruence. *Journal of Pragmatics*, 31(3):339–362.

Sebastian Löbner. 1996. Definite associative anaphora. In S. Botley, editor, *Approaches to Discourse Anaphora: Proceedings of the Discourse Anaphora and Resolution Colloquium (DAARC 96)*, pages 28–39, Lancaster University.

Douglas B. Lenat. 1995. Cyc: A large-scale investment in knowledge infrastructure. *Commun. ACM*, 38(11):33–38, November.

Maciej Ogrodniczuk, Katarzyna Głowińska, Mateusz Kopeć, Agata Savary, and Magdalena Zawisławska. 2015. *Coreference in Polish: Annotation, Resolution and Evaluation*. Walter De Gruyter.

Massimo Poesio and Ron Artstein. 2008. Anaphoric Annotation in the ARRAU Corpus. In Nicoletta Calzolari, Khalid Choukri, Bente Maegaard, Joseph Mariani, Jan Odijk, Stelios Piperidis, and Daniel Tapias, editors, *Proceedings of the 6th International Conference on Language Resources and Evaluation (LREC 2008)*, pages 1170–1174, Marrakech, Morroco. European Language Resources Association.

Massimo Poesio, Renata Vieira, and Simone Teufel. 1997. Resolving Bridging References in Unrestricted Text. In *Operational Factors in Practical, Robust Anaphora Resolution for Unrestricted Texts*, pages 1–6.

Massimo Poesio, Rodolfo Delmonte, Antonella Bristot, Luminita Chiran, and Sara Tonelli. 2004. The VENEX corpus of anaphora and deixis in spoken and written Italian. Unpublished manuscript. Available at `cswww.essex.ac.uk/poesio/publications/VENEX04.pdf`.

Massimo Poesio. 2000. The GNOME annotation scheme manual. Technical report, University of Essex, United Kingdom.

Ellen F. Prince. 1981. Toward a taxonomy of given-new information. In P. Cole, editor, *Syntax and semantics: Vol. 14. Radical Pragmatics*, pages 223–255. Academic Press, New York.

Marta Recasens, Antònia Martí, and Mariona Taulé. 2007. Where Anaphora and Coreference Meet. Annotation in the Spanish CESS-ECE Corpus. In *Proceedings of RANLP 2007, Borovets, Bulgaria*, pages 504–509

Marta Recasens, Antònia Martí, and Constantin Orasan. 2012. Annotating Near-Identity from Coreference Disagreements. In Nicoletta Calzolari (Conference Chair), Khalid Choukri, Thierry Declerck, Mehmet Uğur Doğan, Bente Maegaard, Joseph Mariani, Asuncion Moreno, Jan Odijk, and Stelios Piperidis, editors, *Proceedings of the Eight International Conference on Language Resources and Evaluation (LREC 2012)*, Istanbul, Turkey, may. European Language Resources Association (ELRA).

Laure Vieu and Michel Aurnague. 2007. Part-of relations, functionality and dependence. In Michel Aurnague, Maya Hickmann, and Laure Vieu, editors, *The categorization of spatial entities in language and cognition*, volume 20 of *Human Cognitive Processing*, pages 307–336. John Benjamins Publishing Company.

Morton E. Winston, Roger Chaffin, and Douglas J. Herrman. 1987. A Taxonomy of Part-Whole Relations. *Cognitive Science*, 11(4):417–444.

Šárka Zikánová, Eva Hajičová, Barbora Hladká, Pavlína Jínová, Jiří Mírovský, Anja Nedoluzhko, Lucie Poláková, Kateřina Rysová, Magdaléna Rysová, and Jan Václ. 2015. *Discourse and Coherence. From the Sentence Structure to Relations in Text*. Institute of Formal and Applied Linguistics.

Beyond Identity Coreference:
Contrasting Indicators of Textual Coherence in English and German

Kerstin Kunz
Universität Heidelberg
Heidelberg, Germany

Ekaterina Lapshinova-Koltunski
Universität des Saarlandes
Saarbrücken, Germany

José Manuel Martínez
Universität des Saarlandes
Saarbrücken, Germany

`kerstin.kunz@iued.uni-heidelberg.de`
`{e.lapshinova,j.martinez}@mx.uni-saarland.de`

Abstract

This paper focuses on the interaction of chains of coreference identity with other types of relations, comparing English and German data sets in terms of language, mode (written vs. spoken) and register. We first describe the types of coreference and the chain features analysed as indicators of textual coherence and topic continuity. After sketching the feature categories under analysis and the methods used for statistical evaluation, we present the findings from our analysis and interpret them in terms of the contrasts mentioned above. We will also show that for some registers, coreference types other than identity are of great importance.

1 Introduction

This paper presents the findings from an empirical analysis of different types of coreference chains in a corpus of English and German written and spoken registers. The motivation lying behind our study is twofold.

First, our objective is to analyse the interaction between typical relations of coreference identity and other relations in chains, e.g. type-instance, part-whole, etc. Example (1) illustrates a coreference chain consisting of the antecedent *town* and anaphors expressed via It/it, and a lexical chain with the elements *town, Reigate, London, village, place, Banstead*, establishing relations of type/(co-)instance (e.g. *town – Reigate/London*), hyper-/hyponymy (*place – village/town*).

(1)   *I live in a <u>town</u> called <u>Reigate</u>. <u>It</u>'s between <u>London</u> and the countryside which is quite nice. It takes us about 25 minutes to get to <u>London</u> on the train. I say <u>it</u>'s a <u>town</u>, <u>it</u>'s more of a <u>village</u>. <u>It</u>'s quite small. <u>It</u>'s very nice actually, <u>it</u>'s a nice <u>place</u> to live. And I grew up in a <u>place</u> called <u>Banstead</u> which is fairly close to <u>Reigate</u>.*

We focus on the features of such chains, including the type of the semantic relations, the distance between chain elements, the number of chains as well as chain length. Hence, the focus is not on the formal types of anaphors and antecedents but on the relations themselves. These features serve as indicators of how coherence and topic continuity are overtly expressed in texts.

Second, another aim of this study is to analyse specific properties of textual coherence. The intention here is to see which factor plays a more important role for variation in coherence: language (English vs. German), mode of production (written vs. spoken) or register (political essays, interviews, popular scientific texts and fictional texts containing dialogues).

Knowledge about these coherence types may advance automatic multilingual coreference resolution, which is, however, beyond the scope of this study.

2 Related Work

Most existing studies concentrate on the properties of anaphors and antecedents only, describing their structural and functional properties. Some of them,

Proceedings of the Workshop on Coreference Resolution Beyond OntoNotes (CORBON 2016), co-located with NAACL 2016, pages 23–31,
San Diego, California, June 16, 2016. ©2016 Association for Computational Linguistics

mostly theoretical, e.g. (Ariel, 2001; Kibrik, 2011), are related to the model of referential choice based on the degree of referent salience. Algorithms describing the degree of salience were presented by Hajičová et al. (2006); Lambrecht (1994), Strube & Hahn (1999), etc.

There also exists a considerable amount of large-scale annotated data for coreference, anaphoric relations, event anaphora, bridging relations and so on, compiled mostly for automatic anaphora resolution (MUC-6 (1995), MUC-7 (1997) or ACE NIST (Doddington et al., 2004) and more recently CoNNL 2011 (Pradhan et al., 2011). However, most of these corpora are monolingual and cannot be applied for a multilingual analysis, as they do not contain comparable registers across languages. For instance, the largest coreference corpus for English is OntoNotes (Technologies, 2006) containing several genres. For German, the TüBa-D/Z corpus (Telljohann et al., 2012) was annotated with semantic and coreference information, but contains newspaper texts only.

Besides, the number of studies that base their analysis on corpora annotated with chains, e.g. as described in (Zikánová et al., 2015; Lapshinova-Koltunski and Kunz, 2014a) , is rather small in contrast to those just using the annotation of relations. Yet, an extensive comparison from a multilingual perspective is missing.

3 Phenomena under analysis

Our focus therefore is on the textual relations set up in what we call **chains** in our study. A chain minimally consists of a tie between an anaphor and an antecedent, yet many chains are larger and contain several anaphors. We mainly distinguish two types of chains: **coreference chains** and **lexical chains**.

The coreference chains in our framework not only include relations of identity between **entities**, as between *town* and *it* in example (1) above, but also **abstract** and **situation anaphora** as in (2), where *That* refers to the underlined preceding clause.

(2)   *They may cry, and <u>we find it very hard to find out why</u> ... That's difficult.*

The formal types of anaphors annotated in coreference chains are mainly function words (i.e. grammatical types of cohesion) and include personal and possessive pronouns, demonstrative determiners, demonstrative pronouns, the definite article, and local and temporal adverbs (*here, there, now, then*). The annotated antecedents may include NPs, clauses, clause complexes (see example (2)) or even larger textual chunks.

The lexical chains analysed in this study contain lexical relations between nominal antecedents and anaphors (nouns or nominal compounds), which vary in terms of the semantic relation between the chain elements. Relations include repetitions as between *London - London*, *place - place*, hyperonymy as between *place - town* and *place - village* in example (1) in Section 1 above and others. They are comparable to what is called **bridging** or **indirect anaphora** in the state-of-the-art literature.

Note that the two types of chains may interact as in example (3), where coreference relations are set up between the two grammatical anaphors (the demonstrative pronoun *this* and the definite article *the*) to the antecedent *reward system*. In addition, a lexical relation of hyper-/hyponymy holds between *this system* (hyperonym) and a relation of repetition between *the system* and this antecedent.

(3)   *Neurobiologists have long known that the euphoria induced by drugs of abuse arises because all these chemicals ultimately boost the activity of the brain's <u>reward system</u>: a complex circuit of nerve cells, or neurons, that evolved to make us feel flush after eating or sex... At least initially, goosing <u>this system</u> makes us feel good... But new research indicates that chronic drug use induces changes in the structure and function of <u>the system</u>'s neurons...*

The chain features of coreference and lexical cohesion analysed in this study include: 1) **chain length** concerns the number of elements in a coreference or a lexical chain; 2) **chain number** concerns the number of different coreference and lexical chains per text; 3) **chain distance** is the distance in tokens between different elements in the same chain. 4) **semantic relation** is the type of semantic relation between adjacent chain elements. The types analysed in this study are: 1) identity, for all elements in a coreference chain; and all kinds of other relations, namely: 2) repetition, 3) antonym, 4) synonym, 5) hyperonym, hyponym and cohyponym, 6) holonym, meronym, comeronym, 7) type, instance, coinstance. Apart from analysing each of these features separately we also study their interaction.

4 Methods and resources

4.1 Research questions

The chain features described in Section 3 indicate how coherence is created and how and to which degree topics are distributed throughout the texts. For instance, we may find long coreference chains in combination with a small distance between the respective chain elements. This points to high **topic continuity in terms of certain referents**. Furthermore, **topic continuity within one domain** is expressed by long lexical chains with small distance between elements. Small chains and low distance in combination with a high number of different chains hints at a high degree of **topic variation**, i.e. that text producers often jump from one topic to another. By contrast, long chains and high distances between elements indicates **topic interaction** i.e. that there are several important topics which are interwoven. Moreover, repetition in combination with coreference points to low **semantic variation** whereas relations of lexical cohesion such as type-instance and meronymy point to high variation.

We are additionally interested in which contrasts are more pronounced, those concerning language, mode or register (see Section 1) and which of the analysed features mainly contribute to these contrasts.

4.2 Data

For the research aims within this study, we use a data set containing texts of both written and spoken discourse. The written part was extracted from the corpus described in (Hansen-Schirra et al., 2012), whereas the spoken subcorpus was extracted from the corpus described in (Lapshinova-Koltunski et al., 2012). The whole corpus is annotated on various linguistic levels, including parts-of-speech (POS), chunks, clauses, sentences, and various devices of cohesion, i.e. coreference, discourse relations, elliptical constructions and substitution annotated as

described by Lapshinova & Kunz (2014b)[1]. Relations of coreference other than identity (synonymy, antonymy, hyponymy, etc.) were annotated for the subset of the data analysed in this study. The registers included are political essays (ESSAY), popular scientific articles (POPSCI), fictional excerpts (FICTION) and transcribed interviews (INTERVIEW). ESSAY and POPSCI represent written discourse, INTERVIEW represents spoken discourse, whereas FICTION is on the borderline, as it contains both written and spoken elements in the form of dialogues. INTERVIEW and FICTION additionally share narrative elements. The details on the analysed subset are provided in Table 1.

register	EO		GO	
	texts	tokens	texts	tokens
ESSAY	23	27171	20	31407
FICTION	10	36996	10	36778
INTERVIEW	9	30057	12	35036
POPSCI	8	27055	9	32639

Table 1: Corpus description.

4.3 Visualisation techniques

We use various techniques to investigate the distributional characteristics of subcorpora in terms of occurrences of the features described in Section 3 and to answer the questions in Section 4.1.

Box plots are used to visualise a summary of the distribution underlying a particular sample and to compare central measure values and spread of the data across groups. Special attention is given to the median (second quartile) and the IQR (range between the first and third quartile). Box plots have lines extending vertically from the boxes (whiskers) indicating variability outside the upper and lower quartiles. We use notched box plots to see if the differences between the variables are significant: if the notches of two box plots overlap, there is no evidence that their medians differ (Chambers et al., 1983). The means are also plotted for the sake of completeness. The evidence from box plots is confirmed with two-way factorial **ANOVA** tests for the significance of the differences between languages

---

[1] More information about the corpus and how to gain access to it can be found at `http://hdl.handle.net/11858/00-246C-0000-0023-8CF7-A`.

(English vs. German), registers (ESSAY vs. FIC-TION, etc.) and the interaction between these two variables. η^2 is calculated to show the variance explained by the variables and their interaction.

Mosaic plots are used to visualise a table and to examine the association between the variables. For each cell, the height of bars is proportional to the observed relative frequency. The colours indicate the standard deviation of the expected count in chi-square testing (or standardised residuals). If row and column variables are completely independent (no association), the mosaic bars for the observed values are aligned to the mosaic bars for the expected values. In case of an association, the bars are coloured according to the standardised residuals. Standardised residual is a measure of the strength of the difference between observed and expected values, and thus, a measure of how significant your cells are to the chi-square value. This helps to see which cells are contributing the most to the value.

Correlation plots are used to visualise correlations between various variables under analysis. For this, we calculate row and column profiles. The profile of a given row/column is calculated by taking each row/column point and dividing by the sum of all row/column points. Then, the squared distance is computed between each row/column profile and the other rows/columns in the table, resulting in a distance matrix (a kind of correlation matrix), which can be visualised with a correlation plot.

Correspondence analysis (CA) is a multivariate technique to observe similarities and differences between the variables under analysis using an entire set of features in interaction. It enables us to see how certain features are grouped together and where the biggest differences and similarities lie, see (Venables and Smith, 2010; Baayen, 2008; Greenacre, 2007) for details. Moreover, we are able to trace the interplay of categories of the cohesive devices under analysis. The output is plotted into a two dimensional graph. The position of the points indicates the relative importance of a feature for a subcorpus.

5 Results

5.1 Chain length

Figure 1 visually summarises the average chain length distributions across languages and registers

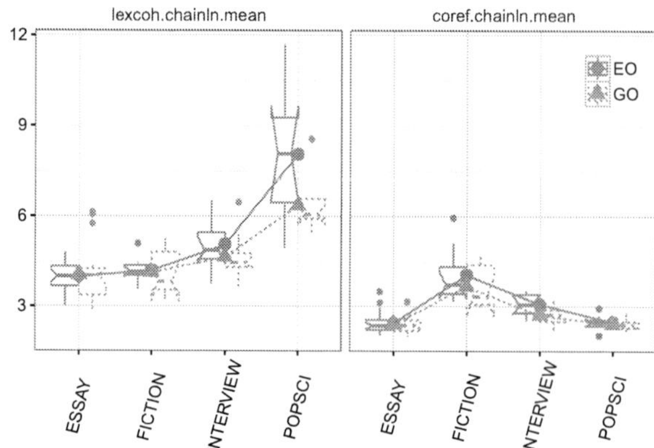

Figure 1: Average length chain: lexical cohesion vs. coreference.

for lexical and coreference chains. Regarding **lexical chains**, the data shows a significant difference between registers ($\not> .05$) and for the interaction *language:register*, whereas the difference between languages is not significant (see p values in Table 2). The register featuring the longest lexical chains and a more distinctive behaviour is POPSCI, while the other registers tend to show ($\approx 50\%$) shorter chains and differences are not so marked. As for **coreference chains**, only the difference between registers is statistically significant (see Table 3). FICTION is the register showing the longest coreference chains and the clearest difference when compared to the other registers. η^2 in Tables 2 and 3 confirms that the independent variable *register* is the factor explaining a higher proportion ($\approx 60\%$) of the variation observed for both types of chains, whereas the effect of *language* and the interaction *language:register* is negligible.

	p	η^2
language	0.0512459	0.02
register	0.0000000	0.59
language:register	0.0135995	0.04

Table 2: Two-way factorial ANOVA significance tests and effect sizes for lexical chains.

	p	η^2
language	0.0488657	0.02
register	0.0000000	0.60
language:register	0.4213339	0.01

Table 3: Two-way factorial ANOVA significance tests and effect sizes for coreference chains.

5.2 Chain number

Figure 2 shows a significant difference between registers for **lexical chains** with respect to the number of chains, and for the interaction *language:register* ($\not> .05$). The register featuring the highest number of lexical chains is FICTION, at the other end of the spectrum we find ESSAY ($\approx 33\%$ of FICTION), both registers show a clearcut difference when compared with INTERVIEW and POPSCI, which are located somewhere in the middle. Although the difference between languages is not significant (see p values in Table 4), there is an interesting difference in terms of register ranking. As for **coreference chains**, the picture is almost the same. We observe a slightly lower number of coreference chains than lexical chains. Nevertheless, the difference is not so marked as with chain length. η^2 in Tables 4 and 5 confirms that the independent variable *register* is the factor explaining a higher proportion ($\approx 50\%$ for lexical chains, $\approx 60\%$ for coreference) of the variation observed for both types of chains, whereas the effect of *language* and the interaction *language:register* is negligible.

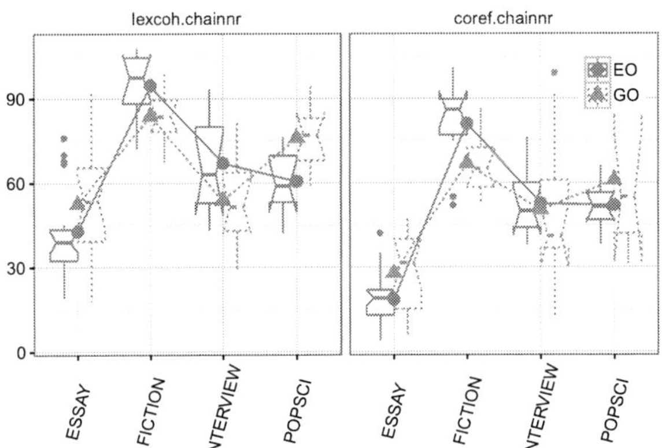

Figure 2: Number of chains: lexical cohesion vs. coreference.

	p	η^2
language	0.5652659	0.00
register	0.0000000	0.47
language:register	0.0060930	0.06

Table 4: Two-way factorial ANOVA significance tests and effect sizes for lexical chains.

	p	η^2
language	0.4941296	0.00
register	0.0000000	0.62
language:register	0.0338786	0.03

Table 5: Two-way factorial ANOVA significance tests and effect sizes for coreference chains.

5.3 Chain distance

Regarding **lexical chains**, Figure 3 shows a significant difference between registers, taking into account the average distance between elements of the chains. By contrast, the difference between languages is not significant (see p values in Table 6). The register showing the greatest average distance between elements in lexical chains is FICTION, at the other end of the spectrum we find ESSAY ($\approx 50\%$ of FICTION), both registers disassociate from INTERVIEW and POPSCI, which are located somewhere in the middle. **Coreference chains** show a completely different picture this time: Differences between registers are again significant. However, FICTION and INTERVIEW stand out as the registers with the highest distance between elements of chains, ESSAY is again the register showing the lowest distance, and POPSCI is situated in the middle. Quite remarkably, there clearly is a higher spread of the distributions for **coreference** than for **lexical chains** denoted by the IQR and the standard deviation reaching proportions up to 1 to 3 in some cases. The magnitude and range of the values is very similar for both lexical and coreference chains. Finally, η^2 in Tables 6 and 7 confirms that the independent variable *register* is the factor explaining a higher proportion of the variation observed for both lexical chains ($\approx 60\%$) and to a less extent for coreference ($\approx 30\%$), whereas the effect of *language* and the interaction *language:register* is negligible.

	p	η^2
language	0.5291255	0.00
register	0.0000000	0.61
language:register	0.1872871	0.02

Table 6: Two-way factorial ANOVA significance tests and effect sizes for lexical chains.

5.4 Combination of chain features

First, we prove if there is an association between the variables under analysis using a mosaic plot illus-

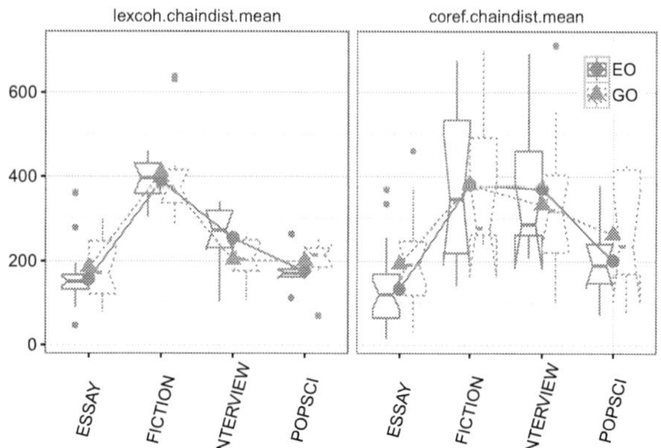

Figure 3: Average chain distance: lexical cohesion vs. coreference.

	p	η^2
language	0.3216957	0.01
register	0.0000001	0.32
language:register	0.5594535	0.02

Table 7: Two-way factorial ANOVA significance tests and effect sizes for coreference chains.

trated in Figure 4.

Blue colour indicates that the observed value is higher than the expected value if the data were random, whereas red colour specifies that the observed value is lower. The number of lexical chains is very important in both English and German for ESSAY, distance between elements in coreference chains plays a great role in INTERVIEW (however, more in English than in German). The distance between elements in lexical chains is strong in FICTION (however, more in German than in English). Overall, this confirms our observations in Sections 5.1, 5.2 and 5.3 above.

We then produce a correlation plot on the basis of squared distances as explained in 4.3 above. The size and the colour of the circle in the plot is proportional to the magnitude of the distance between register profiles, see Figure 5.

We see that cross-lingual differences between registers (e.g. EO-ESSAY vs. GO-ESSAY) are smaller than intralingual distances between registers of one language (e.g. GO-FICTION vs. GO-ESSAY). This, again, confirms our observations in the previous Sections, where we saw a prevalence of the variable *register* in the variation in our data.

Next, we analyse the association between chain

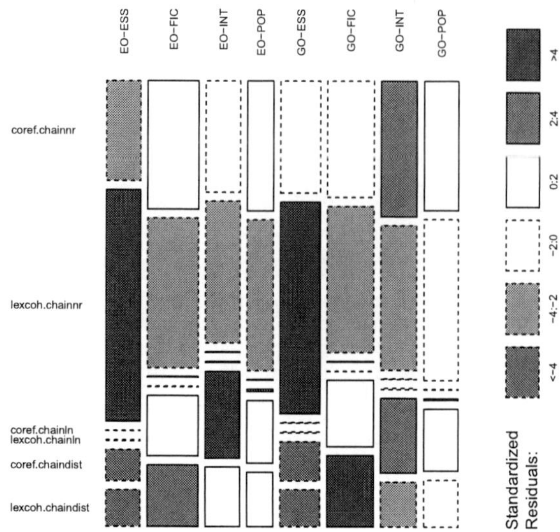

Figure 4: Standardized residuals for chain features.

properties and the registers, which is possible with a correlation graph on the basis of log-likelihood ratio (calculated on the basis of observed and expected values of chi-squared test), see Figure 6. Blue colour of the cell means a positive value and a log(ratio) that is higher than 0, whereas red colour would mean a negative value with a log(ratio) below 0. Cell size and colour intensity indicate the strength of the association.

As seen in Figure 6, all chain features are positively associated with all registers of both languages though there are certain preferences. For instance, length of lexical chains is of special importance in POPSCI, especially in English, whereas their number is more specific for English and German ESSAY. Distance between elements in chains play a greater role for INTERVIEW and FICTION, as already seen above (see Figure 4).

5.5 Semantic relations

For the semantic relations under analysis (see Section 4.1 above), we start with the association between the variables proved with a mosaic plot illustrated in Figure 7.

This plot clearly shows that identity relations are more important in both fictional registers, repetitions in English essays and interviews, hyponymy and meronymy relations are more typical for both popular-scientific registers. Fictional texts in both languages show strong preferences for using coref-

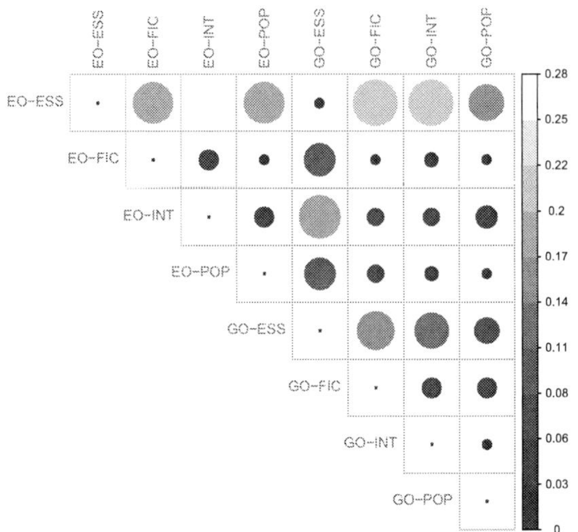

Figure 5: Correlations between language-register profiles.

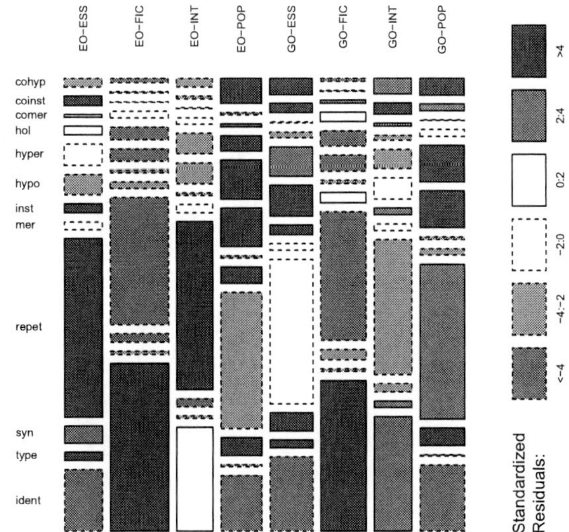

Figure 7: Standardized residuals for semantic relations.

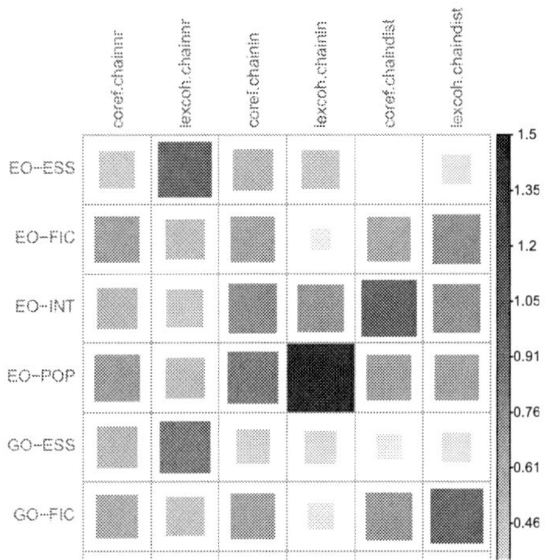

Figure 6: Associations between chain features and registers.

erence, whereas this semantic type is much less important for political essays and popular-scientific articles. In general, the coloured patterns for registers of both languages seem to be similar, which confirms the observation on the strength of registerial contrast in our data.

Next, we analyse the correlations between register profiles in our data (based on distance matrix), visualised in Figure 8.

Again, cross-lingual differences between registers are smaller here. At the same time, the intralingual differences between registers seem to be greater in English than in German, since the circles are bigger on the left upper part of the plot. This confirms the observations from our previous analyses on lexical

cohesion, in which we used a set of shallow lexical features (TTR, LD, most frequent words, etc.). As for coreference, an opposite effect was observed in (Kunz and Lapshinova-Koltunski, 2015) for the same language pair.

Analysing association between semantic relations and the registers in a correlation plot (Figure 9) produced on the basis of log-likelihood ratio, we see that our previous observations are confirmed here too: relations of identity are strongly associated with FICTION, hyponymy and meronymy with POPSCI. Instance-type relations are typical for ESSAY.

In general, the registers with week identity associations (ESSAY and POPSCI) tend to show a strong association to other relations, i.e. hyper-/hyponymy, type-instance, etc., whereas semantic relations tend to show a lower association (FICTION and partly INTERVIEW) when the identity association is strong. This means that for certain registers (e.g. narrative ones), chain relations other than identity play a minor role.

5.6 Feature combination

In the last analysis step, we combine all the features under analysis , to map the correlations between them, as well as between registers applying CA, see Figure 10.

The plot provides us with two multilingual subcorpora groupings: FICTION and INTERVIEW on the left side, and ESSAY and POPSCI on the right

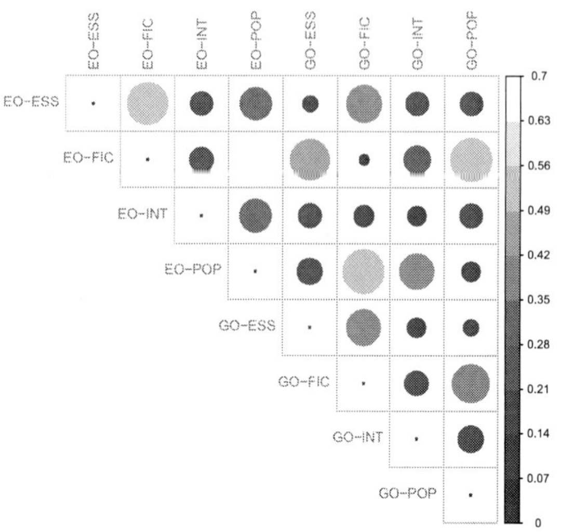

Figure 8: Correlations between language-register profiles.

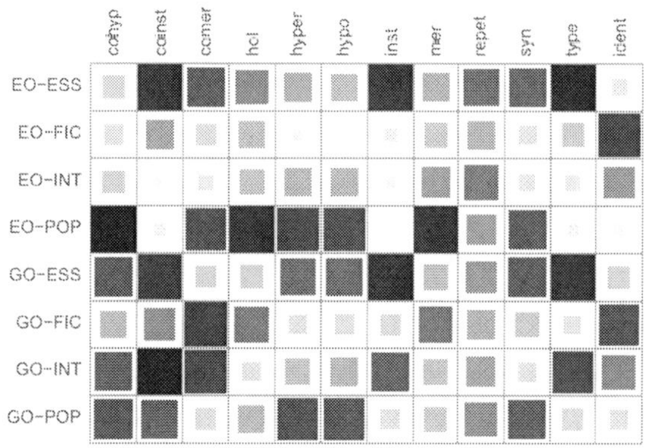

Figure 9: Associations between semantic relations and registers.

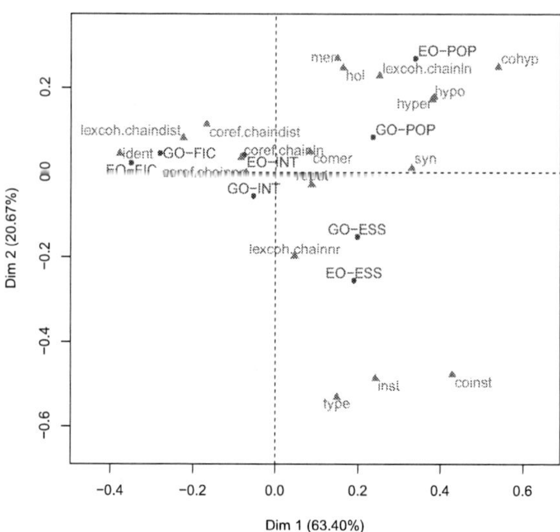

Figure 10: Correspondence analysis for all features.

side. This suggests a subdivision according to mode: written vs. spoken. In terms of features, those related to lexical cohesion are on the right side of the x-axis, and coreference-related ones on the left side. However, the distance between elements of lexical chains seems to have a correlation with the relation of identity and its chain properties, especially with the distance between elements of coreference chains (as their points are situated close to each other on the plot). Length and number of coreference chains also have a correlation and are especially important for interviews. We also observe groupings of the subtypes of semantic relations on the plot, e.g. meronym and holonym; hyperonym, hyponym and cohyponym; type, instance and coinstance.

6 Discussion

Altogether, registerial differences are more pronounced than language differences, at least for the language pair English-German. The differences and similarities observed between the registers seem to reflect typical situational configurations, some of which pointing to differences between written and spoken discourse.

In POPSCI, we find a relatively low number of long lexical chains in which the distance between elements is relatively low, in combination with a medium number of short coreference chains with low distance. This goes along with relatively high semantic variation and few repetitions, as compared to the other registers. The chain features express continuity within one topic domain and a detailed development of these topics, reflecting the intention of information distribution. In ESSAY, we observe the lowest frequencies for chain number, chain length and distance in both coreference and lexical chains, pointing to a generally lower textual coherence and much topic variation. The frequent use of repetitions serve the communicative goal of persuasion. FICTION is characterized by a high number of short lexical chains and long coreference chains, with a high distance between elements of the two chain types, and with much semantic variation in lexical chains. Thus there is a focus on specific referents reflecting a narrative style together with

30

extensive use of lexical resources available in the two languages. INTERVIEW features longer chains than ESSAY and POPSCI but shorter ones than FICTION, a medium number of chains which is below FICTION and a chain distance as high as in FICTION for coreference. Apart from that, INTERVIEW equals ESSAY in low distance in lexical chains and frequent use of repetitions. This however may rather be attributed to constraints of short term memory capacity in a spoken context rather than the intention to manipulate opinions as in ESSAY.

Last but not least, our findings show that identity is not the only and most important coreference relation to build textual coherence, at least for some registers. This all the more calls for an extensive exploration of such relations in future analyses.

References

M. Ariel. 2001. Accessibility theory: An overview. In T. Sanders, J. Schliperoord, and W. Spooren, editors, *Text representation: Linguistic and psycholinguistic aspects*, pages 29–87. John Benjamins Publishing, Amsterdam, Philadelphia.

R. Harald Baayen. 2008. *Analyzing Linguistic Data. A Practical Introduction to Statistics Using R*. Cambridge University Press.

John Chambers, William Cleveland, Beat Kleiner, and Paul Tukey. 1983. *Graphical Methods for Data Analysis*. Wadsworth.

G. Doddington, A. Mitchell, M. Przybocki, L. Ramshaw, S. Strassel, and R. Weischedel. 2004. Automatic content extraction (ace) program – task definitions and performance measures. In *Proceedings of LREC-2004: 4th International Conference on Language Resources and Evaluation*, Lisbon, Portugal, May 24-30.

Michael J. Greenacre. 2007. *Correspondence analysis in practice*. Chapman & Hall/CRC, Boca Raton.

E. Hajičová, B. Hladká, and L. Kučová. 2006. An annotated corpus as a test bed for discourse structure analysis. In *Proceedings of the Workshop on Constraints in Discourse*, pages 82–89, Maynooth, Ireland. National University of Ireland.

Silvia Hansen-Schirra, Stella Neumann, and Erich Steiner. 2012. *Cross-linguistic Corpora for the Study of Translations. Insights from the Language Pair English-German*. de Gruyter, Berlin, New York.

A. A. Kibrik. 2011. *Reference in discourse*. Oxford University Press, Oxford.

Kerstin Kunz and Ekaterina Lapshinova-Koltunski. 2015. Cross-linguistic analysis of discourse variation across registers. *Special Issue of Nordic Journal of English Studies*, 14(1):258–288.

K. Lambrecht. 1994. *Information structure and sentence form. Topic, focus and the mental representation of discourse referents*. Cambridge University Press, Cambridge.

Ekaterina Lapshinova-Koltunski and Kerstin Kunz. 2014a. Annotating cohesion for multillingual analysis. In *Proceedings of the 10th Joint ACL - ISO Workshop on Interoperable Semantic Annotation*, Reykjavik, Iceland, May. LREC.

Ekaterina Lapshinova-Koltunski and Kerstin Kunz. 2014b. Annotating cohesion for multillingual analysis. In *Proceedings of the 10th Joint ACL - ISO Workshop on Interoperable Semantic Annotation*, Reykjavik, Iceland, May. LREC.

Ekaterina Lapshinova-Koltunski, Kerstin Kunz, and Marilisa Amoia. 2012. Compiling a multilingual spoken corpus. In Tommaso Raso Heliana Mello, Massimo Pettorino, editor, *Proceedings of the VIIth GSCP International Conference: Speech and corpora*, pages 79–84, Firenze. Firenze University Press.

S. Pradhan, L. Ramshaw, M Mitchell, M. Palmer, R. Weischedel, and N. Xue. 2011. Conll-2011 shared task: Modeling unrestricted coreference in ontonotes. In *Proceedings of the Fifteenth Conference on Computational Natural Language Learning: Shared Task*.

M. Strube and U. Hahn. 1999. Functional centering: Grounding referential coherence in information structure. *Computational Linguistics*, 25(3):309–344.

BBN Technologies. 2006. *Coreference Guidelines for English OntoNotes – Version 6.0*. Linguistic Data Consortium. BBN Pronoun Coreference and Entity Type Corpus.

H. Telljohann, E. Hinrichs, S. Kbler, H Zinsmeister, and K. Beck. 2012. Stylebook for the tübingen treebank of written german (tüba-d/z). Technical report, Tübingen, Germany. Revised Version.

William N. Venables and David M. Smith. 2010. *An Introduction to R. Notes on R: A Programming Environment for Data Analysis and Graphics*.

Š. Zikánová, E. Hajičová, B. Hladká, Jínová P., J. Mírovský, A. Nedoluzhko, L. Poláková, K. Rysová, M. Rysová, and J. Václ. 2015. *Discourse and Coherence. From the Sentence Structure to Relations in Text*. ÚFAL, Prague, Czech Republic.

Exploring the steps of Verb Phrase Ellipsis

Zhengzhong Liu
Language Technologies Institute
Carnegie Mellon University
Pittsburgh, PA 15213, USA
liu@cs.cmu.edu

Edgar Gonzàlez and **Dan Gillick**
Google Research
1600 Amphitheatre Parkway
Mountain View, CA 94043, USA
{edgargip, dgillick}@google.com

Abstract

Verb Phrase Ellipsis is a well-studied topic in theoretical linguistics but has received little attention as a computational problem. Here we propose a decomposition of the overall resolution problem into three tasks—target detection, antecedent head resolution, and antecedent boundary detection—and implement a number of computational approaches for each one. We also explore the relationships among these tasks by attempting joint learning over different combinations. Our new decomposition of the problem yields significantly improved performance on publicly available datasets, including a newly contributed one.

1 Introduction

Verb Phrase Ellipsis (VPE) is the anaphoric process where a verbal constituent is partially or totally unexpressed, but can be resolved through an antecedent in the context, as in the following examples:

(1) His wife also [antecedent *works for the paper*], as **did** his father.

(2) In particular, Mr. Coxon says, businesses are [antecedent *paying out a smaller percentage of their profits and cash flow in the form of dividends*] than they **have** historically.

In example 1, a light verb **did** is used to represent the verb phrase *works for the paper*; example 2 shows a much longer antecedent phrase, which in addition differs in tense from the elided one. Following Dalrymple et al. (1991), we refer to the full verb expression as the "antecedent", and to the anaphor as the "target".

VPE resolution is necessary for deeper Natural Language Understanding, and can be beneficial for instance in dialogue systems or Information Extraction applications.

Computationally, VPE resolution can be modeled as a pipeline process: first detect the VPE targets, then identify their antecedents. Prior work on this topic (Hardt, 1992; Nielsen, 2005) has used this pipeline approach but without analysis of the interaction of the different steps.

In this paper, we analyze the steps needed to resolve VPE. We preserve the target identification task, but propose a decomposition of the antecedent selection step in two subtasks. We use learning-based models to address each task separately, and also explore the combination of contiguous steps. Although the features used in our system are relatively simple, our models yield state-of-the-art results on the overall task. We also observe a small performance improvement from our decomposition modeling of the tasks.

There are only a few small datasets that include manual VPE annotations. While Bos and Spenader (2011) provide publicly available VPE annotations for Wall Street Journal (WSJ) news documents, the annotations created by Nielsen (2005) include a more diverse set of genres (e.g., articles and plays) from the British National Corpus (BNC).

We semi-automatically transform these latter annotations into the same format used by the former. The unified format allows better benchmarking and will facilitate more meaningful comparisons in the future. We evaluate our methods on both datasets, making our results directly comparable to those published by

Proceedings of the Workshop on Coreference Resolution Beyond OntoNotes (CORBON 2016), co-located with NAACL 2016, pages 32–40,
San Diego, California, June 16, 2016. ©2016 Association for Computational Linguistics

Nielsen (2005).

2   Related Work

Considerable work has been done on VPE in the field of theoretical linguistics: e.g., (Dalrymple et al., 1991; Shieber et al., 1996); yet there is much less work on computational approaches to resolving VPE.

Hardt (1992; 1997) presents, to our knowledge, the first computational approach to VPE. His system applies a set of linguistically motivated rules to select an antecedent given an elliptical target. Hardt (1998) uses Transformation-Based Learning to replace the manually developed rules. However, in Hardt's work, the targets are selected from the corpus by searching for "empty verb phrases" (constructions with an auxiliary verb only) in the gold standard parse trees.

Nielsen (2005) presents the first end-to-end system that resolves VPE from raw text input. He describes several heuristic and learning-based approaches for target detection and antecedent identification. He also discusses a post-processing substitution step in which the target is replaced by a transformed version of the antecedent (to match the context). We do not address this task here because other VPE datasets do not contain relevant substitution annotations. Similar techniques are also described in Nielsen (2004b; 2004a; 2003a; 2003b).

Results from this prior work are relatively difficult to reproduce because the annotations on which they rely are inaccessible. The annotations used by Hardt (1997) have not been made available, and those used by Nielsen (2005) are not easily reusable since they rely on some particular tokenization and parser. Bos and Spenader (2011) address this problem by annotating a new corpus of VPE on top of the WSJ section of the Penn Treebank, and propose it as a standard evaluation benchmark for the task. Still it is desirable to use Nielsen's annotations on the BNC which contain more diverse text genres with more frequent VPE.

3   Approaches

We focus on the problems of target detection and antecedent identification as proposed by Nielsen (2005). We propose a refinement of these two tasks, splitting them into these three:

1. **Target Detection (T)**, where the subset of VPE targets is identified.

2. **Antecedent Head Resolution (H)**, where each target is linked to the head of its antecedent.

3. **Antecedent Boundary Determination (B)**, where the exact boundaries of the antecedent are determined from its head.

The following sections describe each of the steps in detail.

3.1   Target Detection

Since the VPE target is annotated as a single word in the corpus[1], we model their detection as a binary classification problem. We only consider modal or light verbs (*be, do, have*) as candidates, and train a logistic regression classifier ($\mathbf{Log}^T$) with the following set of binary features:

1. The POS tag, lemma, and dependency label of the verb, its dependency parent, and the immediately preceding and succeeding words.

2. The POS tags, lemmas and dependency labels of the words in the dependency subtree of the verb, in the 3-word window, and in the same-size window after (as bags of words).

3. Whether the subject of the verb appears to its right (i.e., there is subject-verb inversion).

3.2   Antecedent Head Resolution

For each detected target, we consider as potential antecedent heads all verbs (including modals and auxiliaries) in the three immediately preceding sentences of the target word[2] as well as the sentence including the target word (up to the target[3]). This follows Hardt (1992) and Nielsen (2005).

We perform experiments using a logistic regression classifier ($\mathbf{Log}^H$), trained to distinguish correct antecedents from all other possible candidates. The set of features are shared with the Antecedent Boundary Determination task, and are described in detail in Section 3.3.1.

---

[1] All targets in the corpus of Bos and Spenader (2011) are single-word by their annotation guideline.

[2] Only 1 of the targets in the corpus of Bos and Spenader (2011), has an antecedent beyond that window.

[3] Only 1% of the targets in the corpus are cataphoric.

However, a more natural view of the resolution task is that of a ranking problem. The gold annotation can be seen as a partial ordering of the candidates, where, for a given target, the correct antecedent ranks above all other candidates, but there is no ordering among the remaining candidates. To handle this specific setting, we adopt a ranking model with domination loss (Dekel et al., 2003).

Formally, for each potential target t in the determined set of targets T, we consider its set of candidates C_t, and denote whether a candidate $c \in C_t$ is the antecedent for t using a binary variable a_{ct}. We express the ranking problem as a bipartite graph $\mathcal{G} = (V^+, V^-, E)$ where vertices represent antecedent candidates:

$$V^+ = \{(t, c) \mid t \in T, c \in C_t, a_{ct} = 1\}$$
$$V^- = \{(t, c) \mid t \in T, c \in C_t, a_{ct} = 0\}$$

and the edges link the correct antecedents to the rest of the candidates for the same target[4]:

$$E = \{((t, c^+), (t, c^-)) \mid (t, c^+) \in V^+, (t, c^-) \in V^-\}$$

We associate each vertex i with a feature vector $\mathbf{x}_i$, and compute its score s_i as a parametric function of the features $s_i = g(\mathbf{w}, \mathbf{x}_i)$. The training objective is to learn parameters $\mathbf{w}$ such that each positive vertex $i \in V^+$ has a higher score than the negative vertices j it is connected to, $V_i^- = \{j \mid j \in V^-, (i, j) \in E\}$.

The combinatorial domination loss for a vertex $i \in V^+$ is 1 if there exists any vertex $j \in V_i^-$ with a higher score. A convex relaxation of the loss for the graph is given by (Dekel et al., 2003):

$$f(w) = \frac{1}{|V^+|} \sum_{i \in V^+} \log(1 + \sum_{j \in V_i^-} \exp(s_j - s_i + \Delta))$$

Taking $\Delta = 0$, and choosing $\mathbf{g}$ to be a linear feature scoring function $s_i = \mathbf{w} \cdot \mathbf{x_i}$, the loss becomes:

$$f(w) = \frac{1}{|V^+|} \sum_{i \in V^+} \log \sum_{j \in V_i^-} \exp(\mathbf{w} \cdot \mathbf{x}_j) - \mathbf{w} \cdot x_i$$

The loss over the whole graph can then be minimized using stochastic gradient descent. We will denote the ranker learned with this approach as **Rank**^{H}.

---

[4]During training, there is always 1 correct antecedent for each gold standard target, with several incorrect ones.

> **Algorithm 1:** Candidate generation
>
> **Data**: a, the antecedent head
> **Data**: t, the target
> **Result**: B, the set of possible antecedent boundaries $(start, end)$
>
> 1 **begin**
> 2 $a_s \longleftarrow$ SemanticHeadVerb(a);
> 3 $E \longleftarrow \{a_s\}$ // *the set of ending positions*;
> 4   **for** $ch \in$ RightChildren(a_s) **do**
> 5 $e \leftarrow$ RightMostNode(ch);
> 6   **if** $e < t \wedge$ ValidEnding(e) **then**
> 7 $E \longleftarrow E \cup \{e\}$
> 8 $B \longleftarrow \emptyset$;
> 9   **for** $e \in E$ **do**
> 10 $B \longleftarrow B \cup \{(a, e)\}$;

3.3 Antecedent Boundary Determination

From a given antecedent head, the set of potential boundaries for the antecedent, which is a complete or partial verb phrase, is constructed using Algorithm 1.

Informally, the algorithm tries to generate different valid verb phrase structures by varying the amount of information encoded in the phrase. To do so, it accesses the semantic head verb a_s of the antecedent head a (e.g., *paying* for *are* in Example 2), and considers the rightmost node of each right child. If the node is a valid ending (punctuation and quotation are excluded), it is added to the potential set of endings E. The set of valid boundaries B contains the cross-product of the starting position $S = \{a\}$ with E.

For instance, from Example 2, the following boundary candidates are generated for *are*:

- are paying
- are paying out
- are paying out a smaller percentage of their profits and cash flow
- are paying out a smaller percentage of their profits and cash flow in the form of dividends

We experiment with both logistic regression (**Log**^{B}) and ranking (**Rank**^{B}) models for this task. The set of features is shared with the previous task, and is described in the following section.

3.3.1 Antecedent Features

The features used for antecedent head resolution and/or boundary determination try to capture aspects of both tasks. We summarize the features in Table 1. The features are roughly grouped by their type. **Labels** features make use of the parsing labels of the antecedent and target; **Tree** features are intended to capture the dependency relations between the antecedent and target; **Distance** features describe distance between them; **Match** features test whether the context of the antecedent and target are similar; **Semantic** features capture shallow semantic similarity; finally, there are a few **Other** features which are not categorized.

On the last column of the feature table, we indicate the design purpose of the feature: head selection (H), boundary detection (B) or both (B&H). However, we use the full feature set for all three tasks.

4 Joint Modeling

Here we consider the possibility that antecedent head resolution and target detection should be modeled jointly (they are typically separate). The hypothesis is that if a suitable antecedent for a target cannot be found, the target itself might have been incorrectly detected. Similarly, the suitability of a candidate as antecedent head can depend on the possible boundaries of the antecedents that can be generated from it.

We also consider the possibility that antecedent head resolution and antecedent boundary determination should be modeled independently (though they are typically combined). We hypothesize that these two steps actually focus on different perspectives: the antecedent head resolution (**H**) focuses on finding the correct antecedent position; the boundary detection step (**B**) focuses on constructing a well-formed verb phrase. We are also aware that **B** might be helpful to **H**, for instance, a correct antecedent boundary will give us correct context words, that can be useful in determining the antecedent position.

We examine the joint interactions by combining adjacent steps in our pipeline. For the combination of antecedent head resolution and antecedent boundary determination (**H+B**), we consider simultaneously as candidates for each target the set of all potential boundaries for all potential heads. Here too, a

logistic regression model ($\mathbf{Log}^{H+B}$) can be used to distinguish correct (`target, antecedent start, antecedent end`) triplets; or a ranking model ($\mathbf{Rank}^{H+B}$) can be trained to rank the correct one above the other ones for the same target.

The combination of target detection with antecedent head resolution (**T+H**) requires identifying the targets. This is not straightforward when using a ranking model since scores are only comparable for the same target. To get around this problem, we add a "null" antecedent head. For a given target candidate, the null antecedent should be ranked higher than all other candidates if it is not actually a target. Since this produces many examples where the null antecedent should be selected, random subsampling is used to reduce the training data imbalance. The "null" hypothesis approach is used previously in ranking-based coreference systems (Rahman and Ng, 2009; Durrett et al., 2013).

Most of the features presented in the previous section will not trigger for the null instance, and an additional feature to mark this case is added.

The combination of the three tasks (**T+H+B**) only differs from the previous case in that all antecedent boundaries are considered as candidates for a target, in addition to the potential antecedent heads.

5 Experiments

5.1 Datasets

We conduct our experiments on two datasets (see Table 2 for corpus counts). The first one is the corpus of Bos and Spenader (2011), which provides VPE annotation on the WSJ section of the Penn Treebank. Bos and Spenader (2011) propose a train-test split that we follow[5].

To facilitate more meaningful comparison, we converted the sections of the British National Corpus annotated by Nielsen (2005) into the format used by Bos and Spenader (2011), and manually fixed conversion errors introduced during the process[6] (Our version of the dataset is publicly available for research[7].) We use a train-test split similar to Nielsen

---

[5] Section 20 to 24 are used as test data.

[6] We also found 3 annotation instances that could be deemed errors, but decided to preserve the annotations as they were.

[7] `https://github.com/hunterhector/VerbPhraseEllipsis`

Type	Feature Description	Purpose
Labels	The POS tag and dependency label of the antecedent head	H
	The POS tag and dependency label of the antecedent's last word	B
	The POS tag and lemma of the antecedent parent	H
	The POS tag, lemma and dependency label of within a 3 word around around the antecedent	B
	The pair of the POS tags of the antecedent head and the target, and of their auxiliary verbs	H
	The pair of the lemmas of the auxiliary verbs of the antecedent head and the target.	H
Tree	Whether the antecedent and the target form a comparative construction connecting by *so*, *as* or *than*	H&B
	The dependency labels of the shared lemmas between the parse tree of the antecedent and the target	H
	Label of the dependency between the antecedent and target (if exists)	H
	Whether the antecedent contains any descendant with the same lemma and dependency label as a descendant of the target.	H
	Whether antecedent and target are dependent ancestor of each other	H
	Whether antecedent and target share prepositions in their dependency tree	H
Distance	The distance in sentences between the antecedent and the target (clipped to 2)	H
	The number of verb phrases between the antecedent and the target (clipped to 5)	H
Match	Whether the lemmas of the heads, and words in the the window (=2) before the antecedent and the target match respectively	H
	Whether the lemmas of the ith word before the antecedent and $i - 1$th word before the target match respectively (for $i \in \{1, 2, 3\}$, with the 0th word of the target being the target itself)	H&B
Semantic	Whether the subjects of the antecedent and the target are coreferent	H
Other	Whether the lemma of the head of the antecedent is *be* and that of the target is *do* (be-do match, used by Hardt and Nielsen)	H
	Whether the antecedent is in quotes and the target is not, or vice versa	H&B

Table 1: Antecedent Features

	Documents		VPE Instances	
	Train	Test	Train	Test
WSJ	1999	500	435	119
BNC	12	2	641	204

Table 2: Corpus statistics

(2005)[8].

---

[8]Training set is CS6, A2U, J25, FU6, H7F, HA3, A19, A0P, G1A, EWC, FNS, C8T; test set is EDJ, FR3

5.2 Evaluation

We evaluate and compare our models following the metrics used by Bos and Spenader (2011).

VPE target detection is a per-word binary classification problem, which can be evaluated using the conventional precision (Prec), recall (Rec) and F1 scores.

Bos and Spenader (2011) propose a token-based evaluation metric for antecedent selection. The antecedent scores are computed over the correctly identified tokens per antecedent: precision is the number of correctly identified tokens divided by the number of predicted tokens, and recall is the number of correctly identified tokens divided by the number of gold standard tokens. Averaged scores refer to a "macro"-average over all antecedents.

Finally, in order to asses the performance of antecedent head resolution, we compute precision, recall and F1 where credit is given if the proposed head is included inside the golden antecedent boundaries.

5.3 Baselines and Benchmarks

We begin with simple, linguistically motivated baseline approaches for the three subtasks. For target detection, we reimplement the heuristic baseline used by Nielsen (2005): take all auxiliaries as possible candidates and eliminate them using part-of-speech context rules (we refer to this as $\mathbf{Pos}^T$). For antecedent head resolution, we take the first non-auxiliary verb preceding the target verb. For antecedent boundary detection, we expand the verb into a phrase by taking the largest subtree of the verb such that it does not overlap with the target. These two baselines are also used in Nielsen (2005) (and we refer to them as $\mathbf{Prev}^H$ and $\mathbf{Max}^B$, respectively).

To upper-bound our results, we include an oracle for the three subtasks, which selects the highest scoring candidate among all those considered. We denote these as $\mathbf{Ora}^T$, $\mathbf{Ora}^H$, $\mathbf{Ora}^B$.

We also compare to the current state-of-the-art target detection results as reported in Nielsen (2005) on the BNC dataset ($\mathbf{Nielsen}^T$)[9].

6 Results

The results for each one of the three subtasks in isolation are presented first, followed by those of the end-to-end evaluation. We have not attempted to tune classification thresholds to maximize F1.

6.1 Target Detection

Table 3 shows the performance of the compared approaches on the Target Detection task. The logistic regression model $\mathbf{Log}^T$ gives relatively high precision compared to recall, probably because there are so many more negative training examples than positive ones. Despite a simple set of features, the F1 results are significantly better than Nielsen's baseline $\mathbf{Pos}^T$.

---

[9]The differences in the setup make the results on antecedent resolution not directly comparable.

Notice also how the oracle $\mathbf{Ora}^T$ does not achieve 100% recall, since not all the targets in the gold data are captured by our candidate generation strategy. The loss is around 7% for both corpora.

The results obtained by the joint models are low on this task. In particular, the ranking models $\mathbf{Rank}^{T+H}$ and $\mathbf{Rank}^{T+H+B}$ fail to predict any target in the WSJ corpus, since the null antecedent is always preferred. This happens because joint modeling further exaggerates the class imbalance: the ranker is asked to consider many incorrect targets coupled with all sorts of hypothesis antecedents, and ultimately learns just to select the null target. Our initial attempts at subsampling the negative examples did not improve the situation. The logistic regression models $\mathbf{Log}^{T+H}$ and $\mathbf{Log}^{T+H+B}$ are most robust, but still their performance is far below that of the pure classifier $\mathbf{Log}^T$.

6.2 Antecedent Head Resolution

Table 4 contains the performance of the compared approaches on the Antecedent Head Resolution task, assuming oracle targets ($\mathbf{Ora}^T$).

First, we observe that even the oracle $\mathbf{Ora}^H$ has low scores on the BNC corpus. This suggests that some phenomena beyond the scope of those observed in the WSJ data appear in the more general corpus (we developed our system using the WSJ annotations and then simply evaluated on the BNC test data).

Second, the ranking-based model $\mathbf{Rank}^H$ consistently outperforms the logistic regression model $\mathbf{Log}^H$ and the baseline $\mathbf{Prev}^H$. The ranking model's advantage is small in the WSJ, but much more pronounced in the BNC data. These improvements suggest that indeed, ranking is a more natural modeling choice than classification for antecedent head resolution.

Finally, the joint resolution models $\mathbf{Rank}^{H+B}$ and $\mathbf{Log}^{H+B}$ give poorer results than their single-task counterparts, though $\mathbf{Rank}^{H+B}$ is not far behind $\mathbf{Rank}^H$. Joint modeling requires more training data and we may not have enough to reflect the benefit of a more powerful model.

6.3 Antecedent Boundary Determination

Table 5 shows the performance of the compared approaches on the Antecedent Boundary Determination task, using the soft evaluation scores (the results for

	WSJ			BNC		
	Prec	Rec	F1	Prec	Rec	F1
Ora^T	100.00	93.28	96.52	100.00	92.65	96.18
Log^T	80.22	61.34	69.52	80.90	70.59	75.39
Pos^T	42.62	43.7	43.15	35.47	35.29	35.38
Log^{T+H}	23.36	26.89	25.00	12.52	38.24	18.86
Rank^{T+H}	0.00	0.00	0.00	15.79	5.88	8.57
Log^{T+H+B}	25.61	17.65	20.90	21.50	32.35	25.83
Rank^{T+H+B}	0.00	0.00	0.00	16.67	11.27	13.45
Nielsen^T	-	-	-	72.50	72.86	72.68

Table 3: Results for Target Detection

	WSJ			BNC		
	Prec	Rec	F1	Prec	Rec	F1
Ora^H	94.59	88.24	91.30	79.89	74.02	76.84
Rank^H	70.27	65.55	67.83	52.91	49.02	50.89
Prev^H	67.57	63.03	65.22	39.68	36.76	38.17
Log^H	59.46	55.46	57.39	38.62	35.78	37.15
Rank^{H+B}	68.47	63.87	66.09	51.85	48.04	49.87
Log^{H+B}	39.64	36.97	38.26	30.16	27.94	29.01

Table 4: Results for Antecedent Head Resolution

	WSJ			BNC		
	Prec	Rec	F1	Prec	Rec	F1
Ora^B	95.06	88.67	91.76	85.79	79.49	82.52
Log^B	89.47	83.46	86.36	81.10	75.13	78.00
Rank^B	83.96	78.32	81.04	75.68	70.12	72.79
Max^B	78.97	73.66	76.22	73.70	68.28	70.88

Table 5: Soft results for Antecedent Boundary Determination

	WSJ			BNC		
	Prec	Rec	F1	Prec	Rec	F1
Ora^H**+Ora**^{B}	95.06	88.67	91.76	85.79	79.49	82.52
Rank^H**+Log**^{B}	64.11	59.8	61.88	47.04	43.58	45.24
Rank^H**+Rank**^{B}	63.90	59.6	61.67	49.11	45.5	47.24
Log^H**+Log**^{B}	53.49	49.89	51.63	34.77	32.21	33.44
Log^H**+Rank**^{B}	53.27	49.69	51.42	36.26	33.59	34.88
Rank^{H+B}	67.55	63.01	65.20	50.68	46.95	48.74
Log^{H+B}	40.96	38.20	39.53	30.00	27.79	28.85

Table 6: Soft results for Antecedent Boundary Determination with non-gold heads

	WSJ			BNC		
	Prec	Rec	F1	Prec	Rec	F1
$\mathbf{Ora}^T$+$\mathbf{Ora}^H$+$\mathbf{Ora}^B$	95.06	88.67	91.76	85.79	79.49	82.52
$\mathbf{Log}^T$+$\mathbf{Rank}^H$+$\mathbf{Rank}^B$	52.68	40.28	45.65	43.03	37.54	40.10
$\mathbf{Log}^T$+$\mathbf{Rank}^H$+$\mathbf{Log}^B$	52.82	40.40	45.78	40.21	35.08	37.47
$\mathbf{Log}^T$+$\mathbf{Log}^H$+$\mathbf{Rank}^B$	49.45	37.82	42.86	33.12	28.90	30.86
$\mathbf{Log}^T$+$\mathbf{Log}^H$+$\mathbf{Log}^B$	49.41	37.79	42.83	31.32	27.33	29.19
$\mathbf{Pos}^T$+$\mathbf{Prev}^H$+$\mathbf{Max}^B$	19.04	19.52	19.27	12.81	12.75	12.78
$\mathbf{Log}^T$+$\mathbf{Rank}^{H+B}$	54.82	41.92	47.51	41.86	36.52	39.01
$\mathbf{Log}^T$+$\mathbf{Log}^{H+B}$	38.85	29.71	33.67	26.11	22.78	24.33

Table 7: Soft end-to-end results

the strict scores are omitted for brevity, but in general look quite similar). The systems use the output of the oracle targets ($\mathbf{Ora}^T$) and antecedent heads ($\mathbf{Ora}^H$).

Regarding boundary detection alone, the logistic regression model $\mathbf{Log}^B$ outperforms the ranking model $\mathbf{Rank}^B$. This suggests that boundary determination is more a problem of determining the compatibility between target and antecedent extent than one of ranking alternative boundaries. However, the next experiments suggest this advantage is diminished when gold targets and antecedent heads are replaced by system predictions.

6.3.1 Non-Gold Antecedent Heads

Table 6 contains Antecedent Boundary Determination results for systems which use oracle targets, but system antecedent heads. When $\mathbf{Rank}^H$ or $\mathbf{Log}^H$ are used for head resolution, the difference between $\mathbf{Log}^B$ and $\mathbf{Rank}^B$ diminishes, and it is even better to use the latter in the BNC corpus. The models were trained with gold annotations rather than system outputs, and the ranking model is somewhat more robust to noisier inputs.

On the other hand, the results for the joint resolution model $\mathbf{Rank}^{H+B}$ are better in this case than the combination of $\mathbf{Rank}^H$+$\mathbf{Rank}^B$, whereas $\mathbf{Log}^{H+B}$ performs worse than any 2-step combination. The benefits of using a ranking model for antecedent head resolution seem thus to outperform those of using classification to determine its boundaries.

6.4 End-to-End Evaluation

Table 7 contains the end-to-end performance of different approaches, using the soft evaluation scores.

The trends we observed with gold targets are preserved: approaches using the $\mathbf{Rank}^H$ maintain an advantage over $\mathbf{Log}^H$, but the improvement of $\mathbf{Log}^B$ over $\mathbf{Rank}^B$ for boundary determination is diminished with non-gold heads. Also, the 3-step approaches seem to perform slightly better than the 2-step ones. Together with the fact that the smaller problems are easier to train, this appears to validate our decomposition choice.

7 Conclusion and Discussion

In this paper we have explored a decomposition of Verb Phrase Ellipsis resolution into subtasks, which splits antecedent selection in two distinct steps. By modeling these two subtasks separately with two different learning paradigms, we can achieve better performance then doing them jointly, suggesting they are indeed of different underlying nature.

Our experiments show that a logistic regression classification model works better for target detection and antecedent boundary determination, while a ranking-based model is more suitable for selecting the antecedent head of a given target. However, the benefits of the classification model for boundary determination are reduced for non-gold targets and heads. On the other hand, by separating the two steps, we lose the potential joint interaction of them. It might be possible to explore whether we can bring the benefits of the two side: use separate models on each step, but learn them jointly. We leave further investigation of this to future work.

We have also explored jointly training a target detection and antecedent resolution model, but have not been successful in dealing with the class imbalance inherent to the problem.

Our current model adopts a simple feature set, which is composed mostly by simple syntax and lexical features. It may be interesting to explore more semantic and discourse-level features in our system. We leave these to future investigation.

All our experiments have been run on publicly available datasets, to which we add our manually aligned version of the VPE annotations on the BNC corpus. We hope our experiments, analysis, and more easily processed data can further the development of new computational approaches to the problem of Verb Phrase Ellipsis resolution.

Acknowledgments

The first author was partially supported DARPA grant FA8750-12-2-0342 funded under the DEFT program. Thanks to the anonymous reviewers for their useful comments.

References

Johan Bos and Jennifer Spenader. 2011. An annotated corpus for the analysis of VP ellipsis. *Language Resources and Evaluation*, 45(4):463–494.

Mary Dalrymple, Stuart M. Shieber, and Fernando C. N. Pereira. 1991. Ellipsis and higher-order unification. *Linguistics and Philosophy*, 14(4):399–452.

Ofer Dekel, Yoram Singer, and Christopher D. Manning. 2003. Log-linear models for label ranking. In *Advances in Neural Information Processing Systems*, page None.

Greg Durrett, David Hall, and Dan Klein. 2013. Decentralized Entity-Level Modeling for Coreference Resolution. In *Proceedings of the 51st Annual Meeting of the Association for Computational Linguistics*, pages 114–124.

Daniel Hardt. 1992. An algorithm for VP ellipsis. In *Proceedings of the 30th annual meeting on Association for Computational Linguistics*, number January, pages 9–14.

Daniel Hardt. 1997. An empirical approach to VP ellipsis. *Computational Linguistics*, 23(4):525–541.

Daniel Hardt. 1998. Improving Ellipsis Resolution with Transformation-Based Learning. *AAAI Fall Symposium*, pages 41–43.

Leif Arda Nielsen. 2003a. A corpus-based study of Verb Phrase Ellipsis Identification and Resolution. In *Proceedings of the 6th Annual CLUK Research Colloquium*, page Proceedings of the 6th Annual CLUK Research Colloq.

Leif Arda Nielsen. 2003b. Using Machine Learning techniques for VPE detection. In *Proceedings of Recent Advances in Natural Language Processing*, pages 339–346.

Leif Arda Nielsen. 2004a. Robust VPE detection using automatically parsed text. In *Proceedings of the Student Workshop, ACL 2004*, pages 31–36.

Leif Arda Nielsen. 2004b. Verb phrase ellipsis detection using automatically parsed text. In *Proceedings of the 20th international conference on Computational Linguistics - COLING '04*.

Leif Arda Nielsen. 2005. *A corpus-based study of Verb Phrase Ellipsis Identification and Resolution*. Doctor of philosopy, King's College London.

Altaf Rahman and Vincent Ng. 2009. Supervised models for coreference resolution. In *Proceedings of the 2009 Conference on Empirical Methods in Natural Language Processing*, number August, pages 968–977.

Stuart M. Shieber, Fernando C. N. Pereira, and Mary Dalrymple. 1996. Interactions of scope and ellipsis. *Linguistics and Philosophy*, 19(5):527–552.

Anaphoricity in Connectives: A Case Study on German

Manfred Stede and **Yulia Grishina**
Applied Computational Linguistics
FSP Cognitive Science
University of Potsdam, Germany
stede|grishina@uni-potsdam.de

Abstract

Anaphoric connectives are event anaphors (or abstract anaphors) that in addition convey a coherence relation holding between the antecedent and the host clause of the connective. Some of them carry an explicitly-anaphoric morpheme, others do not. We analysed the set of German connectives for this property and found that many have an additional non-connective reading, where they serve as nominal anaphors. Furthermore, many connectives can have multiple senses, so altogether the processing of these words can involve substantial disambiguation. We study the problem for one specific German word, *demzufolge*, which can be taken as representative for a large group of similar words.

1 Introduction

The vast majority of the research on anaphoricity in Computational Linguistics has been done on nominal anaphora; it is arguably the most important for many purposes, and also the most frequent phenomenon. Nonetheless, *event anaphors*[1] are also highly relevant for text understanding, but they have proven to be much more difficult to resolve than nominal anaphors; see, e.g., (Dipper and Zinsmeister, 2012). In this paper, we zoom in on a specific subclass of event anaphors, namely on anaphoric connectives: They pick up an abstract-object antecedent from the previous context, and at the same time signal a semantic or pragmatic coherence relation between that antecedent and their host clause.

---

[1]In this paper, we use *event* anaphora interchangeably with *abstract* anaphora.

A principal distinction between 'anaphoric' and 'structural' connectives has been made by Webber et al. (2003) in the context of Computational Linguistics; similar observations have been made by linguists working on the German 'Handbook of connectives' (Pasch et al., 2003). While structural connectives (conjunctions) take their arguments qua the syntactic configuration they appear in, anaphoric connectives (certain adverbials) pick up their 'external' argument (or the 'Arg1' in the terminology of the Penn Discourse Treebank, PDTB) (Prasad et al., 2008) by means of anaphora resolution. Often, this argument is present in the clause preceding the anaphoric adverbial, but it need not be; Prasad et al. report that in the PDTB, 9% of the 'Arg1' arguments of connectives in fact appear not in the same or in the previous sentence, but farther away. For illustration, here is a fictitious example:

(1) *[Tom didn't go to the café.]*$_{Arg1}$ *It would close soon anyway. [He chose to sit at the beach]*$_{Arg2}$ *[instead]*$_{conn}$.

In English, a few connective adverbials make their anaphoricity explicit, as they contain a morpheme that overtly refers backward: ***therefore, whereby*** etc. In other languages, this phenomenon is more widespread. In this paper, we will especially look at German, where a large number of connectives exhibit such a morpheme; Section 2 will provide an overview. Afterwards, in Section 3, we present a case study on one specific German word, which can act both as a nominal anaphor and as an event anaphor (in which case it is a connective) and thus poses an additional ambiguity problem. Then,

41

Proceedings of the Workshop on Coreference Resolution Beyond OntoNotes (CORBON 2016), co-located with NAACL 2016, pages 41–46,
San Diego, California, June 16, 2016. ©2016 Association for Computational Linguistics

Section 4 discusses the disambiguation task and sketches a path toward a solution.

2 Anaphoric connectives in German

A connective, according to Pasch et al. (2003), is a closed-class lexical item expressing a two-place relation whose arguments denote eventualities and can, in principle, be expressed as full sentences. Connectives do not form a syntactically homogeneous class but contain both conjunctions (coordinate or subordinate) and certain adverbials. Due to this, they are usually regarded as a discourse phenomenon, and there are not many comprehensive linguistic studies that survey the connectives of a language. A notable exception is the aforementioned handbook for German, which lists about 350 different connectives. In terms of machine-readable lexicons, one for German connectives (*DiMLex*) had been introduced by Stede (2002), which in its current version[2] contains 274 entries. For French, *Lex-Conn* (Roze et al., 2012) is slightly bigger (328 entries). For English, a list has been derived from the PDTB corpus, consisting of 100 connectives.

Since our focus here is on German, we worked with *DiMLex* and determined how many connectives have an explicitly-anaphoric morpheme (as explained above). We found 11 different relevant prefixes and suffixes, and their frequencies are: *da-*: 21, *-dessen*: 17, *wo-/wes-*: 11, *hier-*: 7, *-dem*: 7, *dem-*: 6, *des-*: 4, *-dann*: 3, *-dies*: 2, *dessen-*: 1. Thus, in total 79 connectives have one of the morphemes in question, which amounts to 29%.[3]

We went through these explicitly-anaphoric connectives and determined how many of them also have a non-connective reading. This problem of connective ambiguity had been quantified by Dipper and Stede (2006) as applying to 40% of the words, on the basis of an earlier (smaller) version of *DiMLex*. Many connectives have additional readings as discourse particles, verb particles, or nominal anaphors. Since our 79 connectives carry anaphoric

morphemes, ambiguity can hold between nominal anaphor and event anaphor (= connective). We found that this applies to 40 words; for most of them, their other function is that of a relative pronoun. For example:

(2) *Sie schenkte mir ein Buch, <u>womit</u> ich nichts anfangen konnte.*
'She gave me a book, <u>with which</u> I could not do anything.'

(3) *[Sie schenkte mir ein Buch,]$_{Arg1}$ [womit]$_{conn}$ [sie mir einen großen Gefallen tat.]$_{Arg2}$*
'She gave me a book, <u>whereby</u> she did me a big favor.'

3 Case study: *demzufolge*

The 40 words that we identified in the previous section are ambiguous between nominal anaphor and event anaphor. In order to approach the tasks of (a) determining the correct reading in a given context, and (b) finding the antecedent (which for the event anaphor reading corresponds to the Arg1 of the connective), we decided to first inspect one word in detail and chose *demzufolge*.

3.1 Different readings

A good way to map out the ambiguity of *demzufolge* is to collect the variety of its English translations in a parallel corpus. We used InterCorp[4], where the first 50 hits yield the following: *accordingly, as a result, consequently, as a consequence, therefore, that* (as complementizer or relative pronoun), *which* (as relative pronoun), and the null translation. Making this systematic, we see two broad classes of usages:

1. **Nominal anaphor,** a contracted form of *dem zufolge*, which in German can be paraphrased as *laut dem* ('according to which'). We find two syntactic forms:

(a) Introducing a relative clause:

(4) *Ich las ein Buch, demzufolge die Welt in diesem Jahr untergehen wird.*
'I read a book <u>according to which</u> the world will collapse this year.'

(b) Free adverbial:

---

^[2]https://github.com/discourse-lab/dimlex

[3]Most morphemes do not straightforwardly translate to English; they correspond to local, temporal, and event anaphors in dative or genitive case. The phenomenon occurs in other languages as well; in Dutch, for instance, there are connectives like *daarom, daardoor, waardor*; French examples are *après ca, à part ca*.

[4]https://ucnk.ff.cuni.cz/intercorp/

(5) *Ich habe ein interessantes Buch gelesen.*
Demzufolge wird die Welt in diesem Jahr
untergehen.

'I read an interesting book. <u>According
to it</u> the world will collapse this year.'

2. **Connective** with two arguments that denote eventualities. The online grammar *grammis*[5] in its 'grammatical lexicon' section states that it can appear in three different positions, as modeled by topological-field theory:[6]

- *Vorfeld* (pre-field):

    (6) *Peter war der beste Torschütze.*
    Demzufolge bekam er den Pokal.
    'Peter was the best goal scorer. Therefore he received the tophy.'

- *Mittelfeld* (middle-field):
    (...) *Er bekam demzufolge den Pokal.*

- *Nullstelle* (zero position):
    (...) *Demzufolge: Er bekam den Pokal.*

Irrespective of the position, the coherence relation being signalled is 'cause-result' (in the PDTB terminology), and intuitively, we expect this to be the only one; but see below for an exception. When considering various examples, it becomes clear that the readings cannot be easily distinguished at the linguistic surface. To explore this in depth, we thus conducted a (small) corpus study.

3.2 Corpus Study

To investigate the ambiguity and its potential resolution in authentic contexts, we randomly collected 140 instances of *demzufolge* (using a case-insensitive search) from the DWDS corpus[7]. 50 are from the print and online editions of the weekly paper *Die Zeit* (1946-2014), and 90 from the 'Kernkorpus 20', a genre-balanced corpus of 20th-century German that includes narratives, non-fiction books, scientific text, and some newspaper text. The extracted material for each instance was a window of

three sentences, the second one of which contains the target word *demzufolge*. Henceforth, we call the two collections 'zeit50' and 'kernel90', respectively.

As our first step, to get an initial overview, one author of this paper annotated kernel90: For each instance of *demzufolge* we marked its antecedent and identified the syntactic type. These are the frequencies of the various antecedent types (we also indicate the English translation equivalent of *demzufolge*):

- NP antecedent: 42 (47%)
  Roles of *demzufolge*:
    - relative pronoun ("according to which"): 33 (37%)
    - other function ("therefore"): 9 (10%)
- VP antecedent ("therefore"): 19 (21%)
- S antecedent ("therefore"): 29 (32%)
  Subtypes:
    - one or more full sentences: 22 (24%)
    - sentential complement: 4 (4%)
    - sentences in coordinate structures: 2 (2%)
    - subordinate sentence: 1 (1%)

The relatively balanced distributions between syntactic antecedent types and also between readings/translations (33 non-connectives; 57 connectives) shows that disambiguation cannot be avoided by means of a simple majority baseline.

Next, we were interested in inter-annotator agreement regarding class (non-/connective), connective sense (PDTB taxonomy) and extension of the two arguments. One author of this paper and two trained annotators, who are familiar with German connectives but previously had not studied *demzufolge* in particular, labelled the 50 instances in zeit50. We can subsume the non-/connective decision under the sense labeling, where a non-connective receives the sense 'none'. Another special label annotators could use was 'missing context', indicating that a judgement is not possible because of the restricted context information available.

Results: With three annotators, there are 150 pairs of annotations to be compared. 103 (69%) of the decision pairs were completely identical (i.e., two annotators agreed on the connective sense and on the extensions of both arguments). For the senses, there were 25 cases of pairwise disagreement, and the vast majority (21) concerned the non-/connective

---

[5]http://hypermedia.ids-mannheim.de

[6]Very briefly, the finite verb and the other parts of the predicate constitute the *Satzklammer* ('sentence bracket'). The middle-field is inside the bracket; the pre-field precedes the left bracket; the zero position precedes the pre-field.

[7]www.dwds.de

distinction. 'Missing context' was used on only one instance (by two annotators). Among the connective senses, 'cause-result' was used 39 times, and 'specialization' four times. Given these two relations plus 'none' and 'missing context', we can see sense labeling as a four-way classification task, and we computed the chance-corrected Fleiss-κ for the 3 raters, which is 0.55.

The presence of the 'specialization' sense seems to contradict our initial expectation of non-ambiguity. But, upon reflection, 'specialization' indeed can be quite compatible with a causal or justifying relation, so this is not an extraordinary finding. To illustrate, here is one (abbreviated) instance that received the 'specialization' sense:

(7) *[Im ARD-Deutschlandtrend liegt Merkel in der Wählergunst deutlich hinter ihren möglichen Herausforderern Steinbrück und Steinmeier.]*$_{Arg1}$ *[Bei einer Direktwahl des Regierungschefs würde sie [demzufolge]*$_{conn}$ *im Duell gegen Steinbrück zurzeit mit 37 zu 48 Prozent klar unterliegen.]*$_{Arg2}$
'In the ARD poll, Merkel clearly lags behind her challengers Steinbrück and Steinmeier. In a direct election of the chancellor, she would <u>thus</u> currently lose to Steinbrück with 37 against 48 percent.'

When the disagreement on senses pertains to the non-/connective reading, it – unsurprisingly – correlates with disagreement on Arg1 extension. Overall, among the 150 pairs of instance annotations, there are 32 disagreements on Arg1 extension, and 18 on Arg2 extension. Both of these disagreements are largely restricted to the connective usage, which illustrates the finding (also well-known from the PDTB) that the extension of the spans of causal relations can be quite vague: Is the Arg1 just the preceding clause or sentence, or more than that? For Arg2, as indicated, disagreement is relatively rare. However, our results on argument extension are preliminary, as the annotators had only a three-sentence extract from the host texts to make their judgements.[8] In a larger study, these annotations need to be done on full texts.

---

[8]This is the reason why we did not measure chance-corrected agreement on span extension, as it could be done for example along the lines of (Krippendorf, 2004).

It is interesting to note that the non-/connective distribution differs between zeit50 and kernel90. In the former, the annotators labeled 34±2 instances as non-connectives, i.e., 68%. In kernel90, the corresponding figure is 37%. We attribute this difference to the genres: zeit50, as stated earlier, is taken from a newspaper, including its online edition, which to a large extent presents "instant news" that often involve citing other sources, so that the "according to which" reading is much more prominent than the "therefore" reading of *demzufolge*.

4 Toward disambiguation and resolution

Interpreting *demzufolge* and the 39 similar German words involves two subproblems: Disambiguate the reading (connective or non-connective), and resolve the argument(s) – either the antecedent of the NP-anaphor, or the two arguments of the connective.

For disambiguation, before embarking on full-fledged feature-based classification, it is advisable to check whether standard POS tagging can (partially) solve the problem. To this end, we experimented with two German taggers on the kernel90 set: clevertagger[9], which is integrated in the ParZu parser (Sennrich et al., 2009), and the tagger of the MATE tools (Bohnet, 2010). Both were used with their standard models, which for ParZu was trained on the TüBa-D/Z treebank[10] and for MATE on a dependency-converted version of the TIGER treebank[11]. They both make use of the STTS tagset[12] but in different versions. For our purposes, it is relevant that they use PROAV and PROP, respectively, for the German pronominal adverbs (contractions of a pronominal form and a preposition). Table 1 shows the tag distribution for the four groups of antecedent types; in each group, the top line gives the MATE results and the bottom line those of ParZu. The "other" column conflates a few obvious mistaggings as finite verb, adjective, etc. For the 29 instances with 'S' antecedents, both parsers failed to produce output in some cases (MATE: 5, ParZu: 4).

---

[9]https://github.com/rsennrich/clevertagger
[10]http://www.sfs.uni-tuebingen.de/ascl/ressourcen/corpora/tueba-dz.html
[11]http://www.ims.uni-stuttgart.de/forschung/ressourcen/korpora/tiger.en.html
[12]http://www.ims.uni-stuttgart.de/forschung/ressourcen/lexika/GermanTagsets.en.html

While we cannot really expect a tagger to differentiate between the types of antecedents (thus providing information for anaphora resolution), it is worth testing whether it can predict the non-/connective readings, which here means to split the relative pronoun uses from all others (as shown at the beginning of Sct. 3.2). It turns out that MATE correctly identifies only 6 of 33 relative pronouns (18%) as PRELS. ParZu tags 19 of them (58%) as subordinating conjunctions (KOUS), which is the wrong tag, yet it serves to distinguish them from the connective usages. Closer inspection reveals that 5 of the 6 MATE-PRELS instances are also ParZu-KOUS instances, so that for this task, on the whole ParZu is the better tool. If we assume that the ratios hold for *demzufolge* instances in general, then the upshot of the experiment is: ParZu can partially identify the non-/connective readings of *demzufolge*, when we interpret the KOUS tag as non-connective (with perfect precision, and recall of 19/33 = 58%), and the PROP tag as connective, with a precision of 50/61 (82%) and a recall of 50/57 (94%; counting also the four failed parses). For many purposes, this situation will not be good enough, so that classifiers using "deeper" features, in the spirit of Pitler and Nenkova (2009) have to be built.

Likewise, for the second problem of finding the arguments – of the nominal anaphor or of the connective – deeper features have to be used. Some work on Arg1 identification for English reports results around 80% accuracy based on surface and syntactic features (Elwell and Baldridge, 2008), but it seems not likely that this can be reached for the fairly complicated distinction between NPs, VPs, and sentences for the German connectives we are studying here. The most promising route might be to aim for identifying just the heads of the antecedents, as done for English, e.g., by Wellner and Puste-jovsky (2007); also, it can help to consider semantic features, as proposed by Miltsakaki et al. (2003) for the anaphoric connective *instead*.

5 Summary and outlook

The distinction between structural and anaphoric connectives is well-established, but for the anaphoric ones it is an open question whether those with an explicit anaphoric morpheme be-

antecedent	PROAV PROP	KOUS	PRELS	other
NP (relpro)	22		6	5
	11	19		3
NP (other)	9			
	8			1
VP	19			
	19			
S	24			
	23			2

Table 1: kernel90 dataset: POS tags assigned to *demzufolge* by the parsers MATE (first row in a cell) and ParZu (second row).

have differently from those that do not have one, i.e., whether the group of anaphoric connectives should be split in two for purposes of argument identification. Entangled with this is the problem of non-connective ambiguity: many explicitly-anaphoric connectives also have a second reading as nominal anaphors. As a step toward resolving these issues, we started from a comprehensive lexicon of German connectives and determined that 79 of them have one of 11 different anaphoric morphemes. Of the 79 words, 40 are ambiguous between a connective and non-connective reading. We selected *demzufolge* for a pilot study and built a small corpus of 140 instances annotated with connective senses and argument spans. Experiments with POS taggers revealed that – at least for this word – they can help only to a limited extent for distinguishing the non-/connective readings.

Our next steps are to determine the parallelism between *demzufolge* and the other connectives and then to build sense/argument classifiers for groups of similar connectives. Since there are no large annotated resources for German, we will also look into the possibility of annotation projection, as suggested by Versley (2010) for English-German or Laali and Kosseim (2014) for English-French. For the connectives we study, this might be difficult, since English appears to have much fewer (explicitly-)anaphoric connectives; but if projection can also be done for AltLex instances (multi-word expressions in the PDTB), this might be helpful.

Acknowledgements

We thank Tatjana Scheffler and Erik Haegert for their help with corpus annotation, and the anonymous reviewers for their valuable suggestions on improving the paper.

References

Bernd Bohnet. 2010. Top accuracy and fast dependency parsing is not a contradiction. In *Proc. of the 23rd International Conference on Computational Linguistics (COLING)*, pages 89–97, Beijing, China, August.

Stefanie Dipper and Manfred Stede. 2006. Disambiguating potential connectives. In Miriam Butt, editor, *Proc. of KONVENS '06*, pages 167–173, Konstanz.

Stefanie Dipper and Heike Zinsmeister. 2012. Annotating abstract anaphora. *Language Resources and Evaluation*, 46(1):37–52.

Robert Elwell and Jason Baldridge. 2008. Discourse connective argument identification with connective specific rankers. In *Proc. of the IEEE Conference on Semantic Computing (ICSC)*, Santa Clara/CA.

Klaus Krippendorf. 2004. Measuring the reliability of qualitative text analysis data. *Quality and Quantity*, 38(6):787–800.

Majid Laali and Leila Kosseim. 2014. Inducing discourse connectives from parallel texts. In *Proc. of the 25th International Conference on Computational Linguistics (COLING)*, Dublin/Ireland.

Eleni Miltsakaki, Cassandre Creswell, Katherine Forbes, Aravind Joshi, and Bonnie Webber. 2003. Anaphoric arguments of discourse connectives: Semantic properties of antecedents versus non-antecedents. In *Proc. of the 10 Conference of the European Chapter of the ACL*, Budapest.

Renate Pasch, Ursula Brauße, Eva Breindl, and Ulrich Herrmann Waßner. 2003. *Handbuch der deutschen Konnektoren*. Walter de Gruyter, Berlin/New York.

Emily Pitler and Ani Nenkova. 2009. Using syntax to disambiguate explicit discourse connectives in text. In *Proc. of the ACL-IJCNLP 2009 Conference Short Papers*, pages 13–16, Suntec, Singapore.

R. Prasad, N. Dinesh, A. Lee, E. Miltsakaki, L. Robaldo, A. Joshi, and B. Webber. 2008. The Penn Discourse Treebank 2.0. In *Proc. of the 6th International Conference on Language Resources and Evaluation (LREC)*, Marrakech, Morocco.

Charlotte Roze, Laurence Danlos, and Philippe Muller. 2012. Lexconn: A French lexicon of discourse connectives. *Discours*, 10.

Rico Sennrich, Gerold Schneider, Martin Volk, and Martin Warin. 2009. A new hybrid dependency parser for German. In C. Chiarcos, R. Eckart de Castilho, and M. Stede, editors, *From Form to Meaning: Processing Texts Automatically. Proc. of the Biennial GSCL Conference 2009*, Tübingen. Narr.

Manfred Stede. 2002. DiMLex: A lexical approach to discourse markers. In A. Lenci and V. Di Tomaso, editors, *Exploring the Lexicon - Theory and Computation*. Edizioni dell'Orso, Alessandria.

Yannick Versley. 2010. Discovery of ambiguous and unambiguous discourse connectives via annotation projection. In *Proceedings of Workshop on Annotation and Exploitation of Parallel Corpora (AEPC)*, Tartu, Estonia.

Bonnie Webber, Matthew Stone, Aravind Joshi, and Alistair Knott. 2003. Anaphora and discourse structure. *Computational Linguistics*, 29(4):545–587.

Ben Wellner and James Pustejovsky. 2007. Automatically identifying the arguments of discourse connectives. In *Proc. of the 2007 Joint Conference on Empirical Methods in Natural Language Processing and Computational Natural Language Learning (EMNLP-CoNLL)*, pages 92–101, Prague, Czech Republic.

Abstract Coreference in a Multilingual Perspective:
a View on Czech and German

Anna Nedoluzhko
Charles University in Prague
Malostranske nam. 25
CZ-11800 Prague, Czech Republic
nedoluzko@ufal.mff.cuni.cz

Ekaterina Lapshinova-Koltunski
Saarland University
A2.2 University Campus
D-66123, Saarbrücken, Germany
e.lapshinova@mx.uni-saarland.de

Abstract

This paper aims at a cross-lingual analysis of coreference to abstract entities in Czech and German, two languages that are typologically not very close, since they belong to two different language groups – Slavic and Germanic. We will specifically focus on coreference chains to abstract entities, i.e. verbal phrases, clauses, sentences or even longer text passages. To our knowledge, this type of relation is underinvestigated in the current state-of-the-art literature.

1 Introduction

The main aim of this study is to enhance knowledge on abstract coreference in a multilingual perspective. One of the examples of abstract coreference in German is given in (1). Here, the anaphoric pronoun *dies [this]* referes to the whole preceding sentence and not to nominal phrases (NPs) or pronouns, which are analysed in most studies on coreference.

(1)   *Gleichzeitig brauchen wir mindestens eine Verdoppelung des Wohlstands.* Wenn wir *die Armutsgegenden der Erde anschauen, weiß jeder sofort, dass <u>dies</u> das Mindeste an moralischer Herausforderung ist. [At the same time, we need to double the current level of prosperity. One look at the poor regions throughout the world is enough to make anyone realize that <u>this</u> is the most urgent moral challenge we face].*

Although there exists a number of analyses of such cases (see Section 2), the majority of studies are monolingual or they do not include Germanic and Slavic languages. Information on differences between Czech and German in terms of abstract coreference will be beneficial to contrastive linguistics, translation studies and multilingual natural language processing.

The paper is organised as follows: related work and the definition of the phenomena under analysis are presented in Section 2, data and research questions are detailed in Section 3, followed by the analysis in Section 4. The discussion of the outcome and future work are provided in Section 5.

2 Related Work

There are a number of works on coreference relations other than identity, i.e. concerning references to abstract entities or extended reference. Most of them concentrate on the analysis of abstract anaphora. For instance, Botley (2006) distinguishes three main types of abstract anaphora: "label" anaphora, which encapsulates stretches of text (following Francis (1994)); "situation" anaphora and "text deixis". Following Fraurud (1992), "situation" anaphora is classified into eventuality and factuality. Hedberg et al. (2007), Navarretta & Olsen (2008), and Dipper & Zinsmeister (2009) present a similar distinction concerning "situation" anaphora subtypes. Dipper & Zinsmeister (2009) provide a survey of corpus-based studies on this topic, structur-

47

Proceedings of the Workshop on Coreference Resolution Beyond OntoNotes (CORBON 2016), co-located with NAACL 2016, pages 47–52,
San Diego, California, June 16, 2016. ©2016 Association for Computational Linguistics

ing them according to the form of anaphoric expressions (demonstratives, personal pronouns, etc.) and antecedents (verbal phrases, clauses, arbitary sequences or larger sequences). Most of these studies take into account only some particular forms of anaphors and antecedents, e.g. Hedberg et al. (2007) and Müller (2008) concentrate exclusively on *it, this* and *that*. The analyses of Müller (2008), Kučová & Hajičová (2004) and Pradhan et al. (2007) are limited to coreference to verbal phrases. Viera et al. (2005), Hedberg et al. (2007) and Poesio & Artstein (2008) concentrate on arbitary sequences. Byron (2003), Poesio & Artstein (2008) as well as Navarretta & Olsen (2008) include clauses into their analysis. The only work known to us that provides a description of coreference to various forms of abstract antecedents is (Taulé et al., 2008).

Dipper & Zinsmeister (2009) also describe the languages involved in the studies on abstract coreference. It is obvious that English predominates over other languages. Multilingual approaches are presented in (Vieira et al., 2005), (Navarretta and Olsen, 2008) and (Taulé et al., 2008) only and do not involve the language pair analysed in the present paper.

We analyse properties of abstract anaphora and antecedents from a multilingual perspective comparing Czech and German. Coreference to abstract entities such as events, states, situations, facts and propositions are referred to as *abstract coreference*. These include coreference to (i) verbal phrases as in example (2-a), where *these purposes* refers to *answering of these questions*, (ii) finite clauses and sentences as in example (1) above, in which the German demonstrative pronoun *dies [this]* refers to the whole preceding sentence, and (iii) larger text passages and discontinuous strings as in example (2-b). Here, the modified NP *these goals* refers to the three preceding sentences.

(2)   a.   *Polling is essential for answering both of these questions. ...the technique most frequently employed for these purposes is the "cross-sectional" survey.*

       b.   *Germany is seeking to achieve a 40% reduction of greenhouse gases in Germany by 2020, assuming the EU commits to a reduction of 30%. The German renewable energy act sets a new target of 20% electricity from renewables by 2020. Germany's Sustainable Strategy intends to halve overall energy consumption by 2050. The scale of effort needed to meet these goals demonstrates the degree of commitment of both our nations.*

Anaphoric expressions referring to abstract entities in our approach include mostly pronouns, nouns, nominal groups and pronominal adverbs.

3   Data and Research Questions

For our analysis, several texts of written discourse (essays) with comparable topics on economic, political and social issues have been selected.

For the German data, 8 texts were excerpted from the corpus CroCo (Hansen-Schirra et al., 2012), comprising 12243 tokens and 645 sentences in total. The corpus is annotated on several levels, which include morphological, syntactic, structural and textual information. The information on the latter was annotated with the help of semi-automatic procedures described by Lapshinova-Koltunski & Kunz (2014). Textual information is represented in the form of cohesive devices, such as coreference, connectives, substitution, ellipsis and lexical cohesion. The annotated structures contain information about morpho-syntactic features of devices (including antecedents) and allow yielding information on the chain features, i.e. number of elements in chains, distance between chain elements, etc. Annotation of textual coreference contains not only relations of identity between entities but also abstract and situation anaphora. Therefore, we may have coreference to nominal phrases (NPs) along with coreference to clauses, clause complexes or sentences as the one illustrated in example (1) above.

The Czech texts were taken from the Prague Dependency Treebank (PDT 3.0, (Bejček et al., 2013)). They are annotated with morphological, analytical and tectogrammatical information, whereas each sentence is represented as a dependency tree structure. The tectogrammatical layer of PDT 3.0 also contains annotation of information structure attributes, textual coreference of different types, bridging relations and PDTB-style discourse relations (discourse connectives, the discourse units linked by them, and semantic relations between these units), see (Poláková et al., 2013) for details. Since texts are shorter in the Czech data than in the German data, 15 texts were excerpted to arrive at a similar number of tokens and sentences (11399 and 628 respectively).

Although these two data sets were annotated within two different frameworks, the data on the abstract entities are comparable, since they contain information on the structural types of antecedents (if they are clauses, sentences or longer segments), as well as the structural and functional types of referring devices, i.e. demonstratives or other linguistic means. The comparability of the data was proved and discussed in Lapshinova et al. (2015).

4   Analyses

The total number of abstract coreference, i.e. the cases where anaphoric devices point on antecedents other than nominal groups or pronouns, is similar in the analysed Czech and German texts: 63 and 68 respectively. However, the scopus of the segments they refer to demonstrates variation, as seen from Table 1.

In the German data, the most occurring cases of abstract anaphors (ca. 66%) refer to segments of one sentence, whereas in the Czech texts, there are more cases of coreferences with longer segments (ca. 48%). On the one hand, these difference may have a technical origin. By marking references to longer segments in the data for Czech, annotators did not have to mark the antecedent, which could result in a greater number of abstract anaphors in Czech in general. On the other hand, this could also mean that the authors of texts in Czech summarise larger textual passages more often than those of the German texts.

For the structural types of antecedents, we observe a general tendency of demonstratives to refer to abstract entities in both languages. 72% of all demonstrative heads in our German data refer to abstract entities, whereas 39% do so in the Czech data. They are compensated by modified nominal phrases (with a demonstrative modifier) whose proportion estimates ca. 37% out of all modified NPs in the Czech texts.

Now, we will have a look at various types of anaphoric means that are used in both languages to refer to non-nominal antecedents, see Table 2.

In Czech, most of the explicitly expressed references to clauses (except for one) are realized by a demonstrative pronoun *ten [it/this]*. This is quite expectable, because these are mostly references to clauses within the same sentence, so the antecedent is close to anaphor and should be neither repeated nor emphasized by other demonstratives, cf. example (3), where *ten [it/this]* refers to the immediately preceding antecedent *proč jejich počet naopak ve statistikách nezdůrazňovat [why not to emphasize their number in statistics]*. The remaining sentence is the case of nominalisation (*pokles [decline]*) in example (4), used without a demonstrative pronoun, also because the antecedent clause immediately precedes the anaphoric noun.

(3)   *Cizinci   podstatně   přispěli   k   německému hospodářskému   a   kulturnímu   vývoji, proč jejich počet naopak ve statistikách nezdůrazňovat a tím veřejně uznat jejich   zásluhy   o   německou   hospodářskou   a politickou   demokracii?   [Foreigners   have contributed   significantly   to   the   German economic   and   cultural   development,   so why not to emphasize their number in statistics, and to acknowledge their merit of the German economic and political democracy by this?*

(4)   *Dnes se tento počet snížil na asi půl milionu, jenže   důvodem   poklesu   je   především skutečnost,   že   ten,   kdo   není   zaměstnán déle než rok, již podporu nedostane. [Today, that number dropped to about half a million, but the reason for the decline is the fact that anyone who is not employed for more than a year, gets no support anymore.]*

In some cases (ca. 16%), reference to abstract entities in Czech is expressed by a non-modified NP. In coreference chains in German, these are mostly named entities which never refer to abstract entities.

German shows a clear preference for demonstrative heads (like *dies* in example (1) in Section 1 above) to refer to abstract entities (ca. 65%). Another device within this category is a pronominal adverb, e.g. *dazu, dabei* which represents a com-

	German		Czech	
	abs.	in %	abs.	in %
to clauses	5	7.35	13	20.63
to sentences	45	66.18	20	31.75
to bigger segments	18	26.47	30	47.62
total	68	100.00	63	100.00

Table 1: Number of anaphors referring to the antecedents other than NP and pronoun and their subtypes

	German		Czech	
	abs.	in %	abs.	in %
demonstrative head (*dies, dazu/ ten [this]*)	44	64.71	28	44.44
demonstrative modifier + NP (*diese Frage/ tato otzka [this question]*)	16	23.53	17	26.98
bare NP	0	0.00	10	15.87
temporal/local (*hier, da, nun/ tam, tady [here, there, now]*)	3	4.41	4	6.35
personal pronoun (*er, sie [he she]*, etc.)/ zero anahora	3	4.41	2	3.17
comparative	2	2.94	2	3.17
total	68	100.00	63	100.00

Table 2: Distribution of anaphora types referring to abstract entities in German and Czech

position of a preposition and the definite article, and is very common in German. Most of them in our data (over 55%) refer to sentences or even larger segments, although NPs can also be their antecedents, see example (5).

(5)   *Diese "Euro-Münzhaushaltsmischung" kostet 20 DM. Dafür bekommt man 20 Münzen zwischen 1 Cent und 2 Euro. [This household set of euro coins will cost 20 marks. For this, you get 20 coins between 1 cent and 2 euros in value].*

Anaphoric expressions in the form of nominal phrases modified by a demonstrative pronoun or a definite article, mostly contain a general noun, e.g. *Weise [way]* in example (6).

(6)   *Die neue deutsche Truppe wurde vollständig in die militärischen Strukturen der Nato integriert. Auf diese Weise konnte das Ziel erreicht werden. [The new German units were fully integrated into NATO military structures. In this way it was possible to achieve the goal of...]*

This structure can refer both to longer segments as in example (6), and to clauses as in example (7), where we have an infinitive clause as an antecedent of *dieses Feld [this area].*

(7)   *Es ist eine der wichtigsten Aufgaben des Staates, die Erhaltung des freien Wettbewerbs sicherzustellen. Versagt der Staat auf diesem Felde, dann ist es bald um die soziale Marktwirtschaft geschehen. [Protecting free competition is one of the state' s most important tasks. If the state fails in this area, the social market economy will soon be lost].*

In all cases observed in our data, devices referring to abstract entities occur immediately in the following segment (either a clause or a sentence). No cases of longer distances were discovered in the data at hand.

5   Discussion and future work

In this paper, we present preliminary results of cross-lingual analysis of variation in abstract coreference. We analysed a small portion of texts in two languages that are not very close typologically using data sets annotated within two different frameworks. Our findings show that the differences of typological character (absence of definiteness or pro-drops) have also influence on the preferences for certain functional or structural types expressing coreference. We believe that the knowledge on the difference observed here is important for various areas of linguistics, including contrastive studies, translatology and multilingual NLP, especially machine translation. For instance, when translating from Czech into German, demonstrative heads should be used for summarisation of sentences or longer text segments instead of full nominal phrases. It would be interesting to have a look at translations from Czech to German (e.g. using a discriminative translation model of *it* designed in Novak et al. (2013)) to see if we would also see changes in the preferences for abstract anaphora in translated German, as it was shown by Zinsmeister et al. (2012) for the translations from English into German. The authors show that although demonstrative heads are more common for the originally authored texts in German, translated German reveals a higher number of personal heads expressed with *es*, the direct translation of the English *it* which is used in English for coreference to abstract entities. Both translation scholars and machine translation developers should be aware of such differences to avoid production of texts which sound less natural for the target language.

In our future work, we will also consider if the observed phenomena are genre- or domain-dependent. Coreference to abstract entities seems to be specific for the data at hand: abstract anaphora refer to the most central concepts in the analysed discourse. However, we need to have a look at further genres and domains, as well as at larger number of texts, for the evidence for this assumption.

6 Acknowledgement

We acknowledge the support from the Grant Agency of the Czech Republic (grant 16-05394S). This work has been using language resources developed and stored and distributed by the LINDAT/CLARIN project of the Ministry of Education, Youth and Sports of the Czech Republic (project LM2015071). The work on this project was partially supported by the grant "Multilingual Corpus Annotation as a Support for Language Technologies" (LH14011, Ministry of Education, Youth and Sports). The project GECCo has been supported through a grant from the Deutsche Forschungsgemeinschaft (German Research Society).

References

Eduard Bejček, Eva Hajičová, Jan Hajič, Pavlína Jínová, Václava Kettnerová, Veronika Kolářová, Marie Mikulová, Jiří Mírovský, Anna Nedoluzhko, Jarmila Panevová, Lucie Poláková, Magda Ševčíková, Jan Štěpánek, and Šárka Zikánová. 2013. Prague dependency treebank 3.0.

Simon Botley. 2006. Proceedings of the 10th Joint ACL - ISO Workshop on Interoperable Semantic Annotation. *International Journal of Corpus Linguistics*, 11(1):73–112.

Donna Byron. 2003. Annotation of pronouns and their antecedents: A comparison of two domains. Technical report, University of Rochester.

Stefanie Dipper and Heike Zinsmeister. 2009. Proceedings of the third linguistic annotation workshop (law iii).

Gill Francis. 1994. Labelling discourse: an aspect of nominal group lexical cohesion. In Malcolm Coulthard, editor, *Advances in Written Text Analysis*, pages 83–101, London:Routledge.

Kari Fraurud. 1992. Situation reference: What does it refer to? In *GAP Working Paper*, Fachbereich Informatik, Universitat Hamburg.

Silvia Hansen-Schirra, Stella Neumann, and Erich Steiner. 2012. *Cross-linguistic Corpora for the Study of Translations. Insights from the Language Pair English-German.* de Gruyter, Berlin, New York.

Nancy Hedberg, Jeanette K Gundel, and Ron Zacharski. 2007. Directly and indirectly anaphoric demonstrative and personal pronouns in newspaper articles. *Proceedings of DAARC*, pages 31–36.

Lucie Kučová and Eva Hajičová. 2004. Coreferential Relations in the Prague Dependency Treebank. In *Proceedings of the 5th International Conference on Discourse Anaphora and Anaphor Resolution Colloquium*, pages 97–102, San Miguel. Edies Colibri.

Ekaterina Lapshinova, Anna Nedoluzhko, and Kerstin Kunz. 2015. cross languages and genres: Creating a universal annotation scheme for textual relations. In Ines Rehbein and Heike Zinsmeister, editors, *Proceedings of the Workshop on Linguistic Annotations, NAACL-2015*, Denver, USA.

Ekaterina Lapshinova-Koltunski and Kerstin Kunz. 2014. Annotating cohesion for multillingual analysis. In *Proceedings of the 10th Joint ACL - ISO Workshop on Interoperable Semantic Annotation*, Reykjavik, Iceland, May. LREC.

M.C. Müller. 2008. *Fully Automatic Resolution of It, this and that in Unrestricted Multi-party Dialog.* Ph.D. thesis, University of Tübingen.

Costanza Navarretta and Sussi Olsen. 2008. Annotating abstract pronominal anaphora in the DAD project. In *Proceedings of LREC-08*.

Michal Novák, Anna Nedoluzhko, and Zdeněk Žabokrtský. 2013. Translation of "it" in a deep syntax framework. In Bonnie L. Webber, editor, *51st Annual Meeting of the Association for Computational Linguistics Proceedings of the Workshop on Discourse in Machine Translation*, pages 51–59, Sofija, Bulgaria. Bălgarska akademija na naukite, Omnipress, Inc.

Massimo Poesio and Ron Artstein. 2008. Anaphoric Annotation in the ARRAU Corpus. In *International Conference on Language Resources and Evaluation (LREC)*, Marrakech, Morocco, May.

Lucie Poláková, Jiří Mírovský, Anna Nedoluzhko, Pavlína Jínová, Šárka Zikánová, and Eva Hajičová. 2013. Introducing the prague discourse treebank 1.0. In *Proceedings of the 6th International Joint Conference on Natural Language Processing*, pages 91–99, Nagoya, Japan. Asian Federation of Natural Language Processing, Asian Federation of Natural Language Processing.

S. Pradhan, L. Ramshaw, R. Weischedel, J. MacBride, and L. Micciulla. 2007. Unrestricted coreference: Identifying entities and events in ontonotes. In *Proceedings of the IEEE-ICSC*.

Mariona Taulé, Maria Antònia Martí, and Marta Recasens. 2008. Ancora: Multilevel annotated corpora for catalan and spanish. In *LREC*.

Renata Vieira, Susanne Salmon-Alt, Caroline Gasperin, Emmanuel Schang, and Gabriel Othero. 2005. Coreference and anaphoric relations of demonstrative noun phrases in multilingual corpus. *Anaphora Processing: linguistic, cognitive and computational modeling*, pages 385–403.

Heike Zinsmeister, Stefanie Dipper, and Melanie Seiss. 2012. Abstract pronominal anaphors and label nouns in german and english: selected case studies and quantitative investigations. *Translation: Computation, Corpora, Cognition*, 2(1).

Antecedent Prediction Without a Pipeline

Sam Wiseman and **Alexander M. Rush** and **Stuart M. Shieber**
School of Engineering and Applied Sciences
Harvard University
Cambridge, MA, USA
{swiseman,srush,shieber}@seas.harvard.edu

Abstract

We consider several antecedent prediction models that use no pipelined features generated by upstream systems. Models trained in this way are interesting because they allow for side-stepping the intricacies of upstream models, and because we might expect them to generalize better to situations in which upstream features are unavailable or unreliable. Through quantitative and qualitative error analysis we identify what sorts of cases are particularly difficult for such models, and suggest some directions for further improvement.

1 Introduction

Most recent approaches to identity coreference resolution rely on a set of pipelined features generated by relatively accurate upstream systems. For instance, the CoNLL 2012 coreference datasets (Pradhan et al., 2012), which are based on the OntoNotes corpus (Hovy et al., 2006), make available both gold and predicted parse, part-of-speech, and named-entity information for each sentence in the corpus. While recent systems have managed to improve on the state of the art in coreference resolution by taking advantage of such information (Durrett and Klein, 2013; Wiseman et al., 2015; Björkelund and Kuhn, 2014; Fernandes et al., 2012; Martschat and Strube, 2015), we might be interested in systems that do not use pipelined features for several reasons: first, pipelined systems are known to accumulate errors throughout the stages of the pipeline. Second, unpipelined models do not need to contend with the intricacies of the various systems in the pipeline,

which may have little impact on the target task. Finally, models that do not require pipelined features may be more applicable to regimes in which upstream features are unavailable or unreliable, such as those arising from predicting coreference in low-resource languages or in social media text. Indeed, to the extent that it is easier to obtain coreference annotations than it is to obtain (for instance) parse annotations in such regimes, an unpipelined strategy may be particularly practical.

Accordingly, in this paper we consider systems that attempt to move beyond OntoNotes by making coreference predictions without access to pipelined features, using only a document's words and sentence boundaries. In the hopes of shedding light on whether this is a viable strategy, we consider, as a case study, how well coreference systems without access to upstream features can perform on English. Given the amount of research that has gone into resolving English coreference resolution *with pipelined features*, by also considering the English "unpipelined" setting we can expect to get a rather accurate sense of how much we sacrifice by ignoring these features. Moreover, in addition to the benefits of unpipelined models noted above, the proposed line of research is congenial to the recent trend in NLP of using as few hand-engineered features as possible (as advocated, for instance, in Collobert et al. (2011)).

We report preliminary experiments on the subtask of antecedent prediction (defined in Wiseman et al. (2015) and reviewed below) on the CoNLL 2012 English dataset in this unpipelined setting. In particular, we will assume that we have automatically

Proceedings of the Workshop on Coreference Resolution Beyond OntoNotes (CORBON 2016), co-located with NAACL 2016, pages 53–58,
San Diego, California, June 16, 2016. ©2016 Association for Computational Linguistics

extracted mentions from a document, but that no other pipelined information is available. We emphasize that this is a strong assumption (since pipelined features, such as parse trees, are often used to extract mentions), and so what follows should be interpreted as an attempt to obtain an upper bound on the performance possible in such a setting. We conclude by analyzing the errors made by the proposed unpipelined systems, and discussing how these systems might be made more competitive.

1.1 Problem Setting

As above, we will assume we are given a set of documents from which we are able to automatically extract mentions. We denote by $\mathcal{X}$ the set of these automatically extracted mentions. For a mention $x \in \mathcal{X}$, let $\mathcal{A}(x)$ denote the set of mentions appearing before x in the document, and let the set $\mathcal{C}(x) \subseteq \mathcal{A}(x)$ denote the mentions appearing before x that are coreferent with x. The problem of antecedent ranking involves trying to predict an antecedent $y \in \mathcal{C}(x)$ for only those x for which $\mathcal{C}(x) \neq \emptyset$, that is, for only those x that have coreferent antecedents. We will moreover require that in making these antecedent predictions no pipelined features are used. In particular, we will assume that "unpipelined" systems have access only to a document's mention-boundaries, to the sets $\mathcal{C}(x)$ for each $x \in \mathcal{X}$ (when training), to the words in each document, and to the document's sentence boundaries.

Whereas recent coreference systems typically make use of syntactic information, named-entity tags, word-lists containing type information (e.g., number, gender, animacy), and speaker information (Durrett and Klein, 2013; Björkelund and Kuhn, 2014; Lee et al., 2013), given the aforementioned restrictions, the only common coreference features that remain legal are word-based features and "distance" features. Distance features are typically defined in terms of the number of words, mentions, or sentences between a mention and a candidate antecedent (Durrett and Klein, 2013), and such features can presumably be defined accurately in many settings without the use of upstream systems.

2 Models

We will use a very simple mention-ranking style model for our antecedent prediction. Mention-ranking models make use of a scoring function $s(x, y)$ that scores the compatibility between a mention x and a candidate antecedent y, and they predict the antecedent to be $y^* = \arg\max_{y \in \mathcal{C}(x)} s(x, y)$. We will define s as

$$s(x, y) = \boldsymbol{u}^\top \tanh \left(\boldsymbol{W} \begin{bmatrix} \boldsymbol{\Phi}_c(x) \\ \boldsymbol{\Phi}_c(y) \\ \boldsymbol{\Phi}_d(x, y) \end{bmatrix} + \boldsymbol{b} \right),$$

where $\boldsymbol{\Phi}_c$ extracts relevant word-based features from a mention and its context, and $\boldsymbol{\Phi}_d$ extracts distance based features between x and y. Thus, the scoring function s is defined by applying a standard multi-layer perceptron (MLP) to the (vertically) concatenated outputs of the functions $\boldsymbol{\Phi}_c$ and $\boldsymbol{\Phi}_d$. In particular, $\boldsymbol{W}$ represents the weight matrix of the MLP's first hidden layer, $\boldsymbol{b}$ the corresponding bias vector, and $\boldsymbol{u}$ the vector of weights projecting the first hidden layer into a scalar score. The exact dimensions of these weights will become clear in what follows.

In defining $\boldsymbol{\Phi}_c$ we will view a mention x spanning M words as a sequence of real vectors $\boldsymbol{x}_1, \ldots, \boldsymbol{x}_M$, with each $\boldsymbol{x}_m \in \mathbb{R}^D$ obtained by looking up the m'th word in x in an embedding matrix $\boldsymbol{E} \in \mathbb{R}^{D \times |\mathcal{V}|}$, where $\mathcal{V}$ is our fixed vocabulary. Accordingly, let $\boldsymbol{X}_{1:M} \in \mathbb{R}^{D \times M}$ be the matrix formed by concatenating the embeddings of the words in a mention (in order). Analogously, let $\boldsymbol{X}_{-K:-1} \in \mathbb{R}^{D \times K}$ be the concatenation of the embedding-vectors corresponding to the K words preceding x on the left (padded where necessary), and $\boldsymbol{X}_{M+1:M+K}$ the concatenation of the embedding-vectors corresponding to the K words following x on the right (padded where necessary).

For simplicity, we will require $\boldsymbol{\Phi}_c$ to take the following form:

$$\boldsymbol{\Phi}_c(x) = \begin{bmatrix} \boldsymbol{h}(\boldsymbol{X}_{1:M}) \\ \boldsymbol{h}(\boldsymbol{X}_{-K:-1}) \\ \boldsymbol{h}(\boldsymbol{X}_{M+1:M+k}) \end{bmatrix},$$

where $\boldsymbol{h}(\boldsymbol{X}_{i:j})$ is some function of the matrix $\boldsymbol{X}_{i:j}$. That is, $\boldsymbol{\Phi}_c(x)$ simply concatenates a representation of the words of x with representations (respectively) of the K words preceding and following x.

For example, consider the following passage from the development portion of the CoNLL 2012 English development data, from which the final example in Table 1 is taken, and in which we have highlighted a particular mention we might like to predict an antecedent for:

> Suddenly we realized water came into the engine room and it was rising and they started to pump, of course, and they pumped and pumped and **the water** came more and more and more. (bn/cnn/cnn_0410)

If we are interested in predicting coreferent antecedents for "the water," which we will denote by x, then we will have $M = 2$, and $\boldsymbol{X}_{1:2}$ will be a matrix in $\mathbb{R}^{D\times 2}$ with its first column equal to the embedding (in $\boldsymbol{E}$) for "the," and its second column equal to the embedding for "water." Since in predicting x we will likely also want to take into account some of its surrounding context, we will also form matrices corresponding to the K words to the left and to the right (respectively) of x. Thus, if we set $K = 1$, we will form $\boldsymbol{X}_{-1:-1}$ as the matrix in $\mathbb{R}^{D\times 1}$, which consists of the embedding for "and," and we would define $\boldsymbol{X}_{M+1:M+1}$ analogously. Given the aforementioned $\boldsymbol{X}$ matrices, we define $\boldsymbol{\Phi}_c$ by vertically concatenating the output of applying a function $\boldsymbol{h}$ to each of these matrices.

We now consider three approaches to defining $\boldsymbol{h}(\boldsymbol{X}_{1:M})$, in increasing order of complexity:

Max-Over-Time Model: Define $\boldsymbol{h}(\boldsymbol{X}_{1:M})$ to be in $\mathbb{R}^D$, with $\boldsymbol{h}(\boldsymbol{X}_{1:M})_d = \max_{1\leq j\leq M}(\boldsymbol{X}_{1:M})_{dj}$, for each $d = 1,\dots,D$.[1]

Convolutional Model: We follow Kim (2014) in generating F feature maps of $M - h + 1$ features by applying a (non-linear) filter to each h-length window of $\boldsymbol{X}_{1:M}$, and then max-pooling over time. Thus, $\boldsymbol{h}(\boldsymbol{X}_{1:M}) \in \mathbb{R}^F$.

LSTM Model: We define $\boldsymbol{h}(\boldsymbol{X}_{1:M})$ to be in $\mathbb{R}^H$, where $\boldsymbol{h}(\boldsymbol{X}_{1:M})$ is the M'th hidden state of an LSTM (Hochreiter and Schmidhuber, 1997) run over the vectors $\boldsymbol{x}_1,\dots,\boldsymbol{x}_M$ in $\boldsymbol{X}_{1:M}$.

---

[1] We found the max-pooling described here to be more effective than mean-pooling.

To define $\boldsymbol{\Phi}_d$ we first define indicator features (represented as one-hot vectors), which (respectively) bucket the number of mentions and the number of sentences between a mention and a candidate antecedent into 11 discrete buckets, following Durrett and Klein (2013). We therefore have 22 distance indicator features in total, and they are used to index into an embedding matrix $\boldsymbol{A} \in \mathbb{R}^{D_d \times 22}$. Accordingly, $\boldsymbol{\Phi}_d(x,y) \in \mathbb{R}^{D_d}$ represents the sum of the (two) distance embeddings obtained from $\boldsymbol{A}$ in this way. This approach resembles that of Sukhbaatar et al. (2015).

3 Experiments

3.1 Methods

We conduct antecedent-ranking experiments on the development portion of the CoNLL 2012 English corpus. Mentions were extracted using the Berkeley Coreference System (Durrett and Klein, 2013). We set $K = 4$ in forming word-windows, and we trained by optimizing the margin ranking-loss defined in Wiseman et al. (2015) using mini-batch Adagrad (Duchi et al., 2011).

For the convolutional model, we used windows of size 1, 2, and 3, and 40 filters for each. We set D_d, the dimensionality of the distance feature embeddings which constitute the columns of $\boldsymbol{A}$, to 20. We used the `element-rnn` RNN package (Léonard et al., 2015) to implement the LSTM, and we set the LSTM's hidden-layer size to 200. All models used 300 hidden units in the final layer (represented by $\boldsymbol{W}$), and we used Dropout for regularization. All hyperparameters including window size were tuned on the development set.

For all models we initialized $\boldsymbol{E}$, the word embedding matrix, with word vectors obtained from `word2vec` (Mikolov et al., 2013), and so $\boldsymbol{E} \in \mathbb{R}^{300\times|\mathcal{V}|}$, where $\mathcal{V}$ is the vocabulary consisting of words in the training or development sets (plus an unknown word token). $\boldsymbol{E}$ was updated during training. For the Max-Over-Time Model we found it beneficial to untie the embedding matrices used to embed the words in the mention, before the mention, and after the mention, giving 3 separate embedding matrices. For the Convolutional and LSTM Models, performance was at least as good when using a single embedding matrix.

x	Correct Antecedent Prediction	Convolutional Antecedent Prediction
the Straits [Foundation]	the Straits [Foundation]	the Straits [Association]
those Jewish [sacrifices]	the [sacrifices]	the [people] of Israel
the [water]	[water]	their sinking fishing [boat]

Table 1: Example mentions x which the baseline MLP correctly predicts (middle column), but the Convolutional Model (right column) does not. Heads of each mention (unseen by the Convolutional Model) are in brackets.

Model	Acc.
Wiseman et al. (2015)	82.58
Max-Over-Time Model	70.92
Convolutional Model	72.65
LSTM Model	77.40

Table 2: Accuracy of models described in text (and baseline) on predicting antecedents on CoNLL Development set.

	Errors		
	HM	No HM	Pron.
Wiseman et al. (2015)	588	522	1146
Max-Over-Time Model	1513	608	1646
Convolutional Model	1358	607	1577
LSTM Model	1028	537	1362
Total Mentions	4677	973	7302

Table 3: Errors of models described in text on CoNLL 2012 development set. Mentions are partitioned column-wise as nominal or proper with (previous) head match in the document (HM), nominal or proper with no previous head match in the document (No HM), and pronominal.

3.2 Results

We are particularly interested in determining in what situations a word-and-distance model underperforms models with access to more sophisticated information. In Table 2 we compare the antecedent-prediction accuracy of the three models defined above with the antecedent ranking performance of the model described in Wiseman et al. (2015), which uses an MLP over pipelined coreference features. We will refer to this latter model as the "baseline MLP." We see that the word-and-distance models underperform, though the LSTM model comes within 5.2% of the baseline MLP. (It is also worth noting here that without the distance features Φ_d all models are significantly less accurate, with accuracies decreasing by over 15 percentage points).

4 Discussion

In Table 3 we examine, using an analysis similar to that in Durrett and Klein (2013), where the unpipelined models go wrong. There, we partition mentions column-wise into nominal or proper mentions that have a head-match with some previously occurring mention, nominal or proper mentions that do not, and pronominal mentions. (Note that whereas parse information must be used to detect heads, this is only used in our analysis, and none of the three models introduced here have access to this information).

Let us first consider the Convolutional Model, which underperforms the baseline in all categories, but does particularly badly in predicting antecedents for mentions for which a previous mention in the text has the same head.

Why is this? Further analysis shows that almost 84% of the HM examples that are correctly predicted by the baseline MLP but incorrectly predicted by the Convolutional Model involve the baseline MLP predicting an antecedent with an exact head-match to the current mention, and the Convolutional Model predicting a non-head-match antecedent. We show some representative examples in Table 1, where we bracket the head of each mention. As is evident from Table 1, the model is picking antecedents that are semantically reasonable, but which do not have a head match. The reason the Convolutional Model makes these errors is presumably that it is not able to tell what the head of each mention is (because it sees only the words in the mention, and the word-windows preceding and following). The baseline MLP, however, does have access to the heads of each mention, and so can learn that head-match is a discriminative feature.

As we move to the LSTM model, we find that errors decrease in all categories, though follow largely the same pattern. Indeed, over 78% of the LSTM

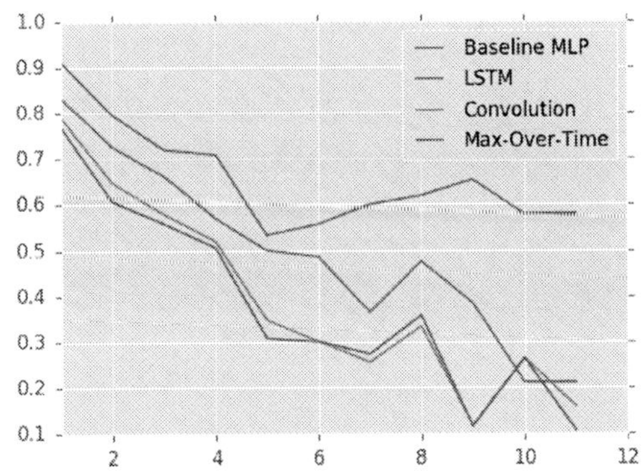

Figure 1: Percentage of antecedents in the CoNLL 2012 development set predicted correctly, by mention length.

model's errors in the HM category also involve predicting a non-head-match antecedent when the baseline MLP correctly predicts a head-match antecedent. Thus, it seems the LSTM model too could benefit from better head-finding. As additional evidence for this hypothesis, in Figure 1 we plot the percentage of correctly predicted antecedents in the CoNLL 2012 development set as the length of the current mention x increases. (Only mention-lengths occurring ≥ 10 times in the development set are reported). We see that the accuracy of both the Convolutional and LSTM models (as well as that of the Max-Over-Time model) generally decreases as the mention-length increases, though that of the baseline MLP model does not. Of course, it stands to reason that finding heads is more difficult in longer mentions, which may explain this trend.

When it comes to the other major category of errors in Table 3, namely, errors on pronominal mentions, it is more difficult to diagnose a single underlying cause of error. In particular, the unpipelined models' errors tend to involve either predicting antecedents that are inconsistent in terms of gender or number, or, interestingly, predicting non-pronominal antecedents when the baseline MLP predicts a pronominal antecedent. While it is certainly the case that the baseline MLP has access to gender information that the unpipelined models do not, it is not as clear why these unpipelined models learn to disprefer predicting pronominal antecedents for pronominal mentions, and this issue requires further investigation.

5 Conclusion

The results presented above suggest that a major factor holding word-and-distance-only models back from competing with models that have access to pipelined features is their inability to find mention-heads and, more generally, to take advantage of syntactic features. While the fact that such models would benefit from syntactic information is not surprising, the examples in Table 1 suggest that even coarse notions of head-finding may be sufficient to improve performance. Accordingly, one might imagine that alignment or attention models (such as that of Bahdanau et al. (2014)) that attempt to model coarse head-information would be useful in such cases.

References

Dzmitry Bahdanau, Kyunghyun Cho, and Yoshua Bengio. 2014. Neural machine translation by jointly learning to align and translate. *arXiv preprint arXiv:1409.0473*.

Anders Björkelund and Jonas Kuhn. 2014. Learning structured perceptrons for coreference Resolution with Latent Antecedents and Non-local Features. *ACL, Baltimore, MD, USA, June*.

Ronan Collobert, Jason Weston, Léon Bottou, Michael Karlen, Koray Kavukcuoglu, and Pavel Kuksa. 2011. Natural Language Processing (almost) from Scratch. *The Journal of Machine Learning Research*, 12:2493–2537.

John Duchi, Elad Hazan, and Yoram Singer. 2011. Adaptive Subgradient Methods for Online Learning and Stochastic Optimization. *The Journal of Machine Learning Research*, 12:2121–2159.

Greg Durrett and Dan Klein. 2013. Easy Victories and Uphill Battles in Coreference Resolution. In *Proceedings of the 2013 Conference on Empirical Methods in Natural Language Processing*, pages 1971–1982.

Eraldo Rezende Fernandes, Cícero Nogueira Dos Santos, and Ruy Luiz Milidiú. 2012. Latent Structure Perceptron with Feature Induction for Unrestricted Coreference Resolution. In *Joint Conference on EMNLP and CoNLL-Shared Task*, pages 41–48. Association for Computational Linguistics.

Sepp Hochreiter and Jürgen Schmidhuber. 1997. Long short-term memory. *Neural Comput.*, 9:1735–1780.

Eduard Hovy, Mitchell Marcus, Martha Palmer, Lance Ramshaw, and Ralph Weischedel. 2006. Ontonotes: the 90% Solution. In *Proceedings of the human language technology conference of the NAACL, Compan-*

ion Volume: Short Papers, pages 57–60. Association for Computational Linguistics.

Yoon Kim. 2014. Convolutional neural networks for sentence classification. In *Proceedings of the 2014 Conference on Empirical Methods in Natural Language Processing, EMNLP*, pages 1746–1751.

Heeyoung Lee, Angel Chang, Yves Peirsman, Nathanael Chambers, Mihai Surdeanu, and Dan Jurafsky. 2013. Deterministic Coreference Resolution based on Entity-centric, Precision-ranked Rules. *Computational Linguistics*, 39(4):885–916.

Nicholas Léonard, Yand Waghmare, Sagar ad Wang, and Jin-Hwa Kim. 2015. rnn: Recurrent Library for Torch. *arXiv preprint arXiv:1511.07889*.

Sebastian Martschat and Michael Strube. 2015. Latent structures for coreference resolution. *TACL*, 3:405–418.

Tomas Mikolov, Ilya Sutskever, Kai Chen, Greg S Corrado, and Jeff Dean. 2013. Distributed representations of words and phrases and their compositionality. In *Advances in neural information processing systems*, pages 3111–3119.

Sameer Pradhan, Alessandro Moschitti, Nianwen Xue, Olga Uryupina, and Yuchen Zhang. 2012. Conll-2012 Shared Task: Modeling Multilingual Unrestricted Coreference in OntoNotes. In *Joint Conference on EMNLP and CoNLL-Shared Task*, pages 1–40. Association for Computational Linguistics.

Sainbayar Sukhbaatar, Jason Weston, Rob Fergus, et al. 2015. End-to-end memory networks. In *Advances in Neural Information Processing Systems*, pages 2431–2439.

Sam Wiseman, Alexander M. Rush, Stuart M. Shieber, and Jason Weston. 2015. Learning anaphoricity and antecedent ranking features for coreference resolution. In *Proceedings of the 53rd Annual Meeting of the Association for Computational Linguistics (ACL)*, pages 1416–1426.

Bridging Corpus for Russian in comparison with Czech

Anna Roitberg
IMPB of IPM RAS
School of Linguistics HSE RSU
Moscow, Russia
aroytberg@lpm.org.ru

Anna Nedoluzhko
Charles University in Prague
Malostranske nam. 25
CZ-11800 Prague
nedoluzko@ufal.mff.cuni.cz

Abstract

In this paper, we present a syntactic approach to the annotation of bridging relations, so-called *genitive bridging*. We introduce the Ru-GenBridge corpus for Russian annotated with genitive bridging and compare it to the semantic approach that was applied in the Prague Dependency Treebank for Czech. We discuss some special aspects of bridging resolution for Russian and specifics of bridging annotation for languages where definite nominal groups are not as frequent as e.g. in Romance and Germanic languages. To verify the consistency of our method, we carry out two comparative experiments: the annotation of a small portion of our corpus with bridging relations according to both approaches and finding for all relations from the RuGenBridge their semantic interpretation that would be annotated for Czech.

1 Motivation

Anaphora plays an important role in understanding textual cohesion and coherence. Clark (1975) divides anaphoric relations into two classes, distinguishing direct and indirect anaphora. Direct anaphora (coreference) takes place between language expressions referring to the same discourse entity. In the case of indirect interferences (also called *bridging*), the antecedent is not mentioned but associated with some expression in the previous text. These are, for instance, relations between *two people – the woman* and *murdered – the murderer* in Clark's Example (1) and (2) below:

(1)   *I met **two people** yesterday. **The woman** told me a story.* (Clark, 1975)

(2)   *John **was murdered** yesterday. The **murderer** got away.* (Clark, 1975)

Generaly speaking, a *bridging relation* can be understood as an inference about two non-coreferential expressions introduced in a text that are related in some particular way that is not explicitly stated, but this relation contributes essentially to the text coherence. This Clark's definition of bridging relations, as vague as it is, led to different notions of bridging being used in different approaches. For example, in (Clark, 1975), non-identity semantic relations between entities are classified into three groups: indirect reference by association, indirect reference by characterization and rhetorical relations. For the time being, there is no generally accepted classification of bridging relations. The basic principle accepted in most of the existing approaches is that a list of bridging relations is based on types of semantic relations. Thus, typical examples of bridging are anaphoric relations between entities, which at the same time are e.g. in meronymic relations as represented in Example (3).

(3)   *There were some **fruits** on the table. John took **an apple**.*

However, such interpretation sounds very vague. If bridging relations are expected to rely on semantics, we have at least two questions to answer before we begin to apply a systematic classification or annotation of language data. First, we have to decide which kinds of relations we are interested in, how

Proceedings of the Workshop on Coreference Resolution Beyond OntoNotes (CORBON 2016), co-located with NAACL 2016, pages 59–66,
San Diego, California, June 16, 2016. ©2016 Association for Computational Linguistics

detailed the classification should be and which relations should be ignored. Second, we have to delimit the boundaries between semantic language-based relations and the relations which are recognized based on the world knowledge or extralinguistic context. Both problems are complicated tasks, the final decision mostly depends on the purpose of the analysis, amount of data and the resources available. To avoid these problems, we decided to choose a syntactic approach to bridging relations, instead of the traditional semantic one. We annotate so-called *genitive bridging*: the case where two elements (an anchor/antecedent and a bridging element/anaphor) can form a genitive construction, where the anchor is marked with the genitive case in Russian. In Example (4), the anchor is *dom [house]*, the bridging element is *stenah [walls]*, and the genitive construction that can be formed is *stenah doma_Gen [the walls of the house]*.

(4)   *U nego byl milyj **dom** s plyuš':om na **stenah** (doma). [He has a nice **house** with ivy climbing the **walls** (of the house).]*

We believe that this approach will improve the consistency of the annotated data and will allow us to create a more reliable corpus for the prepared computational experiments.

This work describes an ongoing project, with the data annotated within the new syntactic approach (RuGenBrigde corpus). To the best of our knowledge, this approach has not been applied to any large-scale data annotation yet, so we do not have any corroboration of its reliability. To prove the advantages of our approach, it is necessary to (i) provide the empirical verification of the quality of our annotation scheme through double annotation and measuring the inter-annotator agreement and (ii) to compare our annotations to other bridging annotation approaches. This paper addresses the second task. We decided to compare our annotations to bridging relations annotation in the Prague Dependency Treebank (PDT, Bejček et al., (2013)). There are several reasons for this choice:

- PDT is one of a restricted number of corpora with a large-scale annotation of bridging relations;

- The texts in PDT are in Czech, which is a Slavic language with many structural (grammatical and syntactic) similarities, e.g. it has the similar declination system, so the genitive bridgings are expected in the same way as in Russian; like Russian, Czech lacks the grammatical category of definiteness;

- The bridging annotation approach used in PDT is claimed to be purely semantic (Zikánová et al., 2015), thus the comparison is especially interesting;

- The number and the types of bridging relations applied in PDT is an average compared to state-of-the-art bridging approaches applied.

The paper is structured as follows: after observing the related work in 1.1, we present the RuGenBrigde corpus for Russian (Section 2) and bridging annotation in Czech (Section 3); we compare the annotation schemes in Section 4. Further, in Section 5, we describe two experiments that have been carried out on the Russian texts: (i) the application of Czech and Russian annotation schemes on the same texts and (ii) the annotation of all pairs from RuGenBrigde corpus with possible PDT bridging relations marks. We discuss the results in Section 6.

1.1   Related work

There are two main annotation approaches. The first (and more popular) is based on semantic constraints on bridging relations. This approach is close to Clark's reference by association. Such bridging interpretation is used in the studies of Asher and Lascarides (1998), applying the segmented discourse representation theory to bridging relations, corpus annotations by M. Poesio for English and Italian (cf. Poesio (2000), Poesio et al. (2004); Poesio and Arstein (2008)), M. Recasens (Recasens et al., 2007) for Spanish and Catalan, Zikánová et al. (2015) for Czech; the semantic approach is also used in Lüngen (2008), Gardent (2003) and so on. The typical relations of the semantic approach are meronymic part–whole and set–subset relations, co-hyponymy (*mother – father* as family members), relations of belonging (e.g. a person and his/her clothes), relations between the situation and its participants (*murder – murderer*), some symptomatic relations (*fever – illness*) and so on.

Alternatively, there are a few corpora, where there are no strict semantic constraints on bridging relations, and all types of "associative" relations between nominal groups are taken into account. This approach is realized e.g. in (Hou et al., 2013).

It should also be noted that usually the term bridging relation is used for definite nominal groups, see e.g. (Löbner, 1998) or (Poesio and Artstein, 2008). However, the same kind of implicit anaphoric linking is also possible with indefinite or quantifying or even generic nominal groups, cf. distribution statistics in (Hou et al., 2013). For instance, in Example (5), a bridging relation can be observed between the Czech generic nominal group *nový VW Golf [the new VW Golf]*[1] and an indefinite nominal group *jedním novým golfem [one of the new Golfs]* (one arbitrary car of this category).

(5)   *Nový VW Golf je vybaven motorem o síle 110 kW... Dostali jsme možnost se jedním novým golfem projet.* (PDT, cit. from (Zikánová et al., 2015) [*The new VW Golf is equipped with an engine power 110 kW... We had an opportunity to ride in one of the new Golfs.*]

2   Annotation of bridging relations in Russian

Here, we present a new corpus RuGenBrigde, the first corpus annotated with bridging relations for Russian. We develop this corpus for training and testing automatic bridging detection and resolution systems. In the present stage of the project, RuGen-Brigde consists of 207 news texts[2] (35,841 tokens), most texts contain 100 - 250 words each. The corpus was annotated with automatic part of speech tagging by FreeLing.[3] The bridging cases were annotated manually using BRAT annotation tool[4].

2.1   Bridging in genitive constructions

Unlike most approaches defining bridging relations in terms of semantic and pragmatic categories, in the

Russian corpus, we use rather syntactic than semantic criteria. We focus mainly on the cases of bridging in genitive construction, so-called, *genitive bridging*. This is the case where the dependent nominal group of the construction is marked with the genitive case in Russian, the head NP has no case restrictions. For instance, in Example (6), there is a genitive bridging relation between *voditel' [driver]* and *avtobus [bus]* , because it is understood as *voditel' avtobusa_Gen [the driver of the bus]*.

(6)   *V **avtobuse** nachalsya pozhar.* **Voditel'** (avtobusa) *sam potušil ogon'.* [*The fire broke out in **the bus**. **The driver** (of the bus) put out the fire by himself.*]

In fact, we capture bridging relations in genitive constructions if an anaphor of bridging pair may have a dependent NP in genitive case, but it is mostly not expressed in the sentence because the potential dependent NP was used recently earlier in the text and it is still actualized in the mind of the reader. For example, by *driver* in Example (6), an addressee can easily infer that the driver of *the bus* mentioned in the previous sentence is meant.

The most typical semantics of Russian genitive constructions is the 'part–whole' relation in a broad sense, where the whole is marked by genitive case (*glaza ubijcy_Gen [eyes of the murderer]*). Other frequent cases are expressions, where a head is a deverbal noun with a genitive participant *vybory prezidenta_Gen [elections of the president]*, measure nouns *barel' nefti_Gen [barrel of oil]* etc.

2.2   Annotation scheme for Russian

Nouns or nominal groups are subjects to annotation. We adhere to the principle of the minimum possible markable: if possible, annotators tag a bare noun, the whole noun phrase is annotated only in the case when it is the minimum possible name of the entity. Thus, in *my beautiful dog*, the markable *dog* is annotated, but in *The Ministry of Justice*, the whole phrase is annotated as a markable because all the words compose the name of the organization.

In RuGenBridge, the following types of bridging relations are annotated:

1. Bridging relations in genitive constructions (type BRIDGE). See Examples (4) and (6)

---

[1]Golf is a type of car made by Volkswagen.
[2]News from www.polit.ru site
[3]http://nlp.lsi.upc.edu/freeling/
[4]http://brat.nlplab.org

above. There are 362 cases of type BRIDGE in our corpus.

2. We also annotate some cases which are very close to the genitive bridging, but genitive construction in Russian is not possible there, for purely syntactic reasons. We use NON-GEN mark for such pairs, see the relation between *Russian Federation* and *Syberia* in Example (7). This type is especially common with the named entities. There are just 8 cases of NON-GEN in our corpus.

(7)   *Pravitel'stvo **Rossijskoj Federacii** vneslo na rassmotrenie (...) Etot proekt takže sposobstvuet razvitiju **Sibiri**. [The Government of the **Russian Federation** brings a bill (...) This bill also promotes the development of **Syberia**.]*

It should be noted, that our annotation scheme is oriented on the language properties of Russian, primarily on the properties of Russian genitive constructions. The ability to form a genitive construction is a very important criterion for the annotators by marking bridging relations in the corpus; in fact, they are guided by it. So, in Example (8) below[5] we annotate the bridging relation *bag – mum*, because *sumka mamy_Gen [mum's bag]* is grammatical in Russian; the link *bag – supermarket* would not be annotated, because **sumka supermarketa_Gen" [*supermarket's bag]* is ungrammatical.

(8)   *The **mum** came from a **supermarket** and got lost in her Facebook. The **bag** is still in the doorway.*

The statistics of the annotated types in RuGenBrigde is presented in Table 2 in Section 5.2, together with the results of comparison experiments.

Apart from the annotation of bridging relations, three most frequent types of annotated NPs are manually marked with special labels in our corpus: (i) GEO (157 cases) for all geographic names (*Moscow, Atlantic Ocean, Thailand* etc.), (ii) ORG (35 cases) for official organizations, both proper and current names (*ministry, policy, LifeNews* etc.) and (iii) POST (22 cases) for political positions (*pres-*

---

ident, deputy etc.). The ORG mark in RuGen-Bridge is comparable to the NORP (Nationality, Organizations and Political organizations) category in OntoNotes (Stoyanov et al., 2011), but we do not include Nationalities, e.g. we do not mark *Swedes* as ORG in Example (9).

(9)   *Swedes usually drink coffee in the morning.*

3 Annotation of bridging relations in Czech

Bridging relations in Czech are annotated on the Prague Dependency Treebank (PDT). This is a large-scale annotation on ca. 50000 sentences of news texts. Apart from bridging, other textual phenomena (syntactic structure, ellipsis, coreference, discourse relations, information structure, etc.) are annotated, see (Poláková et al., 2013). The classification of bridging relations in PDT is based on semantic and pragmatic principles. The annotation preserves distinctions between the following groups: (1) meronymy relations between a part and a whole (subtypes PART-WHOLE and WHOLE-PART, as e.g. in *face – eyes*), (2) the relation between a set and its subsets or elements of the set (subtypes SUBSET-SET and SET-SUBSET, as in *a group of students – some students – a student*), (3) the relation between an entity and a singular function on this entity (subtypes P-FUNCT and FUNCT-P, as in *company – director*) (4) the relation between coherence-relevant discourse opposites (type CONTRAST, as in *black flags – white flags*), (5) non-coreferential explicit anaphoric relation (type ANAPH, as in *first world war – at that time*) and (6) further underspecified group REST consisting of six other bridging subtypes (e.g. relations between family members, event – argument, locality – inhabitant, etc.).

Unlike in RuGenBrigde, bridging relations in PDT connect not only the individual nominal groups but the whole coreference chains. Thus, once postulating a bridging relation between two elements of different coreference chains, it should not be marked again for coreferential expressions later in text. Another significant distinction is the principle of the *maximum* possible markables (all dependency subtrees of antecedent and bridging elements are considered to be markables).

---

[5]We thank our reviewer for this example.

4 Comparison of annotation schemes

The difference of annotation schemes is immediately related to the scope and nature of the corpora. Our goal here is not to compare the corpora: it is useless to compare a big and richly annotated corpus with a small and a focused one, which is still in the early stage of its development. Thus, the comparison concerns only the relevant points.

4.1 Characteristics of markables

The first relevant point concerns properties of markables and the scope. The scope is different: RuGenBrigde chooses the minimum and PDT the maximum scope of the markables. On the other hand, both approaches consider some referential adjectives as markables, first of all those which are derived from locational nouns (e.g. *USA – American*). Only referential and abstract nouns can be annotated in the Czech corpus, non-referential nouns are not concerned. For example, such nouns as measures, points etc. are considered to be non-referential, so bridging relations can not be marked in pairs like *barrel – oil* or *point – share price*. Opposite to this, in the Russian corpus, both referential and non-referential nouns can take part in bridging relations. So, in examples like (10) below, bridging relations will be marked in Russian corpus and will not be marked in Czech corpus.

(10)   *Oil futures contracts rose by 1.79% and settled at $45.54 per **barrel** (of oil) on Friday.*

4.2 Inventory of relations

Bridging annotation in the Czech corpus is a part of discourse level annotation, the semantics of relations was taken into account (Nedoluzhko and Mírovský, 2011) and the corpus is meant to be multi-purpose. The Russian corpus is primarily aimed to create training and testing data for an automatic resolution system. For this reason, semantic classification of relations is not so important. Nevertheless, syntactic constraints inevitably produce some semantic constrains. For instance, the Russian genitive construction is typically used for marking possessive relations (broadly defined). The most common examples of this construction include: *sumka mamy [the mom's bag], stena doma [the wall of the house], hvost kota [cat's tail]* and so on. On the other hand,

examining the list of the most frequent genitive construction examples in Russian National Corpus[6], we can observe three groups of non-possessive cases: (i) the first group consists of expressions with nouns derived from verbs: *uvol'nenie nachal'nika [termination of the boss], pohorony aktera [funeral of an actor]*; (ii) the second group contains expressions with measure words, e.g. *liter, kilogram*; and (iii) the third group represents mostly government positions, such as *ministr inostrannyh del [foreign secretary, lit. minister of foreign affairs]*.

Hence, we cannot say that the genitive constraint is identical to the possessive constraint: there is a finite list of semantic relations between the anchor and the bridging element. Moreover, this set of possible semantic relations seems to be comparable to some types of Czech bridging relations. The bridging anaphora of types PART-WHOLE (WHOLE-PART) and SET-SUB (SUB-SET) are often the cases of general possession, and FUNCT-P (P-FUNCT) are often the cases of government positions.

5 The experiments - application of the PDT and RuGenBrigde schemes

Starting the annotation of Russian corpus, we supposed that elements of annotated pairs will form semantic relational classes similar to those annotated within semantic approaches to bridging relations as the result. So, we expected to catch such cases as part–whole (*krysha doma_Gen [roof of the house]*) or possessive (*sumka mamy_Gen [mom's bag]*) relations. With such a result, systematic syntactic approach could reflect the semantic aspect of bridging relations. To test this hypothesis, we decided to apply a semantically oriented annotation scheme to the Russian texts. For the reasons stated in Section 1, we have chosen the PDT annotation scheme. In what follows, we describe two experiments in application of the PDT scheme for Russian.

5.1 Experiment 1: application of PDT and RuGenBrigde schemes for a subset of RuGenBrigde

In the first experiment, we have annotated 8 documents in Russian with the PDT and RuGenBrigde

---

[6]http://www.ruscorpora.ru

schemes in parallel with two annotators. One annotator used the PDT semantic approach and another annotator used the syntactic approach of the RuGenBrigde corpus. Contrary to the expectative closeness of semantics between the relation sets, there is a very low coincidence between the annotated pairs. The results are shown in Table 1.

Czech annotation scheme		Russian annotation scheme	
TOTAL	69	TOTAL	22
CONTRAST	6	BRIDGE	22
FUNCT-P	3		
P-FUNCT	11		
PART-WHOLE	3		
SET-SUB	5		
SUB-SET	13		
WHOLE-PART	18		
REST	10		

Table 1: Comparison of Russian and Czech annotation schemes on 8 documents from RuGenBrigde

We have 69 bridging pairs with the PDT annotation scheme and only 22 with the Russian one. Furthermore, there are only 7 coincidence cases where anchor and bridging element of the pair are the same, notably that 3 (of the 7) cases belong to one sentence (man and his body parts).

One of the reasons for such difference is that genitive bridging in Russian corpus is allowed in only one direction, where the bridging element (to which the genitive form of the anchor can be potentially added) follows the anchor in text. In Czech, both directions (e.g. PART_WHOLE and WHOLE_PART) are possible. The second reason is that relations between proper names (e.g. *Washington – USA*) are allowed in the PDT scheme and are very seldom in RuGenBrigde. There is only one class of these relations: names of regions may be linked with name of countries, as in case of *Moscow region – Russia* described in Section 2.2 above).

The results of the experiment evidence that the semantic approach is more broad-based than our genitive syntactic approach. However, we believe that syntactic approach could be more systematic and clear for annotation, thus presenting a more reliable data for automatic resolution systems. To test this statement we are intending to annotate our data with more annotators in the near future. On the other hand, this experiment displayed that syntactic approach brights out specific bridging relation types, which are not identified in the semantic approach. For this reason, we decided to conduct another experiment and to examine the cases, which seem to be difficult to catch while applying a semantic annotation scheme.

5.2 Experiment 2: application of the PDT types to all possible RuGenBrigde genitive bridgings

This experiment is aimed to find out which semantic relations are more frequent among the cases of genitive bridging. As another task, we want to distinguish and classify the cases that are not overlapped by the set of PDT semantic relations.

In this experiment, we checked out all cases of genitive bridging in the RuGenBrigde corpus, and for all pairs where it was possible, we added the relations that would be annotated within the PDT annotation framework. As the result, for 430 bridging pairs annotated with genitive bridging (types BRIDGE, COREF-BRIDGE or NON-GEN), we have 165 pairs annotated with the PDT tags and 265 pairs remained without the PDT tags. Table 2 shows the numerical results of the experiment.

Czech annotation marks		Russian annotation marks	
AllPDT	152	AllRuGenBridge	370
PART-WHOLE	73	BRIDGE	362
P-FUNCT	55	NON-GEN	8
SET-SUBSET	8		
REST	16		

Table 2: All relation marks for Russian RuGenBridge pairs

As shown in Table 2, PART-WHOLE (*house – roof*) and FUNCT-P (*Russia – prime-minister*) are significantly more frequent than other PDT relations. 218 pairs which were not annotated with PDT marks can be further sub-classified into the following groups:

1. Anchors are geographical names, bridging elements (56 pairs) can be further divided into two subclasses:

   (a) something is located in this geographic object (*Moscow – hospitals*), or

(b) something is concerned with this geographic object (*Russia – budget*).

2. Among the rest 162 pairs, we detected the following types:

    (a) object – its possessor (*flat – landloard*),

    (b) object – something belonging to this object, but not the part of the object (*aerodrome – airplane*),

    (c) expressions with the names of measures (*oil – barrel*),

    (d) collocations, mostly deverbative nouns (*rates – increase*).

The measure group (2c) reflects the Russian language-specific feature: measure words require genitive dependents, so this bridging relation can be really considered as purely syntactic. Most of examples in the last group (2d) are of syntactic nature (more detail in Section 6).

6 Discussion

Let us now analyze some characteristics of bridging relations which make the output of the syntactic annotation approach. Looking at the semantics of expressions taking part in the bridging relations in ReGenBridge, we can see that there is a significant number of antecedents referring to geographic names: among the total of 370 cases, 135 antecedents (36,5% of all bridging relations in the corpus) are marked with the GEO label. These are mostly names of the countries and the relations can be often interpreted as part-whole bridging relations in the Prague annotation scheme (e.g. country – part of this country, region, etc. make up 41 cases, or 31% of GEO antecedents). Another frequent correlation between the GEO antecedents in the PDT bridging types is the type FUNCT, these are often relations between the name of the country and some unique function on it, e.g. *USA - ministry of foreign affairs* (34 cases, or 25% of GEO antecedents in our corpus). We note that the relations where GEO labels in genitive bridging annotation correspond to PART-WHOLE and FUNCT-P in PDT primarily reflect the world knowledge. This speaks against the purity of the Prague semantic annotation. On the other hand, as mentioned above, the borderline between the world knowledge and semantics is quite fuzzy.

The remainder cases of the GEO antecedents (59 cases) could not be annotated with any of the PDT bridging types.[7] Looking at these pairs in more detail, we can see that the anaphoricity between the entities is not given by a semantic relation, but rather by a textual structure and referent activation practices. Typically for the news genre, events are located in a specific place that is introduced once and remains activated for the whole description (e.g. once introducing Russia, we speek about budget, hospitals and schools there without repetitions like *hospitals of Russia, schools of Russia* and so on). In this way, redundant repetitions are avoided, and this also speaks for the discourse origin of bridging anaphora.

Considering genitive bridgings which did not find any semantic interpretation within the PDT annotation scheme (218 out of 370 cases), we notice that anaphoricity of many pairs is given by situational relationships within the texts. These relations do not have semantic nature, so they can be hardly included in any dictionaries of ontologies. On the other hand, they are not purely pragmatic. They are text-given: being introduced at the beginning, they are further used as known and accepted. In this respect, the general phenomenon of bridging relations (and our genitive bridging is a subset of them) can be considered to be deictic and may be related to the category of definiteness or contextual boundness of expressions in text, where the variables are also introduced and further used in text as known.

An additional interesting point that is given by the comparison of genitive bridging approach to the PDT annotation scheme is that it gives the possibility to test the consistency of the PDT annotation. In some cases, we found problematic the borderlines between SET-SUBSET and FUNCT bridging types (cf. the problematic point of uniqueness in *parliament – deputies* (no annotation to parliament) *parliament – premier* (P-FUNCT to *parliament*, because premier in the parliament is unique)). Also, we met a number of cases which were not annotated

---

[7]These are mostly the cases of multiple objects located in a place marked with a GEO antecedent, e.g. *Russia – schools, banks, hospitals, parks*, etc.

in PDT, however they could be interpreted in terms of PDT semantic relations, for example the pair *defendant – criminal case* was not annotated although it can be considered as 'event – argument' and annotated within the REST subtype. Additionally, we found that the pairs 'a geographic name – something located there' are very common, but such cases were not included in the PDT annotation scheme.

7 Conclusion

In this paper, we introduced the syntactic approach to bridging annotation and presented some preliminary investigations on its semantic interpretation. The comparison has shown that genitive bridging provides an opportunity to find out new functional types of bridging relations with respect to textual structure. We believe that this approach is more consistent than semantic annotation of bridging, because it is based on formal criteria and it does not require fixing a borderline between semantics and the world knowledge. However, the paper presents the ongoing research which is in the first half of its development. Our immediate goals for the future work are (i) to annotate the existing corpus with two annotators and a supervisor, and to measure the inter-annotator agreement, (ii) to extend the corpus and analyze bridging cases attested and (iii) to develop a system for genitive bridging resolution based on the information in the corpus.

Acknowledgments

The study was supported by the Russian Foundation for Basic research (grant No. 15-07-09306), the Grant Agency of the Czech Republic (grant 16-05394S) and Ministry of Education, Youth and Sports (grant LH14011).

References

Nicholas Asher and Alex Lascarides. 1998. Bridging. *Journal of Semantics*, 15(1):83–113.

Eduard Bejček, Eva Hajičová, Jan Hajič, Pavlína Jínová, Václava Kettnerová, Veronika Kolářová, Marie Mikulová, Jiří Mírovský, Anna Nedoluzhko, Jarmila Panevová, Lucie Poláková, Magda Ševčíková, Jan Štěpánek, and Šárka Zikánová. 2013. Prague Dependency Treebank 3.0. Data/software. [cit. 2015_07_22].

Herbert H Clark. 1975. Bridging. In *Proceedings of the 1975 workshop on Theoretical issues in natural language processing*, pages 169–174. Association for Computational Linguistics.

Claire Gardent, Hélène Manuélian, and Eric Kow. 2003. Which bridges for bridging definite descriptions. In *Proceedings of the EACL 2003 Workshop on Linguistically Interpreted Corpora*, pages 69–76.

Yufang Hou, Katja Markert, and Michael Strube. 2013. Global inference for bridging anaphora resolution. In *HLT-NAACL*, pages 907–917.

Sebastian Löbner. 1998. Definite associative anaphora. *manuscript) http://user. phil-fak. uniduesseldorf. de/~ loebner/publ/DAA-03. pdf.*

Harald Lüngen. 2008. RRSet-Taxonomy of rhetorical relations in SemDok. *Interne Reports der DFG-Forschergruppe*, 437.

Anna Nedoluzhko and Jiří Mírovský. 2011. Annotating extended textual coreference and bridging relations in the Prague Dependency Treebank. *Annotation manual. Technical report*, (44).

Massimo Poesio and Ron Artstein. 2008. Anaphoric Annotation in the ARRAU Corpus. In *LREC*.

Massimo Poesio, Rahul Mehta, Axel Maroudas, and Janet Hitzeman. 2004. Learning to resolve bridging references. In *Proceedings of the 42nd Annual Meeting on Association for Computational Linguistics*, page 143. Association for Computational Linguistics.

Massimo Poesio. 2000. Annotating a corpus to develop and evaluate discourse entity realization algorithms: Issues and preliminary results. In *LREC*.

Lucie Poláková, Jiří Mírovský, Anna Nedoluzhko, Pavlína Jínová, Šárka Zikánová, and Eva Hajicová. 2013. Introducing the Prague Discourse Treebank 1.0. In *IJCNLP*, pages 91–99.

Marta Recasens, M Antonia Martı, and Mariona Taulé. 2007. Text as scene: Discourse deixis and bridging relations. *Procesamiento del lenguaje natural*, 39:205–212.

Veselin Stoyanov, Uday Babbar, Pracheer Gupta, and Claire Cardie. 2011. Reconciling ontonotes: Unrestricted coreference resolution in ontonotes with reconcile. In *Proceedings of the Fifteenth Conference on Computational Natural Language Learning: Shared Task*, pages 122–126. Association for Computational Linguistics.

Šárka Zikánová, Eva Hajičová, Barbora Hladká, Pavlína Jínová, Jiří Mírovský, Anna Nedoluzhko, Lucie Poláková, Kateřina Rysová, Magdaléna Rysová, and Jan Václ. 2015. *Discourse and Coherence. From the Sentence Structure to Relations in Text*, volume 14 of *Studies in Computational and Theoretical Linguistics*. Charles University in Prague, Praha, Czechia.

Coreference Resolution for the Basque Language
with BART

Ander Soraluze, Olatz Arregi,
Xabier Arregi, Arantza Díaz de Ilarraza
University of the Basque Country
Donostia - San Sebastián, Spain
{ander.soraluze,olatz.arregi
xabier.arregi,a.diazdeilarraza} @ehu.eus

Mijail Kabadjov, Massimo Poesio
University of Essex
Colchester, UK
{malexa,poesio}
@essex.ac.uk

Abstract

In this paper we present our work on Coreference Resolution in Basque, a unique language which poses interesting challenges for the problem of coreference. We explain how we extend the coreference resolution toolkit, BART, in order to enable it to process Basque. Then we run four different experiments showing both a significant improvement by extending a baseline feature set and the effect of calculating performance of hand-parsed mentions vs. automatically parsed mentions. Finally, we discuss some key characteristics of Basque which make it particularly challenging for coreference and draw a road map for future work.

1 Introduction

Basque is a language spoken by nearly three quarters of a million people, most of which live in the Basque country, a region spanning parts of northern Spain and southwestern France. One of the most surprising findings about the Basque language is that it cannot be linked with any of its Indo-European neighbours in Europe and, hence, has been classified as a language isolate. It differs considerably in grammar from the languages spoken in surrounding regions. It is an agglutinative, head-final, pro-drop, free-word order language (Laka, 1996).

Naturally, the Basque language has also inspired a lot of work in Computational Linguistics with tools for automatically processing it becoming increasingly available (Alegria et al., 1996; Alegria et al., 2002; Alegria et al., 2003; Aduriz and Díaz de Ilarraza, 2003; Alegria et al., 2008). However, as it is

the case with most less-resourced languages, there are tools for the core processing levels, such as tokenisation, sentence splitting, morphological analysis, syntactic parsing/chunking, but much less so for higher semantic levels required in end goal applications such as Question Answering (Morton, 2000), Text Summarisation (Steinberger et al., 2007) or Information Extraction (Def, 1995; Hirschman, 1998). One such intermediate problem which has been underresearched for Basque, and hence, no readily usable tools are publicly available yet, is that of Coreference Resolution (Poesio et al., 2016).

However, preliminary work on Coreference for Basque is starting to emerge (Soraluze et al., 2015), and in this paper we describe our work on extending the coreference resolution toolkit, BART[1] (Versley et al., 2008) to the Basque language. BART benefits from an open architecture and provides a mechanism through language plugins which makes it particularly suitable for adaptations to new languages, and it attained good performance in the shared task on Multilingual Coreference at CoNLL 2012 (Uryupina et al., 2012).

For our experiments we use the EPEC corpus annotated for coreference (Aduriz et al., 2006) and we run experiments across two dimensions. First, we use a baseline model based on (Soon et al., 2001) vs. a model that includes extra features reliably extracted for Basque with the tools at hand. Second, we measure performance on hand-parsed mentions vs. performance on automatically parsed mentions which illustrates the effect of pre-processing quality on the end results.

---

[1]http://www.bart-coref.eu/

67

Proceedings of the Workshop on Coreference Resolution Beyond OntoNotes (CORBON 2016), co-located with NAACL 2016, pages 67–73,
San Diego, California, June 16, 2016. ©2016 Association for Computational Linguistics

One of the key challenges that the Basque language introduces for Coreference is that it uses a genderless system for pronouns. In our experiments we look in more depth around this issue and show the challenges it presents as well as suggest viable solutions to model it with machine learning techniques.

The remainder of this paper is organised as follows: Section §2 briefly surveys related work, Section §3 gives details of EPEC, a coreference corpus, Section §4 describes the extension of BART to Basque, Section §5 presents results and provides a discussion on the challenges for coreference in Basque, and towards the end we draw conclusions and pointers to future work.

2 Related Work

Preliminary work on Coreference for Basque was done by (Soraluze et al., 2015) where they adapt the Stanford coreference resolution system (Lee et al., 2013) to Basque. And there has been a lot of work on extending the BART coreference toolkit to languages other than English. (Poesio et al., 2010) extend it to Italian using the Evalita corpus of Wikipedia articles (Broscheit et al., 2010) work on German using the TüBa-D/Z coreference corpus, (Kopeć and Ogrodniczuk, 2012) develop the Polish plug-in using a subset of the National Corpus of Polish, and finally (Uryupina et al., 2012) run experiments on Arabic and Chinese.

3 Annotated Corpus of Basque

EPEC (Reference Corpus for the Processing of Basque) (Aduriz et al., 2006) is a 300,000 word sample collection of standard written Basque that has been manually annotated at different levels (morphology, surface syntax, phrases, etc.). The corpus is composed by news published in *Euskaldunon Egunkaria*, a Basque language newspaper. It is aimed to be a reference corpus for the development and improvement of several NLP tools for Basque.

Recently, mentions and coreference chains were also annotated by two linguists in a subset of the EPEC corpus which is composed of about 45,000 words. First, automatically annotated mentions obtained by our mention detector were corrected; then, coreferent mentions were linked in clusters. The

mention detector is a set of hand-crafted rules that have been compiled into Finite State Transducers (FST). The FSTs match chunks and clauses provided by the preprocessing tools and identify the mentions and their boundaries. Further discussion about the FSTs' behaviour can be found in (Soraluze et al., 2012).

All the annotation process has been carried out using the MMAX2 annotation tool (Müller and Strube, 2006). The coreference annotation of the EPEC corpus is explained more in detail in (Ceberio et al., 2016).

To adapt BART to Basque, we divided the dataset into three main parts: one for training the system, the other for tuning, and the last for testing. More detailed information about the three parts can be found in Table 1.

	Words	Mentions	Clusters	Singletons
Train	23520	6525	1011	3401
Devel	6914	1907	302	982
Test	15949	4360	621	2445

Table 1: EPEC-coref corpus division information.

4 Extending BART to Basque

BART was originally created for English, but its flexible modular architecture ensures its portability to other languages.

BART consists of five main components: preprocessing pipeline, mention factory, feature extraction module, decoder and encoder. Furthermore, an additional independent *Language Plugin* module handles language specific information and is accessible from any component.

In the adaptation process of BART, we used a preprocessing pipeline of Basque linguistic processors, developed the *Basque Language Plugin* and added new features for coreference resolution specifically geared towards Basque.

4.1 Preprocessing and Mention Detection

The preprocessing pipeline takes raw texts and applies a series of Basque linguistic processors to analyse the texts: i) A morphological analyser that performs word segmentation and PoS tagging (Alegria et al., 1996), ii) A lemmatiser that resolves the ambiguity caused at the previous phase (Alegria et al.,

2002), iii) A multi-word item identifier that determines which groups of two or more words are to be considered multi-word expressions (Alegria et al., 2004), iv) A named-entity recogniser that identifies and classifies named entities (person, organisation, location) in the text (Alegria et al., 2003), v) A chunker, an analyser that identifies verbal and nominal chunks based on rule-based grammars (Aduriz and Díaz de Ilarraza, 2003), vi) A clause tagger, that is, an analyser that identifies clauses, combining rule-based-grammars and machine learning techniques (Alegria et al., 2008).

After the preprocessing step, mentions that are potential candidates to be part of coreference chains are identified using the mention detector explained in Section 3.

Finally, the linguistic information obtained by the preprocessing tools and the mentions identified by the mentions detector are stored in stand-off format of the MMAX2 annotation tool (Müller and Strube, 2006) that BART uses.

4.2 Basque Language Plugin

Developing a Basque language plugin for BART involved building on the system's already existing language plugins, and then translating closed-class words such as pronouns, mapping key part-of-speech tags and adapting lower-level heuristics for finding the head noun in noun phrases, person and number identification, as well as reading features made available by the preprocessing tools.

4.3 Feature engineering for Basque

Some kind of linguistic information from the mention is used by all the features implemented in BART. MentionFactory computes these properties when a language is supported by BART. In the case of a new language, such as Basque, they should be provided as part of the mention representation computed by external preprocessing facilities. So, we added in the MMAX2 files relevant features for coreference resolution in Basque, as are number and lemma.

For our experiments, we trained BART with two different models. The first one, is a simple model, presented by (Soon et al., 2001).[2] The second one,

is an improved version of the first one where more Basque oriented features have been added. The features used in each model are presented in Table 2.

In the two models, gender agreement does not cause any improvement in the scores, as Basque is genderless.[3]

At this point the proposed new features to handle the specificity of Basque are not new and have also been used for other languages (see (Poesio et al., 2016) for details).

5 Experimental Results

We have tested the two models presented in Subsection 4.3 in two different environments. In the first one automatically detected mentions are provided to the models and in the second one the mentions are gold.[4]

The metrics used in our evaluations are MUC (Vilain et al., 1995), B^3 (Bagga and Baldwin, 1998), $CEAF_e$ (Luo, 2005), $CEAF_m$ (Luo, 2005), and BLANC (Recasens and Hovy, 2011). The scores have been calculated using the reference implementation of the CoNLL scorer (Pradhan et al., 2014).

Table 3 presents the results obtained by the two models when automatic mentions are used.

		R	P	F_1
Mention Detection		72.91	74.69	73.79
MUC	Soon	18.37	67.23	28.86
	Basque	35.44	45.53	39.86
B^3	Soon	53.96	72.85	62.00
	Basque	58.10	65.27	61.48
$CEAF_m$	Soon	57.50	58.90	58.19
	Basque	58.67	60.10	59.38
$CEAF_e$	Soon	67.42	52.93	59.31
	Basque	61.63	58.15	59.84
BLANC	Soon	32.29	62.47	36.46
	Basque	38.70	48.81	42.41
CONLL	Soon	-	-	50.05
	Basque	-	-	53.72

Table 3: Scores with automatic mentions.

In the case of automatically detected mentions, Basque model outperforms the Soon baseline model

---

Basque with BART, at this stage we were unable to incorporate all features in the original (Soon et al., 2001) model.

[3]We maintain this feature with the aim of not modifying the (Soon et al., 2001) model.

[4]Since the official CoNLL scorer is used for the evaluation, it also takes care of the alignment between automatically detected mentions and gold ones.

Features		Baseline	Basque
Gender	M_i and M_j agree in gender	√	√
Number	M_i and M_j agree in number	√	√
Alias	Matches abbreviations and name variations	√	√
StringMatch	M_i and M_j have the same surface form	√	√
SemClassAgree	Assesses the semantic compatibility of M_i and M_j	√	√
Appositive	M_i and M_j are in apposition structure	√	√
DistanceSentence	Distance in sentences between M_i and M_j	√	√
LemmaMatch	M_i and M_j have the same surface lemma	×	√
HeadMatch	M_i and M_j have the same head	×	√
StringKernel	Computes the similarity M_i and M_j strings	×	√
DistanceMarkable	Distance in markables between M_i and M_j	×	√
HeadPartofSpeech	M_i and M_j head PoS are the same	×	√

Table 2: Features used for Coreference Resolution in our experiments. M_i is a candidate antecedent and M_j is a candidate anaphor.

according to F_1 on all the metrics except B^3. In CoNLL metric, Basque model has a score of 53.72, which is 3.67 points higher than Soon Baseline, which scores 50.05.[5]

Scores obtained when gold mentions are provided are shown in Table 4.

		R	P	F_1
Mention Detection		100	100	100
MUC	Soon	23.62	78.66	36.34
	Basque	49.49	57.28	53.10
B^3	Soon	74.66	98.00	84.75
	Basque	81.21	87.78	84.37
$CEAF_m$	Soon	75.58	75.58	75.58
	Basque	76.59	76.59	76.59
$CEAF_e$	Soon	91.11	70.29	79.35
	Basque	82.10	77.64	79.81
BLANC	Soon	57.08	89.79	61.68
	Basque	66.78	75.99	70.34
CONLL	Soon	-	-	66.81
	Basque	-	-	72.42

Table 4: Scores with gold mentions.

When gold mentions are used the Basque model also outperforms the Soon baseline according to all the metrics, except B^3. The official CoNLL metric is outperformed by 5.61 points.

Comparing the results obtained when gold mentions are used with those obtained with the automatic mentions, there is a considerable difference. CoNLL F_1 of Soon baseline is 50.05 when automatic mentions are provided, while providing gold mentions this value raises to 66.81, an increase of 16.76. Similar increase in CoNLL F_1 happens with the Basque model. In this case, there is an increase

of 18.7 points, from 53.72 with automatic mentions to 72.42 when gold mentions are used.

We also had a look at the pronoun resolution performance alone, but only MUC scores on automatic mentions as the CoNLL scorer does not provide a break-down of scores per anaphor type, and there was a small gain in performance from the Soon baseline to the Basque model from $F1 = 27.4$ to $F1 = 33.0$, respectively. The gain is due mostly to higher precision, suggesting the additional features in the Basque model help discriminate better erroneously resolved pronouns in the baseline model, however, more work will need to be devoted to improving recall, which is particularly challenging in the case of Basque due to the lack of gender in the Basque pronoun system.

5.1 Error Analysis

In our error analysis we had a look at examples from our corpus covering the following four cases:

Case a. There were errors in the coreference resolution due to errors in the pre-processing which were propagated across the pipeline. Consider example 1, for instance:[6]

(1) **Gold mentions**: [Del Bosquek] prentsaurrekoa eman zuen atzo. [Vicente Del Bosque], [Real Madrileko entrenatzailea] , nahikoa kezkati azaldu zen.
Automatic mentions: [Del Bosquek] prentsaurrekoa eman zuen atzo. [Vicente Del Bosque , Real Madrileko entrenatzailea] , nahikoa kezkati azaldu zen.

Case b. Due to the challenges posed by the genderless pronoun system in Basque, there were pro-

---

[5]The CoNLL metric is the arithmetic mean of MUC, B^3 and $CEAF_e$ metrics.

[6]English translation: "[Del Bosque] gave a press conference yesterday. [Vicente Del Bosque], [Real Madrid coach], appeared quite concerned".

nouns easy to resolve in relative terms which were missed or incorrectly resolved. Example 2 illustrates this:[7]

(2) Lehendakari hautatu zutenetik, [Djukanovicek] aldaketa handia eman dio [bere] ildo politikoari.

Case c. Here with example 3 we illustrate an instance of a challenging cases of pronouns which are currently beyond the scope of our approach:[8]

(3) Gobernuaren bilera honen ondoren, oporretara joango da [Jospin], eta hauek baliatuko ditu, ziur aski , Chevenement kasuaz gogoetak egiteko eta konponbide batekin [bere] jarduerari eusteko.

In this example it is more challenging to resolve correctly the pronoun [bere] "[his]" as [bere] can refer to Jospin or to Chevenement.

Case d. Finally, with example 4 we show an instance of a correctly resolved pronoun by our system:[9]

(4) "[Guk] ez dugu inoiz penaltietan irabazi." Luzapena golik gabe amaitzean, itzal beltz batek estali zuen Arena estadioa . Rijkaard-ek esana zuen arreta bereziz prestatu zituztela penaltiak, "[gure] istoria ez errepikatzeko".

5.2 Discussion

Taking into consideration Basque most relevant grammatical characteristics, in some aspects it is more challenging to resolve coreferences in this language than in others.

Since Basque is an agglutinative language, a given lemma takes many different word forms, depending on the case (genitive, locative, etc.) or the number (singular, plural, indefinite) for nouns and adjectives. For example, the lemma lehendakari ("president") forms the inflections lehendakaria ("the president"), lehendakariak ("the president"), lehendakariari ("to the president"), lehendakariei ("to the presidents"), lehendakariaren ("of the president"), etc. This means that looking only for the given exact word, is not enough for Basque

to resolve coreference when string matching techniques are applied and as we observed in our experiments the use of lemmas is more effective in morphologically rich languages.

Besides the agglutination, there is no grammatical gender in the nominal system. Nouns and adjectives have no distinct endings depending on gender. In addition, there are no distinct forms for third person pronouns in Basque, and demonstratives are used as third person pronominals (Laka, 1996).

This makes it impossible to use gender as a feature in the resolution process which has been proven particularly useful in the resolution of pronouns, for example. Furthermore, the animacy feature cannot be used for pronoun resolution either. In this scenario, distance-based features, like Sentence Distance and Markable distance could be the most effective features for pronoun resolution. Nevertheless, research will have to be devoted to finding other useful features to make up for the lack of gender and animacy.

6 Conclusion

In this paper we presented our ongoing work on Coreference Resolution in Basque. We described the main resource we have been using which is the EPEC corpus annotated with coreferences and we explained how we have been adapting the coreference resolution toolkit, BART, to enable it to process Basque. We ran two levels of experiments one resolving coreferences using the gold mentions and one using automatically parsed mentions and we trained two different models for each, a baseline model based on (Soon et al., 2001) and a Basque model with extended feature set. We showed that the Basque model significantly outperforms the baseline. We also discussed key characteristics of the Basque language which make it particularly challenging for coreference.

Next we plan to investigate more in depth suitable features that can both make up for the lack of gender and animacy and be extracted reliably from unrestricted text. We also plan to run an extrinsic evaluation guaging the effect of coreference on a higher level task.

---

[7]English translation: "Since he was elected as president, [Djukanovic] has greatly changed [his] policy lines".

[8]English translation: "After this government meeting, [Jospin] will go on holidays, and will surely use it to reflect on Chevenement case and to maintain [his] activity with a new solution".

[9]English translation: "[We] have never won on penalties." After the extension finished without goals, a large shadow turn off the stadium. Rijkaard said they prepared penalties with great attention,"so that [our] story would not occur again".

Acknowledgments

This work has been supported by Ander Soraluze's PhD grant from Euskara Errektoreordetza, the University of the Basque Country (UPV/EHU) and by the EXTRECM project, Spanish Government (TIN2013-46616-C2-1-R). The research leading to these results has received funding from the European Union - Seventh Framework Programme (FP7/2007-2013) under grant agreement 610916 SENSEI.

References

Itziar Aduriz and Arantza Díaz de Ilarraza. 2003. Morphosyntactic Disambiguation and Shallow Parsing in Computational Processing of Basque. *Inquiries into the lexicon-syntax relations in Basque*, pages 1–21. University of the Basque Country.

Itziar Aduriz, Maxux Aranzabe, Jose Mari Arriola, Maite Atutxa, Arantza Díaz de Ilarraza, Nerea Ezeiza, Koldo Gojenola, Maite Oronoz, Aitor Soroa, and Ruben Urizar. 2006. Methodology and Steps towards the Construction of EPEC, a Corpus of Written Basque Tagged at Morphological and Syntactic Levels for the Automatic Processing. pages 1–15. Rodopi. Book series: Language and Computers.

Iñaki Alegria, Xabier Artola, Kepa Sarasola, and Miriam Urkia. 1996. Automatic Morphological Analysis of Basque. *Literary & Linguistic Computing*, 11(4):193–203.

Iñaki Alegria, Maxux Aranzabe, Aitzol Ezeiza, Nerea Ezeiza, and Ruben Urizar. 2002. Robustness and Customisation in an Analyser/Lemmatiser for Basque. In *LREC-2002 Customizing knowledge in NLP applications workshop, pages 1-6, Las Palmas de Gran Canaria, 28th May 2002"*.

Iñaki Alegria, Nerea Ezeiza, Izaskun Fernandez, and Ruben Urizar. 2003. Named Entity Recognition and Classification for texts in Basque. In *II Jornadas de Tratamiento y Recuperación de Información*, (JOTRI 2003), pages 198–203, Madrid, Spain.

Iñaki Alegria, Olatz Ansa, Xabier Artola, Nerea Ezeiza, Kepa Gojenola, and Ruben Urizar. 2004. Representation and Treatment of Multiword Expressions in Basque. In *ACL workshop on Multiword Expressions*, pages 48–55.

Iñaki Alegria, Bertol Arrieta, Xavier Carreras, Arantza Díaz de Ilarraza, and Larraitz Uria. 2008. Chunk and Clause Identification for Basque by Filtering and Ranking with Perceptrons. *Procesamiento del Lenguaje Natural*, 41.

Amit Bagga and Breck Baldwin. 1998. Algorithms for Scoring Coreference Chains. In *In The First International Conference on Language Resources and Evaluation Workshop on Linguistics Coreference*, pages 563–566.

Samuel Broscheit, Simone Paolok Ponzetto, Yannick Versley, and Massimo Poesio. 2010. Extending BART to provide a coreference resolution system for German. In *Proceedings of the International Conference on Language Resources and Evaluation, LREC 2010*, Valletta, Malta.

Klara Ceberio, Itziar Aduriz, Arantza Díaz de Ilarraza, and Ines Garcia-Azkoaga. 2016. Coreferential relations in Basque: the annotation process. Theoretical Developments in Hispanic Linguistics. The Ohio State University.

Defense Advanced Research Projects Agency. 1995. *Proceedings of the Sixth Message Understanding Conference (MUC-6)*, San Francisco, CA. Morgan Kaufmann.

Lynette Hirschman. 1998. MUC-7 coreference task definition, version 3.0. In N. Chinchor, editor, *Proceedings of the 7th Message Understanding Conference*. NIST.

Mateusz Kopeć and Maciej Ogrodniczuk. 2012. Creating a Coreference Resolution System for Polish. In *Proceedings of the Eight International Conference on Language Resources and Evaluation (LREC'12)*, Istanbul, Turkey. European Language Resources Association (ELRA).

Itziar Laka. 1996. A Brief Grammar of Euskara, the Basque Language. http://www.ehu.es/grammar. University of the Basque Country.

Heeyoung Lee, Angel Chang, Yves Peirsman, Nathanael Chambers, Mihai Surdeanu, and Dan Jurafsky. 2013. Deterministic Coreference Resolution Based on Entity-centric, Precision-ranked Rules. *Comput. Linguist.*, 39(4):885–916, December.

Xiaoqiang Luo. 2005. On Coreference Resolution Performance Metrics. In *Proceedings of the Conference on Human Language Technology and Empirical Methods in Natural Language Processing*, HLT '05, pages 25–32, Stroudsburg, PA, USA. Association for Computational Linguistics.

Tom Morton. 2000. Coreference for NLP applications. In *Proceedings of the Annual Meeting of the Association for Computational Linguistics (ACL)*.

Christoph Müller and Michael Strube. 2006. Multi-level Annotation of Linguistic Data with MMAX2. In Sabine Braun, Kurt Kohn, and Joybrato Mukherjee, editors, *Corpus Technology and Language Pedagogy: New Resources, New Tools, New Methods*, pages 197–214. Peter Lang, Frankfurt a.M., Germany.

Massimo Poesio, Olga Uryupina, and Yannick Versley. 2010. Creating a coreference resolution system for Italian. In *Proceedings of the Seventh International Conference on Language Resources and Evaluation (LREC'10)*, Valletta, Malta, may. European Language Resources Association (ELRA).

Massimo Poesio, Roland Stuckardt, and Yannick Versley, editors. 2016. *Anaphora Resolution: Algorithms, Resources and Applications*. Springer–Verlag.

Sameer Pradhan, Xiaoqiang Luo, Marta Recasens, Eduard Hovy, Vincent Ng, and Michael Strube. 2014. Scoring Coreference Partitions of Predicted Mentions: A Reference Implementation. In *Proceedings of the 52nd Annual Meeting of the Association for Computational Linguistics (Volume 2: Short Papers)*, pages 30–35. Association for Computational Linguistics.

Marta Recasens and Eduard Hovy. 2011. BLANC: Implementing the Rand index for coreference evaluation. *Natural Language Engineering*, 17(4):485–510.

Wee Meng Soon, Hwee Tou Ng, and Daniel Chung Yong Lim. 2001. A Machine Learning Approach to Coreference Resolution of Noun Phrases. *Computational Linguistics*, 27(4):521–544, December.

Ander Soraluze, Olatz Arregi, Xabier Arregi, Klara Ceberio, and Arantza Díaz de Ilarraza. 2012. Mention Detection: First Steps in the Development of a Basque Correference Resolution System. In *KONVENS 2012, The 11th Conference on Natural Language Processing*, Vienna, Austria.

Ander Soraluze, Olatz Arregi, Xabier Arregi, and Arantza Díaz de Ilarraza. 2015. Coreference Resolution for Morphologically Rich Languages. Adaptation of the Stanford System to Basque. *Procesamiento del Lenguaje Natural*, 55:23–30.

Josef Steinberger, Massimo Poesio, Mijail A. Kabadjov, and Karel Ježek. 2007. Two uses of anaphora resolution in summarization. *Information Processing and Management*. Special Issue on Text Summarisation.

Olga Uryupina, Alessandro Moschitti, and Massimo Poesio. 2012. BART goes multilingual: the UniTN/Essex submission to the CoNLL-2012 shared task. In *Proceedings of the Joint Conference on EMNLP and CoNLL-Shared Task*, Jeju, Korea.

Yannick Versley, Simone Paolo Ponzetto, Massimo Poesio, Vladimir Eidelman, Alan Jern, Jason Smith, Xiaofeng Yang, and Alessandro Moschitti. 2008. BART: a modular toolkit for coreference resolution. In *Proceedings of the 2008 Conference of the Association for Computational Linguistics*, pages 9–12.

Marc Vilain, John Burger, John Aberdeen, Dennis Connolly, and Lynette Hirschman. 1995. A Model-theoretic Coreference Scoring Scheme. In *Proceedings of the 6th Conference on Message Understanding*, MUC6 '95, pages 45–52, Stroudsburg, PA, USA. Association for Computational Linguistics.

Error analysis for anaphora resolution in Russian: new challenging issues for anaphora resolution task in a morphologically rich language

Svetlana Toldova **Ilya Azerkovich** **Anna Roytberg**

National Research University Higher School of Economics

21/4, Staraya Basmannaya Ulitsa, 105066, Moscow, Russia

`toldova@yandex.ru, cvi@yandex.ru, iazerkovich@gmail.com`

Alina Ladygina

Eberhard Karls Universität Tübingen

Geschwister-Scholl-Platz,

72074, Tübingen, Germany

`aladygina@yahoo.com`

Maria Vasilyeva

Lomonosov Moscow State University

1 Humanities Building, 1-51 Leninskie Gory,

GSP-1, 119991, Moscow, Russia

`linellea@yandex.ru`

Abstract

This paper presents a quantitative and qualitative error analysis of Russian anaphora resolvers which participated in the RU-EVAL event. Its aim is to identify and characterize a set of challenging errors common to state-of-the-art systems dealing with Russian. We examined three types of pronouns: 3rd person pronouns, reflexive and relative pronouns. The investigation has shown that a high level of grammatical ambiguity, specific features of reflexive pronouns, free word order and special cases of non-referential pronouns in Russian impact the quality of anaphora resolution systems. Error analysis reveals some specific features of anaphora resolution for morphologically rich and free word order languages with a lack of gold standard resources.

1 Introduction

Anaphora resolution, or the task of identifying noun-phrase antecedents of pronouns and adjectival anaphors in a text, is an essential step in the text-processing pipeline of NLP. Still, building an anaphora resolution module is challenging for text-mining systems, as it requires a high level of morphological and syntactic analysis at the first stages of the NLP pipeline. Nevertheless, this task has a long history of development and evaluation (e.g. the MUC-6 conference in 1995), and different aspects of anaphora resolution are well studied and have rich resource support, especially for English. However, Russian (as well as other Slavic languages) poses additional challenges for anaphora resolution, in particular, it has rich morphology, free word order and

lacks articles. Furthermore, Russian is a relatively low-resourced language (Toldova et al., 2015) due to the lack of freely distributable gold standard corpora for different NLP tasks.

In our paper, we analyze the performance of Russian anaphora resolvers which participated in the RU-EVAL-2014 evaluation campaign (Toldova et al., 2014). RU-EVAL-2014 was dedicated both to anaphora and coreference resolution, but our study focuses only on anaphora resolution, as there were more participants in this task and the results obtained were more reliable.

The aim of this paper is to present quantitative and qualitative error analysis for different pronoun types (reflexives, 3rd person pronouns and relative pronouns). We identify and characterize a set of challenging errors common to state-of-the-art systems dealing with Russian. Error analysis enables us to compare the efficiency of different NLP approaches and detect errors that occur either due to language-specific issues or system defects that could be fixed.

In Section 2, we discuss the previous experience of anaphora and coreference resolution error analysis that we took into account. In the section 3, we give a short overview of RU-EVAL-2014, describe the data used for evaluation (RuCoref corpus) and the annotation scheme. Then, we briefly describe systems that took part in RU-EVAL-2014, the evaluation principles and systems' general performance. The qualitative and quantitative error analysis presented in section 4 reveals language specific features influencing system performance such as particular types of morphological ambiguity, lack of animacy

74

Proceedings of the Workshop on Coreference Resolution Beyond OntoNotes (CORBON 2016), co-located with NAACL 2016, pages 74–83,
San Diego, California, June 16, 2016. ©2016 Association for Computational Linguistics

opposition in pronouns, some specific features of syntactic binding for reflexives in Russian, special cases of "antecedentless" pronouns (when pronouns show semantic reinterpretation) and others. We also focus on some issues that are common for other languages, such as syntactic ambiguity in the case of NP embedding and some cases of referential conflicts. In Section 5, we present our conclusions.

2 Anaphora resolution error analysis: background

Previous studies on anaphora and coreference resolution errors classified system mistakes using different criteria. For instance, Kummerfeld and Klein (2013) consider only deficiencies in the structure of coreferential chains, such as missing/additional mention, span errors, etc. Some studies investigate precision and recall errors in coreference resolution (Uryupina, 2008; Martschat and Strube, 2014) and report particularly difficult cases, namely, resolving 1st and 2nd person pronouns, identifying and linking the names of organizations, and interpreting specific semantic relations, such as meronymy, hyponymy and hyperonymy.

Few works focus specifically on pronominal anaphora resolution mistakes. Barbu (2002) investigates the performance of several anaphora resolution systems and distinguishes errors regarding pronoun types (personal, possessive, reflexives), distance between an anaphor and its antecedent and syntactic function of the referring expressions. Evans (2002) presents a modified system for anaphora resolution in English and defines more detailed error types, such as pre-processing mistakes (syntactic parsing, erroneous encoding or incorrect annotation of training data), non-trivial syntactic cases (number and gender disagreement), distant antecedents, specific types of anaphora (verbal anaphora, cataphora, inferred antecedent, event anaphora) and referential ambiguity. Both studies show that incorrect syntactic processing and distant antecedents have a considerable impact on the accuracy of the system.

Unfortunately, very few studies examine error types in Slavic languages, although in this field we might expect specific mistakes, since Slavic languages pose particular challenges in anaphora resolution due to a rich morphology and free word order

(Toldova et al., 2015).

3 Data and Systems: RU-EVAL-2014

3.1 Description of the evaluation campaign

RU-EVAL-2014 was the first evaluation campaign that measured the performance of anaphora and corefence resolvers designed for Russian. It relied on similar evaluation events: MUC-7 (Chinchor and Hirschmann, 1997), EVALITA (Poesio and Uryupina, 2011), ARE (Orasan et al., 2008), SemEval (Recasens et al., 2010), CoNLL-2011/2012 (Pradhan et al., 2011; Pradhan et al., 2012). The aim of the campaign was to assess the state-of-the-art in the field for Russian. The majority of teams dealing with Russian are working with disjoint models (cf. RU-EVAL events on pos-tagging and parsing). This leads to a high diversification of standards and annotation schemes. Thus, evaluation principles of the previous campaigns for other languages had to be adapted for this RU-EVAL event, taking into account specific conditions for developing Russian anaphora resolvers. For the evaluation campaign, the gold standard corpus, the Russian Coreference Corpus (RuCor), was created (Toldova et al., 2016).

3.2 RuCor

RuCor consists of two parts, manually annotated for pronominal anaphora and coreference resolution tasks: the learning set and the evaluation set, 185 texts (200 000 tokens) in total. It is comprised of publicly available texts of different genres (from 5 up to 100 sentences): news (45%), essays (21%), fiction (18%), scientific articles (11%) and blog posts (5%). Each text was manually annotated by two annotators, then the annotation was checked by a supervisor. The corpus also contains automatic morphological annotation. The set of tools, developed by S. Sharoff for Russian was used, which includes a tokenizer, a TreeTagger-based part-of-speech tagger (Schmid, 1994), and a lemmatizer, based on CSTLemma (Jongejan and Dalianis, 2009).

For coreference relations, NPs referring to concrete entities were annotated. Toldova and colleagues (2016) also annotated different types of non-referential expressions that were not taken into consideration in the evaluation procedure, such as pred-

75

icative and sitive NPs. As for anaphoric relations, four types of pronouns were annotated: 1) 3rd person pronouns (including 3rd person possessive *jego* 'his/its', *eje* 'her', *ih* 'their'), 2) relative pronoun *kotoryj* 'which', 3) reflexive pronoun (*sebya* 'oneself' and a possessive reflexive pronoun *svoj* 'oneself's'), 4) headless demonstratives. The latter were not taken into consideration in anaphora evaluation. Generic and abstract NPs were annotated if they served as antecedents for those pronouns. The annotation provides morphosyntactic characteristics of an NP (full noun group or a pronoun). In NPs containing modifiers, the semantic head of the group is additionally marked, similarly to MUC-7 methodology (Hirschmann, 1997). All the potential heads are annotated. For example, two heads are annotated for an NP *[[professor] [Vagner]]* (person's occupation and surname). There are several possible analyses for this NP: some systems consider only 'professor' to be the NP head, others —the surname. Moreover, some systems link a pronoun to the full NP, while others link it only to the NP head. Thus, the annotation of several potential heads enables to compare systems with different syntactic and coreferential models.

3.3 Participants

Results presented by six different systems were evaluated in the competition. Originally, there were more participants, but as some systems did not manage to analyze the whole evaluation set, they were excluded from further consideration. The final participant lineup was as follows.

- **An@phora**, a system, developed by M. Ionov and A. Kutuzov. The team presented three different runs: one for rule-based approach, one for a Random Forest algorithm and one for a hybrid algorithm (Kutuzov and Ionov, 2014).

- **Compreno**, a linguistic processor, developed by the ABBYY Corporation. It is built upon a self-developed ontology and widely uses semantic analysis. The system provides deep syntactic analysis, using dependency parser designed by this company (Bogdanov et al., 2014).

- A machine-learning based system presented by

the Institute of System Analysis, below it is referred to as **ISA** (Kamenskaya et al., 2014). The system developers make use of semantic role labeling to improve its performance.

- A system presented by the Open Corpora project (referred to below as **OC**). It uses Tomita-parser for NP extraction and MaltParser for shallow syntactic parsing (Protopopova et al., 2014).

- **Phenomena**, a machine learning based system, developed individually by S. Ponomarev. It relies heavily on semantic and ontological relations and applies a logistic regression classifier. It involves morphological and syntactic analysis provided by the Tomita parser[1].

- **SemSyn**, a rule-based system, built around the syntactic parser (Boyarski et al., 2013).

3.4 Evaluation

In the pronominal anaphora resolution task, performance on only 3 types of pronominal NPs was evaluated: 1) 3rd person pronouns, 2) the relative pronoun (*kotoryj* 'which') and 3) reflexive pronouns. The zero anaphora was not evaluated. As in Evalita-2011 (Poesio and Uryupina, 2011), we used a weak criterion for antecedent identification. It was not required to link a pronoun to its linear closest nonpronominal antecedent. We treat as true positives the pair of a pronoun and any mention belonging to the same coreference chain which matches the corresponding mention in the gold standard. For instance, in (1), the following pairs: '*him – Vagner*', '*him – professor*' or '*him – he*' are allowed.

(1)   *I do not know [Vagner]ᵢ well. Nevertheless, [the [professor]]ᵢ / [he]ᵢ was living nearby, I had met [him]ᵢ just twice.*

The evaluation was based on the principle of lenient matching of NPs: a system antecedent matches an NP in the gold standard corpus (GS) if it includes one of possible heads annotated for this gold standard NP. This makes it possible to compare the results of the systems that differ in principles of antecedent mark-up (cf. NP heads vs. full NPs vs.

---

[1]Properties of this system are presented in a blog post: https://habrahabr.ru/post/229403/

partial NPs). For example, for the NP *[Professor] [Vagner]* the responses, *professor, Vagner* or *professor Vagner* are considered correct. However, the head mismatch in case of embedded NPs as in system response *sumku [mamy]* 'moms bag' for gold standard NP *[mamy]* 'mom' is treated as an error.

We conducted our error analysis based on the systems' responses in the evaluaton set (85 texts, 1600 chains, 2300 pairs). Most of the systems carried out several runs with precision ranging from 36% to 82%. The results are displayed in Table (1).

Run	Algorithm type	P	R	F-measure
sys1	rule-based+onto	0.82	0.70	0.76
sys2	rule-based	0.71	0.58	0.64
sys3	rule-based	0.63	0.50	0.55
sys4	logreg+onto	0.54	0.51	0.53
sys5	svm+sem	0.58	0.42	0.49
sys6	decision tree	0.36	0.15	0.21

Table 1: Evaluation results of RU-EVAL-2014

We present all of the runs. The variation in the results for different runs of one system is not as significant as difference between systems, in spite of the different algorithms employed in different runs.

The rule-based runs generally show better results than those based on machine learning techniques; the top three results are achieved by rule-based systems. Incorporating semantics into analysis leads to better results. The runs involving semantic role labeling, named entity recognition or ontological information achieve higher F-measure scores.

4 Comparative error analysis

The anaphora resolution systems presented in the previous section are a representative sample of the state-of-the-art for anaphora resolution in Russian. Therefore, by analyzing the errors they make, we can uncover remaining challenges in anaphora resolution and analyze qualitative differences between the systems. The results of such an analysis will deepen our understanding of anaphora resolution and will suggest promising directions for further research.

4.1 Error rate analysis for different pronoun classes

In the preliminary analysis, we categorized each error by the pronoun type. Our hypothesis was that syntactic position of a pronoun could influence the error rate. Thus, we distinguished the following classes of anaphoric pronouns: 3rd person pronouns in subject position (nominative case, ***ana_nom***), in direct object position (pronouns in the accusative case, ***ana_acc***), anaphors in prepositional phrases (***ana_pp***[2]) and those in other argument positions (***ana_other***). We also treated possessive 3rd person pronouns (***ana_poss***) as a separate class. As for reflexive pronouns, we split them in two classes: reflexive pronouns proper (***refl***) and reflexive possessives (***refl_poss***), since Russian possessive reflexives have some specific features (cf. Paducheva (1985), see also sections 4.2 and 4.3 for details). Relative pronouns (***rel***) constitute the last class.

Raw frequencies of different pronoun types are presented in table 2. General statistics on error rate is presented in Table 3.

pronoun type	raw frequency
ana_nom	640
ana_acc	217
ana_pp	195
ana_other	174
ana_poss	298
refl	126
refl_poss	294
rel	357
total	2301

Table 2: Statistics on pronoun types

	sys1	sys2	sys3	sys4	sys5	sys6
ana_nom	0.20	0.33	0.43	0.46	0.44	0.72
ana_acc	0.27	0.36	0.43	0.58	0.5	0.75
ana_pp	0.21	0.39	0.46	0.53	0.45	0.77
ana_other	0.23	0.35	0.44	0.45	0.41	0.69
ana_poss	0.20	0.35	0.46	0.42	0.47	0.68
refl	0.20	0.34	0.52	0.83	0.86	0.65
refl_poss	0.17	0.29	0.41	0.55	0.44	0.60
rel	0.19	0.29	0.43	0.55	0.57	0.71
mean	0.21	0.34	0.45	0.55	0.53	0.69

Table 3: Precision error rate for different pronoun types

The raw error rate for different pronoun types depends on system's general performance rather than on the pronoun type. We normalized the error rate

---

[2]Russian personal pronouns have a special stem starting with *n-* in prepositional context (c.f. *vizhu ego* 'saw him' vs. *pokazal na nego* 'point at him').

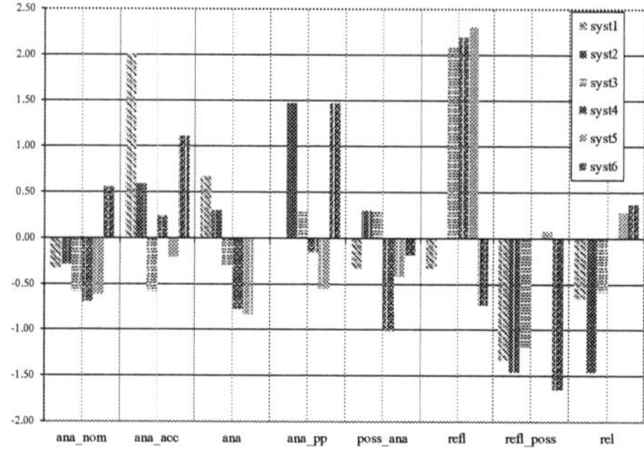

Figure 1: Diagram for different error types across systems

over the system's error rate mean and calculated the deviation (see the comparative diagram in Figure 1). As it can be seen from the diagram, the least problematic cases are possessive reflexives, relatives and 3rd person pronouns in nominative case. The most difficult is the resolution of personal pronouns in accusative case. There is also a tendency for the systems that handle syntactic anaphora (reflexives and the relative pronoun) quite well to have more mistakes in cases of 3rd person pronouns. On the contrary, the systems that are poor at reflexive pronouns analysis outperform the syntax-oriented systems in the discourse anaphora resolution.

We expected that syntactically regulated pronouns (e.g. reflexive and relative pronouns) would be less problematic. This hypothesis was supported, e.g. by (Barbu, 2002), where reflexives are absent in error statistics due to the extremely low rate of such mistakes. But for Russian, contrary to our expectations, the rate of errors in reflexive pronouns had the maximum range across the systems. The high error rate in reflexives is due to the fact that some systems do not take into account the binding theory (see section 4.3.1). However, even those systems that do have a syntactic reflexive resolution model still make mistakes: the lowest error rate for reflexives and possessive reflexives is 20% and 17% for these two types respectively.

It is worth mentioning that relative pronouns in NPs like *kamen, kotoryj* 'the stone which', where the head noun controlling relative clause and the adjacent relative pronoun are coindexed, also present

problems for anaphora resolvers (17% error rate for the best result). The high error number in such cases is due to syntactic homonymy in case of embedded NPs as heads, like in *oblomok kamnja, kotoryj* 'a piece of the stone, that', where two anaphoric pairs are possible 'piece – that' or 'stone – that' (see 4.3.2).

The personal pronouns in Russian (as in other languages) are the most difficult issue. The basic criterion for these pronouns is the antecedent – pronoun agreement in morphological features (Jurafsky and Martin, 2009, p. 803). The Russian error analysis reveals issues with this criterion for morphologically rich languages. A lot of systems' mistakes arose due to particular types of morphological homonymy in both pronouns and antecedent forms (cf. *im* –'he.INSTR' vs. 'they.DAT', NOM.PL vs. GEN.SG in feminine nouns), absence of animacy opposition in pronouns etc. (see 4.2 for details).

4.2 Morphological errors

In this section, we will analyze errors that arise due to specific morphological properties of Russian.

In agglutinative languages, morphology usually provides an additional cue for correct anaphora resoloution (see Soraluze et al. (2015) for Basque), but this is not the case for Russian, as it is relatively more flective and tends to express grammatical meanings cumulatively.

Russian personal and possessive pronouns agree with their antecedent in person and number. The third person singular pronouns and possessives also agree in gender (feminine, masculine and neuter in nominative, neuter and masculine are neutralized in oblique cases). In contrast to English, reflexive pronouns *sebja* and *svoj* do not agree in gender and number with the antecedent, and animacy is not marked in any pronouns.

This animacy deficiency together with the neutralization of some gender contrasts in the pronoun system cause additional problems for anaphora resolvers. Animacy deficiency expands the set of potential candidates: systems have to consider both animate and inanimate nouns. For some anaphora resolvers which lack semantic analysis, it is difficult to rule out potential antecedents of the wrong animacy. This was previously reported by Ionov and Kutuzov (2014). Still, in some contexts an inani-

78

mate reading is more plausible than the animate one. Locative contexts such as *v nem* 'in him' is such an example. But this fact is ignored by systems that are not using deep semantic processing, cf. 2.

(2)   *[Nash proekt]$_i$[3] otkroet dveri vsem talantlivym ljudjam. My budem predlagat uchastvovat v [nem]$_{is}$ vsem, i [Grigoriju Perelmanu]$_s$ v chastnosti.*
        '[Our project]$_i$ is opened to all talented people. We will offer everyone to participate in [it]$_{is}$, and [Grigori Perelman]$_s$ in particular.'

The only argument of verbs such as *udastsja* 'manage, succeed', on the the contrary, is more likely to be animate, like the pronoun *im* 'them' in 3. Yet, the anaphora resolver links *im* to the intervening *administracii* 'administrations' which is also plural, without considering animacy disagreement.

(3)   *... [storonniki]$_i$ oppozitsii nachali zahvatyvat [oblastnye administratsii]$_s$ ... [Im]$_{is}$ udalos' ...'*
        '... Opposition [supporters]$_i$ started to occupy [regional administrations]$_s$... [They]$_{is}$ managed...'

Lack of masculine-neuter gender contrasts leads to ambiguity that is difficult to be resolved, cf. the wordform *nego* might be a genitive form of either pronoun *on* 'he' or *ono* 'it'. In the next example (4), the correct interpretation is neuter, but the resolver chooses a more distant masculine antecedent *chelovek* '(a) man'.

(4)   *[Chelovek]$_s$, zavedshij [oruzhije]$_i$, dolzhen pozabotitsa o tom, chtoby ot [nego]$_{is}$ ne postradali drugie ljudi.*
        'When procuring a [weapon]$_i$, [(a) man]$_s$ must make sure that other people do not fall a victim to [it]$_{is}$.'

Likewise, nominal case-number syncretism misguides the number agreement requirement. An average wordform has 2,5 possible analyses (Toldova et al., 2015), therefore, morphological disambiguation is still problematic. For instance, all feminine nouns and some others have the same wordform for genitive singular and nominative plural, cf. *shkoly* 'school-GEN.SG' or 'school-NOM.PL'. Thus, in

(5), due to incorrect morphological analysis, *shkoly* was chosen as the antecedent for *oni* 'they' instead of a more distant plural NP *dva cheloveka* 'two people'.

(5)   *[Dva cheloveka]$_i$ upali s kryshi doma. Kazhetsja, [shkoly]$_s$. [Oni]$_i$...*
        '[Two people]$_i$ fell from the roof of a building. A [school's]$_s$, it seems. [They]$_{is}$...'

In general, morphological analysis in Russian is done less efficiently than in English. For instance, named entities, such as *Merkel* (Angela Merkel), are often attributed a wrong inflectional class and gender. Besides, even having the correct gender information, some systems choose gender incongruent antecedents for the pronouns, cf. *Vladimirom Putinym* 'Vladimir-INSTR Putin-INSTR' – *ona* 'she'.

To sum it up, Russian rich morphology is an additional source of errors. Some of them are unattested in English anaphora resolution. An anaphora resolver for Russian has to deal jointly with pronoun animacy deficiency, neutralization of gender contrasts in pronouns, nominal case-number syncretism and process novel nouns.

4.3 Syntactic errors

4.3.1 Binding conditions

Errors caused by the violation of syntactic rules were detected in all the systems. The majority of precision mistakes are due to the Binding conditions' violation. Some recall mistakes are due to specificity of binding properties of Russian reflexive pronouns.

Syntactically regulated pronouns, such as reflexives, present no problem for systems in English. E.g. Barbu (2002) reports very low error rate for reflexive pronouns (see also 4.1), as the reflexives do obey the binding conditions: in most cases, the antecedent of a reflexive is in the same clause and occupies the subject position (see (Chomsky, 1981)). In Russian, however, the lowest rate for reflexives is nearly 20% and the range of variation across systems is very high.

Firstly, some mistakes occurred due to difficulties in subject detection. This can be accounted for by free word order and case homonymy in nouns.

---

[3]Here and further, the index i corresponds to the real anaphoric relations, while s is the anaphoric links drawn by the system

Secondly, reflexives in Russian can have antecedents in another clause. Russian reflexives (*sebja, svoj*) allow long distance binding, when they occur in infinite clause or within an NP, since PRO and the NP specifier are transparent for binding (Rappaport, 1986). This often prevents the system from finding the correct antecedent and the participants even ignored reflexive pronouns in embedded infinitive clauses. For example, in (6) the system did not find *svoj* in the infinitive clause, although it has a unique antecedent in the same sentence.

(6) *[Ona]$_i$ vyezzhala redko i [∅]$_i$ umela [PRO]$_i$ zastavit' vysoko tsenit' [svoi]$_i$ poseschenija.*
'[She]$_i$ came out rarely and [∅]$_i$ knew, how to [PRO]$_i$ make others appreciate [her]$_i$ visits.'

There are cases of cataphoric usage of the reflexive possessive *svoj* (in 5% of the contexts). In this case systems fail to match this pronoun as in (7), or incorrectly bind it to the antecedent in the preceding sentence as in (8):

(7) *Za [svoju]$_i$ desjatiletnuju istoriju [kompanija]$_i$ sumela stat glavnym poiskovikom.*
'During [its]$_i$ 10 year history, [(the) company]$_i$ managed to become the main search engine.'

(8) *Zapretit' pravjaschuju partiju predlozhili [deputaty]$_s$. V [svoju]$_{is}$ ochered', [mestnyj parlament]$_i$ podkontrolen pravjaschej partii.*
'[(The) deputy]$_s$ suggested to ban the governing party. In [its]$_{is}$ turn, [(the) local parliament]$_i$ is under the control of the governing party.'

Incorrect binding is attested for personal pronouns as well. According to (Chomsky, 1981), personal pronouns are not bound within their local domain, i.e. this pronoun cannot have an antecedent within the same clause.

(9) *[Sasha]$_i$ ljubit [ego]$_{*i}$ / [sebja]$_{i/*j}$*
'[Sasha]$_i$ loves [him]$_{*i}$ / [himself]$_{i/*j}$.'

Applying the strategy of the nearest antecedent that matches the pronoun grammatical features, some systems choose the antecedent in the same clause, although such a decision leads to an ungrammatical interpretation. On the contrary, several participants bind reflexives to a referring group outside their local domain:

(10) *Eto pokazhet nashe otnoshenije k ["ottsu*

narodov"]$_i$ i tem, [kto]$_s$ pytaetsja [ego]$_{is}$ vykopat'.
'This will show our attitude to ["the father of nations"]$_i$ and those, [who]$_s$ try to dig [him]$_{is}$ out.'

(11) *On$_i$ ne pozvolil sebe$_{is}$ i legchajshego nameka.*
'He$_i$ did not afford himself$_{is}$ the slightest hint.'

Moreover, there are cases of recall mistakes for the reflexive *sebja* in a certain type of idiomatic expressions where it functions not as a proper verb argument, but rather as a middle voice marker, e.g. *pokazat sebja* - 'to come up', *vesti sebja* - 'to behave' (cf. "missing antecedents" type of errors for idiomatic use of pronouns in (Evans, 2002)). Though it is arguable, whether the pronoun has to be linked with the corresponding subject NP, we found out that such a non-standard use of *sebja* caused a number of mistakes for systems.

The high rate of deficiencies in reflexive anaphora resolution highlights the fact that Russian has some specific issues in binding condition modeling. Therefore, the anaphora resolvers need particular heuristics and deeper syntactic analysis in order to handle cases of cataphora and long distance binding.

4.3.2 Parsing errors

Incorrect syntactic parsing influences the results as well. Firstly, we observe errors in matching NP boundaries, especially for NPs with dependent genitive groups, such as *pomoschnik presidenta* 'president's assistant' or *zdanie ministerstva* 'the building of (the) ministry' (the genitive groups are underlined). Several systems incorrectly matched genitives only, ignoring the preceding head of the group and chose them as antecedents.

Secondly, many participants did not recognize multi-word parenthetical words and treat them as PPs or NPs. Consequently, the systems consider the nouns within these expressions as antecedents, in particular, when the nouns appeared at the shortest distance. For example, in (12) the noun *vzgljad* 'view, opinion' is linked to an anaphor, since it is the nearest candidate which agrees in number and gender with the pronoun.

(12) *Na [moj vzgljad]$_s$, [on]$_s$ dolzhen vypolnjat neskolko trebovanij.*

'In [my opinion]$_s$, [he]$_s$ should fulfill some re-
quirements.'

4.3.3 A case of NP embedding

A frequent source of errors is NP embedding. There are two potential antecedents in complex NPs: e.g. possessor vs. full NP in a possessive construction, or NP in a prepositional phrase vs. full NP with a prepositional phrase. In the NP *zdanije ministrestva* 'building of the Ministry' both the possessor and the full NP are potential antecedents for *jego* 'its/his'. The possessor antecedent is a less frequent case, but it is closer to the pronoun. Thus, it is a source for precision mistakes. The same applies to embedding of NPs with prepositional phrases as in *[nash zelenyj sad [nad rekoj]]* '[our green garden [by the river]]'. Especially, it affects the selection of antecedents for relative pronouns(see 4.1). Additionally, grammatical ambiguity influences the correct analysis of such constructions.

4.3.4 Distant antecedent

All the systems limited the position of a potential antecedent to a window of a certain size. If the actual antecedent is located beyond this window, it is ignored by the system. This leads to errors in distant antecedent cases (when antecedents occurred more distant than 2 sentences in the text prior to the pronoun or in the previous paragraph).

According to some reports (Kutuzov and Ionov, 2014; Kamenskaya et al., 2014), setting the maximal window size improves the performance of the system considerably. However, there are rare cases when no appropriate antecedent is located within the fixed window. In (13) reflexive *soboj* should be linked to the personal pronoun *oni*, but instead it is connected to the preposition *pered* 'in front of', which is incorrectly analysed as a homonymous noun *pered* 'front'. Thus, the closest agreement matching antecedent is chosen (a potential antecedent is between a pronoun and its real antecedent), which leads to a precision error.

(13)   *[Ljudi]$_i$, nastroennye ekstremistski, [oni]$_i$, kak pravilo, ljudi ogranichennye i ne otdajut sebe otchet v tom, chto dazhe esli, kak [oni]$_i$ dumajut, [oni]$_i$ stavjat [pered]$_s$ [soboj]$_j$ blagorodnye celi, to, sovershaja terroristicheskie [akty]$_s$, [oni]$_i$s otdaljajutsja...*

'[Extremists]$_i$ are, as a rule, very simple-minded and do not realize that even if [they]$_i$, as [they]$_i$ think, have noble ideas [in front of]$_s$ [themselves]$_i$, by committing terroristic acts [they]$_{is}$ move away...'

Thus, there is a tendency for Russian systems to overestimate the linear distance factor for an antecedent, which shows a lack of salience based models for the anaphora resolution task.

4.4 Opaque or pleonastic antecedents

One of the essential issues for the anaphora resolution task is to distinguish the cases of pronouns that have no antecedent (cf. Evans (2002)). For English and some other European languages, expletives present such a problem. As for Russian, there is no obligatory subject in a clause. Impersonal, indefinite-personal, zero pronoun (pro-pronoun) clauses are possible. However, there are special cases of pleonastic antecedents or cases of non-referential pronouns.

Firstly, there are pronouns used in idioms and lexicalized constructions such as in *Vot to-to i ono*_3sg.Neut.PRON 'Here we go', or in honorific terms as in *Jego*_3SG.PRON.POSS *prevoshoditelystvo* 'His excellency'.

Secondly, the pronoun *svoj* has a lexical meaning 'own', so it does not need an antecedent in such cases as in *Svoja*_REFL.POSS *rubashka blizche k telu* 'self before all'.

Standard cases of discontinuous, inferred and implicit antecedents are another source of precision and recall mistakes for Russian. The former are the cases when a plural pronoun refers to two different discourse disjoint NPs and becomes a new group referent (c.f. two arguments of a verb as in 'Peter met John and they...'). The other types of precision errors in case of number disagreement is the so-called associative plural as in *Masha obizhaetsya chto my ih ne zovem* 'Mary takes offence that we don't invite them (Mary and her friends)'. Thus, there are specific cases of pronoun semantic re-interpretation as non-anaphoric elements (as in *svoj* as 'own' or *kotoryj*) and cases of opaque antecedents (e.g. in the associative plural) that affect the anaphora resolution precision.

5 Conclusion

In this study, we have examined different error types that are characteristic for Russian anaphora resolvers. Russian, as a relatively underresourced language with rich morphology, poses challenging issues, such as a lack of animacy distinctions in pronouns, morphological ambiguity, specific binding conditions and particular cases of non-referential pronouns and opaque antecedents. These issues are relevant for all systems which participated in RU-EVAL-2014 evaluation campaign, despite the difference in their approaches and models. Our findings show that language-specific properties require a joint fine-grained analysis of morphology, syntax and semantics, as well as particular rules for some phenomena, such as binding, in order to achieve efficient anaphora resolution for Russian.

Acknowledgments

The reported study was supported by the Russian Foundation of Basic Research, research project No. 15-07-09306 "Evaluation benchmark for information retrieval".

References

C. Barbu. 2002. Error analysis in anaphora resolution. In *LREC*.

A.V. Bogdanov, S.S. Dzhumaev, D.A. Skorinkin, and A.S. Starostin. 2014. Anaphora analysis based on {ABBYY} compreno linguistic technologies. 13(20).

K. K. Boyarski, E. A. Kanevskij, and Stepukova A. V. 2013. Vyjavlenie anaforicheskih otnoshenij pri avtomaticheskom analize teksta [in russian, 'detection of anaphoric relations in automatic text processing']. *Nauchno-tehnicheskij vestnik informatsionnyh tehnologij, mehaniki i optiki*, 5(87):108–112.

N. Chinchor and L. Hirschmann. 1997. Muc-7 coreference task definition, version 3.0. In *Proceedings of MUC*, volume 7.

N. Chomsky. 1981. *Lectures on Government and Binding*. Foris.

R. Evans. 2002. Refined salience weighting and error analysis in anaphora resolution. *Proceedings of Reference Resolution for Natural Language Procesing*, pages 51–59.

L. Hirschmann. 1997. Muc-7 coreference task definition. version 3.0. In *Proceedings of the 7th Message Understanding Conference (1997)*.

B. Jongejan and H. Dalianis. 2009. Automatic training of lemmatization rules that handle morphological changes in pre-, in-and suffixes alike. In *Proceedings of the Joint Conference of the 47th Annual Meeting of the ACL and the 4th International Joint Conference on Natural Language Processing of the AFNLP: Volume 1-Volume 1*, pages 145–153. Association for Computational Linguistics.

Daniel Jurafsky and James H. Martin. 2009. *Speech and Language Processing (2Nd Edition)*. Prentice-Hall, Inc., Upper Saddle River, NJ, USA.

M.A. Kamenskaya, I.V. Khramoin, and I.V. Smirnov. 2014. Data-driven methods for anaphora resolution of russian texts. 13(20).

J. K Kummerfeld and D. Klein. 2013. Error-driven analysis of challenges in coreference resolution. In *Proceedings of the Conference on Empirical Methods in Natural Language Processing*, pages 265–277.

A. Kutuzov and M. Ionov. 2014. The impact of morphology processing quality on automated anaphora resolution for russian. In *Computational Linguistics and Intellectual Technologies*, volume 13.

S. Martschat and M. Strube. 2014. Recall error analysis for coreference resolution. In *EMNLP*, pages 2070–2081.

C. Orasan, D. Cristea, R. Mitkov, and A. H. Branco. 2008. Anaphora resolution exercise: an overview. In *LREC*.

E. V. Paducheva. 1985. *Vyskazyvanie i ego sootnesnnost' s dejstvitel'nostju [In Russian, 'Utterance and its interrelationship with reality']*. Ripol Klassik.

M. Poesio and O. Uryupina. 2011. Anaphora resolution task at Evalita 2011. In *Working Notes of EVALITA 2011*.

S. Pradhan, L. Ramshaw, M. Marcus, M. Palmer, R. Weischedel, and N. Xue. 2011. Conll-2011 shared task: Modeling unrestricted coreference in ontonotes. In *Proceedings of the Fifteenth Conference on Computational Natural Language Learning: Shared Task*, CONLL Shared Task '11, pages 1–27, Stroudsburg, PA, USA. Association for Computational Linguistics.

S. Pradhan, A. Moschitti, N. Xue, O. Uryupina, and Y. Zhang. 2012. Conll-2012 shared task: Modeling multilingual unrestricted coreference in ontonotes. In *Joint Conference on EMNLP and CoNLL - Shared Task*, CoNLL '12, pages 1–40, Stroudsburg, PA, USA. Association for Computational Linguistics.

E.V. Protopopova, A.A. Bodrova, S. A. Volskaya, I. V. Krylova, A. S. Chuchunkov, S. V. Alexeeva, V. V. Bocharov, and D. V. Granovsky. 2014. Anaphoric annotation and corpusbased anaphora resolution: an experiment. 13(20).

G. C Rappaport. 1986. On anaphor binding in russian. *Natural Language & Linguistic Theory*, 4(1):97–120.

M. Recasens, L. Màrquez, E. Sapena, A. Martí, Ma. Taulé, V. Hoste, M. Poesio, and Y. Versley. 2010. Semeval-2010 task 1: Coreference resolution in multiple languages. In *Proceedings of the 5th International Workshop on Semantic Evaluation*, pages 1–8. Association for Computational Linguistics.

H. Schmid. 1994. Probabilistic part-of-speech tagging using decision trees. In *Proceedings of the international conference on new methods in language processing*, volume 12, pages 44–49. Citeseer.

Ander Soraluze, Olatz Arregi, Xabier Arregi, and Arantza Díaz de Ilarraza. 2015. Coreference resolution for morphologically rich languages. adaptation of the stanford system to basque. *Procesamiento del Lenguaje Natural*, 55:23–30.

S. Toldova, A. Roytberg, A. Ladygina, M. Vasilyeva, I. Azerkovich, M. Kurzukov, G. Sim, D. Gorshkov, A. Ivanova, A. Nedoluzhko, et al. 2014. Ru-eval-2014: Evaluating anaphora and coreference resolution for russian. In *Computational Linguistics and Intellectual Technologies*, volume 13.

S. Toldova, O. Lyashevskaya, A. Bonch-Osmolovskaya, and M. Ionov. 2015. Evaluation for morphologically rich language: Russian nlp. In *Proceedings on the International Conference on Artificial Intelligence (ICAI)*, page 300. The Steering Committee of The World Congress in Computer Science, Computer Engineering and Applied Computing (WorldComp).

S. Toldova, Yu. Grishina, A. Ladygina, M. Vasilyeva, G. Sim, and I. Azerkovich. 2016. Russian coreference corpus. In Francisco Alonso Almeida, Ivalla Ortega Barrera, Elena Quintana Toledo, and Margarita E. Sánchez Cuervo, editors, *Input a Word, Analyze the World*. Cambridge Scholars Publishing.

Olga Uryupina. 2008. Error analysis for learning-based coreference resolution. In *LREC*.

How to Handle Split Antecedents in Tamil?

Vijay Sundar Ram R. and Sobha Lalitha Devi
AU-KBC Research Centre,
MIT Campus of Anna University,
Chennai, India
{sundar, sobha}@au-kbc.org

Abstract

Resolution of the anaphoric entities in natural language text is very much essential to extract the complete information from the text. In this paper, we present a methodology to resolve one of the difficult pronouns, plural pronouns with split antecedents in Tamil. We have used a salience measure based approach with salience factors obtained from sub-categorization information of nouns and selectional restriction rules of the verbs. We have evaluated our approach with Tamil novel corpus and the results are encouraging.

1   Introduction

Anaphoric expressions in natural language text help in bringing cohesion to the text. The resolution of these anaphoric expressions is vital in developing information extraction and understanding systems. Theoretically various anaphoric expressions such as pronominal, reflexives, reciprocals, distributors, one pronoun, definite descriptions, VP anaphora, and zero anaphora are well studied. Automatic resolution engines for various types of anaphors were presented from early 80's of the last century, starting with Hobb's (1978) naïve approach followed by knowledge rich approaches by Carter et al (1987), Carbonll and Brown (1988), and Rich and LuperFoy (1988). These approaches were followed by knowledge poor approaches by Lappin and Leass (1994), Kennedy and Baguraov, Mitkov (1998) etc. Centering theory based approach was introduced by Grosz, Joshi and Kuhn (1979, 1981). The task of anaphora resolution got boosted with various Machine Learning (ML) techniques. The first ML approach was presented by Dagan and Itai (1980) and various ML techniques were later used.

Byron (2001) has mentioned difficult anaphors which are excluded in most of the systems and they are as follows. i) Constructions which are required to interpret pronouns with split antecedents or cataphora. ii) Pronouns with antecedents, different from NPs such as clauses. iii) Pronouns with no antecedents in the discourse such as deictic or generic pronouns. There are very less number of automatic resolution engines for these difficult anaphors. In this paper, we present an algorithm for automatic resolution of one of the difficult anaphors; plural pronouns with split antecedents. We have studied the split antecedents in Tamil, a morphologically rich and verb final South Dravidian language and came up with an algorithm to resolve it. Consider example 1 given below:

Ex 1:

   a) ***nepaal pirathamar   ke. pi. ooli***
     Nepal Prime minister K P Oli
     inthiya pirathamar   moodiyai
     Indian   Prime Minister Modi
     puthu dilliyil canthiththaar.
     New Delhi   meet(V)+past+3h
     (Nepal Prime minister KP Oli met Indian Prime Minister Modi in New Delhi.)

   b) ***avarkal*** ceythiyaalarkalai
     They   press-people(N)
     Ithirabath-aucil   canththinar.
     Hyderabad-House(N)+loc meet(V)+pst+3p
     (They met the press people at Hyderabad House.)

In the above example 1, the plural pronoun 'avarkal' (they) in sentence 1.b, refers to ***nepal pirathamar ke. pi. ooli*** (Nepal Prime minister K P

Proceedings of the Workshop on Coreference Resolution Beyond OntoNotes (CORBON 2016), co-located with NAACL 2016, pages 84–91,
San Diego, California, June 16, 2016. ©2016 Association for Computational Linguistics

Oli) and ***inthiya pirathamar moodiyai*** (Indian Prime Minister Modi), where these two entities have occurred in the subject and object of sentence 1.a.

Split antecedents are well studied in the framework of computational model in various languages and the details are as follows. Kosuga (2014) has presented a study on Japanese reciprocal anaphor 'otagai' with split antecedents. Han et al. (2011) have presented a behavioral study of grammatical status of 'caki' in Korean, which takes split antecedents as referent. Split antecedents were considered for coreference annotation in various languages such as Spanish, Catalan, Italian, English, Polish etc. MATE, AnaCora, and Polish Coreference annotation schema support annotation of split antecedents. There are no published works on Split Antecedents in Indian languages and particularly in Tamil and our work is first of its kind.

Split antecedents are well studied under different constructions. Following are the different constructions explored in English. Split antecedents occur with a relative clause construction as in example 2.

Ex 2:
> Marry met ***a man*** and John met ***a woman who know each other well***. (Mckinney-Bock, 2013)

There are different theoretical solutions for this split antecedents in relative construction. McKinney-Bock et al (2013) have presented a head-external approach and Ning Znang (2007) have proposed a syntactic derivation approach. Split antecedents are dealt with VP-ellipsis construction as in example 3.

Ex 3:
> 'Sally want to sail around the world and Barbara wants to fly to South Africa and they will, if money is available' (Webber 1978)
> 'Sally will sail around the world and Barbara will fly to South Africa'

Gatt and van Deemter (2009) have studied the characteristics of plural pronouns with split antecedents in GNOME corpus. They have studied the similarity and distance between the plural pronoun and their antecedents.

Cristea et al. (2002) have presented a paper investigating the difficult problems that could arise in anaphora resolution and proposed some solutions within the frame work of a general anaphora resolver. They have discussed on the methodology to resolve the plural pronouns with split antecedents. Consider example 4.

Ex 4:
> a) ***John*** waited for ***Maria***.
> b) ***They*** went for pizza.

During the interpretation of the above sentence, a new discourse entity (DE) must be proposed for the group [John, Maria] as soon as the referential expression 'Maria' is parsed. Cristea et al. (2002) came-up with a set of ideas.

a) Groups should have a property of similarity of their elements and that group formation is triggered by a first referent to it.
b) A group is considered only if it is verbalized as such in the text and it does not exist until it is referred to.
c) World knowledge is needed for group identification. We should use similarity measures to identify members of the group.
d) A new DE should be proposed when no match between the current entity and the preceding DE arise above a threshold.

With these introductions to split-antecedents, we continue the paper as follow. The following section describes about Tamil and anaphora resolution works in this language. In the third section, we present our approach to resolve split-antecedents in Tamil using selectional restriction rules, subcategorization information and salience measure (Lappin and Leass, 1994). The fourth section has description on the experiments and evaluation. The paper concludes with a concluding section.

2 Pronoun Resolution in Tamil

Tamil is a morphologically rich and highly agglutinative language. It belongs to Dravidian family of languages. It is a verb final, nominative-accusative and relatively free-word order language. Subject and finite verb has person, number and gender (PNG) agreement. Similarly 3rd person pronoun's

PNG has agreement with its antecedent. 1st person and 2nd person pronouns have number agreement with its antecedents. Among Indian languages, there are a few automatic anaphora resolution works done in languages such as Tamil, Hindi, Bengali, Punjabi and Malayalam. Similar to what was mentioned by Byron (2001), these resolution engines do not attempt the difficult anaphors. One of the earliest anaphora resolution works in Indian languages was 'Vasisth' presented by Sobha (2000, 2002) for Hindi and Malayalam. Considering anaphora resolution in Tamil, there are few works on resolution of third person pronouns. The details are as follows. Sobha (2007) using salience measure, Akilandeshwari et al. (2013) using Conditional Random Fields (CRFs), Balaji et al. (2012) using bootstrapping approach and Ram and Sobha (2013) using Tree-CRFs. Sobha et al.(2014) have presented a generic pronominal resolution engine for resolving pronouns in Indo-Aryan and Dravidian languages. Akilandeshwari et al. (2012) have studied a different construction in Tamil, where the 3rd person pronouns are agglutinated with relative-participle verbs and they have presented a CRFs based approach for resolving these pronouns.

3 Our Approach for Resolution of Plural Pronouns with Split Antecedents

We attempt to resolve the plural pronouns with split-antecedents using selectional restriction rules of the verb, categorizing the nouns based on its sub-categorization information and ranking the possible antecedents using salience factor weights. In the following sub-sections we explain Sub-categorization of nouns and Selectional restriction rules.

3.1 Selectional Restriction Rules

The verbs describe the action or the process in the nature and this allow the verbs to take nouns with specific sub-categorization feature as its syntactic arguments. This is defined as the selectional restriction (SR) rules of a verb. Consider the sentence in example 5.

Ex 5:

raam   aappil   caappittaan.
Ram(N)   apple(N)   eat(V)+past+3sn
'Ram ate an apple'.

Here 'raam' (Ram) has the sub-categorization feature [+animate, +human] and 'aappil' (apple) with [+edible]. The SR features required by the verb 'caappitu' (eat) for selecting its subject and object are [+animate] and [+edible] respectively. If there is a violation in SR rules, the sentence can be syntactically correct but it will not be semantically correct (Arulmozhi 2006). Verb has the right to select its arguments. We have grouped the verbs according to the sub-categorization information of the subject and object nouns. A group of commonly used 1500 verb senses are analyzed and 500 SR rules are derived from these verbs in-house. The SR rules do not cover figurative usage of language. The sub-categorization features of a noun are explained in the next section. A sample rule is shown in Figure 1.

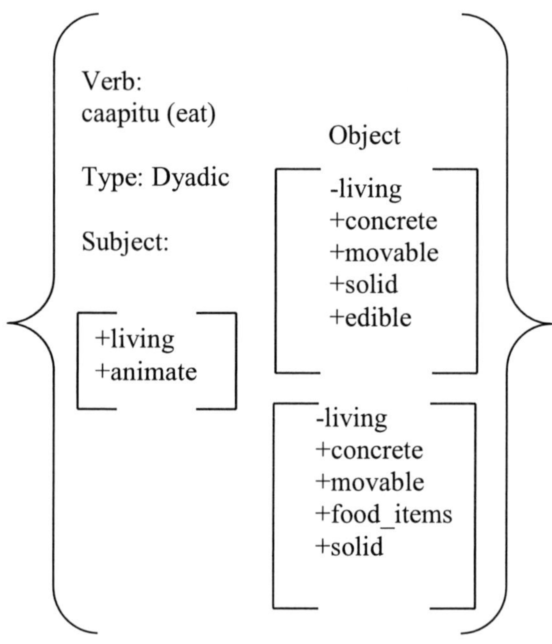

Figure 1: Selectional restriction rule for 'caapitu' (eat).

3.2 Sub-Categorization

Sub-categorization features explain the nature of a noun. Essentially, the arguments of the verb, subject and object are analyzed using these features. These features may include the type of noun, its characteristics, state etc. Sub-categorization information include the features such as [±animate], [±concrete], [±edible] etc (Arulmozhi 2006).

There are totally 104 sub-categorization features. Using the sub-categorization features, which are related to the nouns, the SR features of the verb selects the nouns as its syntactic arguments. We have categoriesed 4500 frequently occurring nouns in Tamil. The Sub-categorization feature for the noun 'aappil' (apple) is presented in Figure 2.

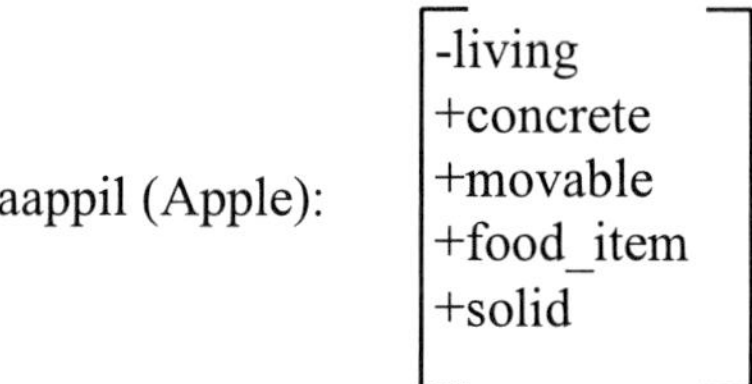

Figure 2: Sub-categorization features of the noun 'aappil' (apple)

These sub-categorization features are used as nodes in building a language ontology. This language ontology is built with respect to the usage of language. Due to this, it deviates substantially from the taxonomy of nature. The sub-categorization features for the nouns can be obtained easily by traversing through various nodes (Arulmozhi, 2006). The nouns are grouped under each node, so we get a coarse to fine grained information of each noun. The ontology starts with [+entity] as the head noun and it divides into [+living] and [-living].

3.3   Resolution of Plural Pronouns

Using the SR rules and the sub-categorization information of nouns we try to resolve the plural pronouns in a two-step process. In the first step we try to group the noun phrases to form groups which can be possible split-antecedents. The nouns are grouped based on the sub-categorization information and following the verb's SR rule restriction rule. Consider examples 6.

Ex 6:
    a)   raam   siitavai   vakuppil
          Ram(N) Sita(N)+acc class(N)+loc
          canthiththaan.
          meet(V)+past+3sm
          (Ram met Sita in the class.)
    b)   avarkal   unavu_vituthikku
          They (plural PRP) hotel (N)+dative
          cenranar.
          go(V)+past+3p
          (They went to the hotel)

Ex 7:
    a)   puunai   pullil
          Cat(N) grass(N)+loc
          vilaiyadi-koNtirunthathu.
          play(V)+progressive
          (The cat was playing on the grass.)
    b)   nay   manalil
          Dog(N) sand(N)+loc
          vilaiyadi-koNtirunthathu.
          play(V)+progressive
          (The dog was playing in the sand.)
    c)   unavai   kaNtathum   avai
          Food(N) on_seeing(V)   they(plural-PRP)
          ooti_vanthana.
          came_running
          (On seeing the food they came running)

In example 6, there are three nouns before the plural pronoun 'avarkal' (they). The sub-categorization of these nouns are as follows:

    a)   raam (Ram):[+living; +animate; +vertebrate; +mammal; +human; -female]
    b)   siita (Sita):[+living; +animate; +vertebrate; +mammal; +human; +female]
    c)   vakkupu (class):[-living; +concrete;-movable; +artifact; +building]

The verb in sentence 6.a and 6.b are 'canthippu' (meet) and 'cel' (go). The SR rules for these verbs are as follows;

    a)   Verb: 'canthippu' (meet)
          Subj: [+living; +animate; +vertebrate; +mammal; +human;]
          Obj: [+living; +animate; +vertebrate; +mammal; +human;]

    b)   Verb: 'cel' (go)
          Subj: [+living; +animate]
          Obj: [-living; +concrete; -movable]

And the plural pronoun 'avarkal' (they) has occurred in the second sentence 6.b. The antecedent of "avarkal" (they) occurs as two separate NPs [raam, siita].

In example 7, there are three nouns before the occurrence of the plural pronoun 'avai' (they). The sub-categorization of these nouns are as follows:

    a) puunai (Cat): [+living; +animate; +vertebrate; +mammal; -human; avion; +carnivorous; +cat_family]

    b) naay (Dog): [+living; +animate; +vertebrate; +mammal; -human; -avion; +carnivorous; +dog_family]

    c) unavu (food): [-living; +concrete; +food_item]

The verbs in sentence 7.a, 7.b and 7.c are 'villaiyatu' and 'ooti_va', where both the verbs take [+living; +animate] as subject argument. And the sentence 8.c has 'avai' (they), plural pronoun. Here the split antecedents are [puunai, naay].

We describe the methodology to perform the resolution of plural pronouns, which do not refer to a plural noun phrase, on text preprocessed with syntactic information such as morphological analysis (Ram et al, 2010), POS tag (Sobha et al, 2010), chunk information, clause boundary (Ram et al, 2012) and named entity (Malarkodi et al, 2012). The morphological analyser gives an indepth analysis of each word, such as root word, suffixes and its labels and person, number and gender (PNG) information. The clause boundary identifier marks the matrix clause and sub-ordinate clause boundaries, which helps in adding positional constraint features.

Following are the steps involved in resolving the plural pronoun. In the first step, we enrich the nouns and the verbs with their sub-categorization information, and SR rules respectively. The named entities (NEs) are mapped to the sub-categorization features, so we get the sub-categorization information using the NE information as described in the example 8.

Ex 8:

    a) Person: [+living; +animate; +vertebrate; +mammal; +human;]

    b) Location: [-living; -moveable; +landscape]

In the second step, when a plural pronoun is encountered in the sentence, the preceding portion of the sentence and two preceding sentences are considered for analysis, as Gatt et al. (2009) have shown that the distance between plural pronouns and their antecedent are very few sentences away.

The noun phrases in the preceding sentences are analysed and grouped to form the possible antecedents. For grouping the NPs, the NPs need to satisfy the following matching conditions.

a) The NPs can be grouped together if they have same sub-categorization information or till the last but one node in the ontology is same. Example [+living; +animate; +vertebrate; +mammal; +human; +female] and [+living; +animate; +vertebrate; +mammal; +human;-female] are considered to be same since both are same till last but one node.

b) Exceptions are as follows:
In the case of NPs with sub-categorization [+living] and do not have [+human], we look for sub-categorization match between the NPs only till [+living; +animate] and such NPs are grouped together.

Following are the steps involved to form possible candidates by grouping the NPs.

    a) Identify the plural pronoun in n^{th} sentence.

    b) Consider sentence n-2th, n-1th and in n^{th} sentence consider the portion preceding to the plural pronoun to form a candidate sentence set.

    c) For each sentence in the candidate sentence set; Noun Phrases in the sentence with conjunct suffix 'um' or conjunct word 'maRRum' (and) are united to form conjunct NPs.
From now onwards the term NPs refers to both NPs and conjunct NPs.

    d) For each sentence in sentence set; if there exists NPs satisfying the matching condition, then the NPs are grouped together.

    e) Group the NPs that occur in same syntactic argument position and satisfy the matching condition across n^{th}, n-1th and n-2th sentences.

S.No	Salience Factors	Weights
1	Same Ontology Nodes	30
2	NPs with following verbs	30
3	NPs with same syntactic argument position	20
4	NPs with different syntactic argument position	10

5	NPs are syntactic argument for verbs having same SR rules	30
6	NPs are syntactic argument for verbs with different SR rules	10
7	NPs in current n^{th} sentence	30
8	NPs in n-1th sentence	20
9	NPs in n-2th sentence	10

Table 1: Salience Factors and their Weights

In the third step, when the possible antecedents are formed by grouping the NPs, they are ranked based on the salience factors derived from the features of NPs such as the sub-categorization information of NPs, the SR rules of verbs followed by the NPs and the syntactic argument position of the NPs in the sentences. The salience factor weights (Lappin and Leass, 1994) are described in table1. The weights for the salience factors are initially manually assigned based on linguistic considerations and fine-tuned through experiments.

4 Experiment, Results and Discussion

To analyse the plural pronouns, we choose a Tamil novel, 'Ponniyin Selvan' which was authored by Kalki, a well-known writer. As mentioned in Section 3.3, we processed the corpus with morphological analyser, POS tagger, chunker, pruner, clause boundary identifier and named entity recognizer. The corpus is made into a column format, where the information from each preprocessing module is added as a column. In the corpus, we considered the first 1000, plural pronouns, 'avarkal' and 'avai'. These pronouns had four different types of antecedents such as plural noun phrase, conjunct NPs, split antecedents and the pronoun 'avarkal' also refers to honorific NP. The distribution of the pronouns with respect to their antecedents is presented in table 2.

S.No	Type of antecedent	Number of occurrence
1	Plural NP	789
2	Conjunct NPs	147
3	Split Antecedents	51
4	Honorific NP	18

Table 2: Distribution of plural pronouns based on their antecedents

In this experiment, we focus on plural pronouns with split antecedents. We considered the sentence having this plural pronoun and its preceding two sentences. In this set of sentences, as mentioned in Section 3.3, we first tag the sub-categorization information for the nouns and SR rules of the verbs. After forming the possible antecedents by grouping NPs, we rank the possible antecedents with the salience factor weights mentioned in Section 3.3 to find the antecedent. The performance evaluation is done with accuracy as the measure. The results are presented in table 3.

S.No	Total number of pronouns with split antecedents	Correctly tagged	Accuracy%
1	51	30	58.82

Table 3: Performance of resolution of plural pronouns with split antecedents

On analyzing the output, we found errors, when the preceding two sentences have similar NPs in the subject position. Consider the following example 9.

Ex 9:
   a) vanthiyathevan   maNtapaththai
       Vanthiyathevan(N) hall(N)+acc
       atainthaan.
       reach(V)+past+3sm
       (Vanthiyathevan reached the hall.)
   b) kunthavai   vaanathiyai
       Kundhavai(N) Vanathi(N)+acc
       azaiththaal.
       call(V)+past+3sf
       (Kundhavai called Vanathi)
   c) avarkal vanthiyathevanai   kaNtu
       they(PN) Vanthiyathevan(N)+acc see(V)
       ciriththanar.
       laugh(V)+past+3pl
       (They on seeing Vanthiyathevan laughed.)

In the above example the possible antecedents for the pronoun 'avarkal' are [vanthiyathevan, kunthavai] and [kunthavai, vaanathiyai]. Here 'vanthiyathevan' and 'kunthavai' have occurred in the subject position and this group of NPs got higher salience score. But [kunthavai, vaanathiyai] is the correct antecedent. This shows the salience weights have to be altered further after analyzing more plural pronouns.

Conclusion

We have presented a methodology to resolve plural pronouns which refer to split antecedents in Tamil. Automatic resolution of split antecedents is less attempted and it is first of its kind in Tamil. Our algorithm works on salience measures, the salience factors for scoring are obtained from the sub-categorization information of the noun phrases and the SR rules of the verbs. We have tested the algorithm on plural pronouns occurred in a Tamil novel. The results are encouraging. We need to test this methodology on a corpus from other domains.

References

Akilandeswari A., Sobha Lalitha Devi. 2013. Conditional Random Fields Based Pronominal Resolution in Tamil. *International Journal on Computer Science and Engineering*, Vol. 5 Issue 6 pp 601 - 610

Akilandeswari A, Bakiyavathi T and Sobha Lalitha Devi, 2012. atu Difficult Pronominal in Tamil. *In: 1ˢᵗ Workshop on Indian Language Data: Resources and Evaluation, Organized under LREC 2012,* Istanbul

Arulmozhi P. 2006. Semantic Tagging for Laguage Processing. *Thesis submitted to Anna University Chennai,* India

Aone C., and McKee D. 1993. A Language-Independent Anaphora Resolution System for Understanding Multilingual Texts. *In proceeding of ACL 1993*, pp 156-163.

Balaji J., Geetha T.V., Ranjani Parthasarathi R., Karky M. 2012.Two-Stage Bootstrapping for Anaphora Resolution *In: Proceedings of COLING 2012*, pp 507–516

Byron, D. 2001. A proposal for consistent evaluation of pronoun resolution algorithms.

Carbonell J. G., and Brown R. D. 1988. Anaphora resolution: A multi- strategy approach. *In: 12ᵗʰ International Conference on Computational Linguistics*, 1988, pp. 96-101

Carter D. 1987. Interpreting anaphors in natural language texts. Chisester: *Ellis Horwood* ltd.

Cristea, D.; Dima, G. E.; Postolache, O. & Mitkov, R. 2002. Handling complex cases of anaphora resolution, In: *4ᵗʰ Discourse Anaphora and Anaphor Resolution Colloquium (DAARC2002)*, University of Lisbon, Portugal, pp. 7-12.

Dagan I., and Itai. A. 1990. Automatic processing of large corpora for the resolution of anaphora references. *In: 13th conference on Computational linguistics*, Vol. 3, Helsinki, Finland, pp.330-332.

Gatt A and Kees van Deemter. 2009. Generating plural NPs in discourse: Evidence from theGNOME corpus. In: *Procs. of COGSCI workshop \Production of Referring Expressions*, Amsterdam

Han, C., Dennis R. S., and Calen W. 2011. An Experimental Study of the Grammatical Status of Caki in Korean. *Japanese/Korean Linguistics 19* (JK 19). Eds. Ho-min S., Haruko C., William O'., Leon S.and Sang Y. C., CSLI, Stanford, 81-94

Hobbs J. (1978). Resolving pronoun references. *Lingua 44*, pp. 339-352.

Joshi A. K., and Kuhn S. 1979. Centered logic: The role of entity centered sentence representation in natural language inferencing. *In: International Joint Conference on Artificial Intelligence.*

Joshi A. K., and Weinstein S. (1981). Control of inference: Role of some aspects of discourse structure – centering. *In: International Joint Conference on Artificial Intelligence,* pp. 385-387.

Kosuge, T. (2014). Japanese Reciprocal Anaphor *Otagai* with Split Antecedents in Disguise and Multi-Dominant Syntactic Structure. *JELS* 31, 319-324.

Lappin S., and Leass H. J. (1994). An algorithm for pronominal anaphora resolution. *Computational Linguistics* 20 (4), pp. 535-561.

Malarkodi C.S and Sobha Lalitha Devi . 2012. A Deeper Look into Features for NE Resolution in Indian Languages. *In: 1ˢᵗ Workshop on Indian Language Data: Resources and Evaluation, Organized under LREC 2012,* Istanbul

McKinney-Bock, K. 2013. Deriving Split-Antecedent Relative Clauses. *University of Pennsylvania Working Papers in Linguistics*: Vol. 19: Iss. 1, Article 14.

Mitkov R. 1998. Robust pronoun resolution with limited knowledge. *In: 17th International Conference on Computational Linguistics* (COLING' 98/ACL'98), Montreal, Canada, pp. 869-875.

Ning Zhang N. 2007. The Syntactic Derivations of Split Antecedent Relative Clause Constructions. *Taiwan Journal of Linguistics* Vol. 5.1, 19-47

Ram R.V.S, Menaka S and Sobha Lalitha Devi. 2010. Tamil Morphological Analyser. In: "Morphological Analysers and Generators", (ed.) Mona Parakh, LDC-IL, Mysore, pp. 1 –18.

Ram R.V.S, Bakiyavathi T, Sindhujagopalan, Amudha K and Sobha Lalitha Devi. 2012. Tamil Clause Boundary Identification: Annotation and Evaluation. *In:1ˢᵗ Workshop on Indian Language Data: Resources and Evaluation, Organized under LREC 2012,* Istanbul

Ram, R.V.S and Sobha Lalitha Devi. 2013. Pronominal Resolution in Tamil Using Tree CRFs. *In Proceedings of 6th Language and Technology Conference, Human Language Technologies as a challenge for Computer Science and Linguistics* - 2013, Poznan, Polan

Rich, E. LuperFoy, S. 1988. Anaphora architecture for anaphora resolution In: *Second Conference on Applied Natural Language Processing (ANLP'88)*, pp. 18-24 Austin, Texas (USA).

Sobha L. and Patnaik B. N. 2000. Vasisth: An Anaphora Resolution System for Indian Languages. *In Proceedings of International Conference on Artificial and Computational Intelligence for Decision, Control and Automation in Engineering and Industrial Applications*, Monastir, Tunisia.

Sobha L. and Patnaik,B.N. 2002. Vasisth: An anaphora resolution system for Malayalam and Hindi. *In Proceedings of Symposium on Translation Support Systems*.

Sobha L. 2007. Resolution of Pronominals in Tamil. Computing Theory and Application, *The IEEE Computer Society Press*, Los Alamitos, CA, pp. 475-79.

Sobha Lalitha Devi and Pattabhi R K Rao T. (2010). "Hybrid Approach for POS Tagging for Relatively Free Word Order Languages", in the Proceedings of Knowledge Sharing Event on Part-Of-Speech Tagging, 25-26th March, 2010, LDC-IL, CIIL, Mysore.

Sobha L., Sivaji B., Ram R.V.S., and Akilandeswari A. 2011. NLP Tool Contest @ICON2011 on Anaphora Resolution in Indian Languages. *In: Proceedings of ICON 2011*.

Webber, B. L. 1978. A Formal Approach to Discourse Anaphora, *Ph.D. thesis, Harvard University.*

When Annotation Schemes Change Rules Help:
A Configurable Approach to Coreference Resolution beyond OntoNotes

Amir Zeldes and Shuo Zhang
Department of Linguistics, Georgetown University
`{amir.zeldes,ssz6}@georgetown.edu`

Abstract

This paper approaches the challenge of adapting coreference resolution to different coreference phenomena and mention-border definitions when there is no access to large training data in the desired target scheme. We take a configurable, rule-based approach centered on dependency syntax input, which we test by examining coreference types not covered in benchmark corpora such as OntoNotes. These include cataphora, compound modifier coreference, generic anaphors, predicate markables, i-within-i, and metonymy. We test our system, called xrenner, using different configurations on two very different datasets: Wall Street Journal material from OntoNotes and four types Wiki data from the GUM corpus. Our system compares favorably with two leading rule based and stochastic approaches in handling the different annotation formats.

1 Introduction

Previous work (Rahman & Ng 2011, Durrett & Klein 2013) has suggested that a trainable coreference resolution approach can outperform rule-based approaches (e.g. Lee et al. 2013) because of its ability to model similar constraints in a lexicalized way that more closely matches training data. However, in many cases the amount of training data required for such approaches is large: if the phenomenon that we wish to include is not annotated in the data, we can only use a trainable system after considerable annotation work to adjust the training set to include it. Permutations of what to include or exclude and how to model each phenomenon, can compound such problems further.[1]

Rule-based approaches (Haghighi & Klein 2009, Lee et al. 2013), by contrast, can more easily add new behaviors, but have been described as "difficult to interpret or modify" (Durrett & Klein 2013: 1971). Although they can achieve results competitive with trainable systems, the hard-wired aspects of rule-based systems are problematic if we wish to adapt to different annotation schemes, languages, and target domains.

The current paper approaches the challenge of different target schemes with a system called *xrenner*: an e**x**ternally configurable **re**ference and **n**on-**n**amed **e**ntity **r**ecognizer. By using a large number of highly configurable mechanisms and rules in easily modifiable text files, with almost no hard-wired language- or domain-specific knowledge, we are able to adapt our system to include or exclude a variety of less standard coreference phenomena, including cataphora, generic indefinite anaphors, compound modifier nominals, predicate markables, clause-nested markables (i-within-i) and metonymy. We test our system on two datasets with very different schemes: Wall Street Journal data from OntoNotes (Hovy et al. 2006), which does not include the above cases, and a small test corpus, GUM (Zeldes 2016), which captures these phenomena and more.

---

[1] These limitations also apply to low resource languages (e.g. Sikdar et al. 2013 for Bengali) and domain adaptation (e.g. biomedical data, Apostolova et al. 2012, Zhao & Ng 2014), where large tailored training data is unavailable.

92

Proceedings of the Workshop on Coreference Resolution Beyond OntoNotes (CORBON 2016), co-located with NAACL 2016, pages 92–101,
San Diego, California, June 16, 2016. ©2016 Association for Computational Linguistics

2   The phenomena

Because of its size and quality, OntoNotes has become an established training and test set for coreference resolution. However, the OntoNotes annotation scheme (BBN Technologies 2007) does not cover several potentially useful and interesting phenomena, such as cataphora, predicatives, indefinite generic coreference, common noun compound modifiers, metonymy, and nested coreference.[2] These are illustrated below with cases from OntoNotes, which are not actually annotated in the corpus:

(1) **Cataphora:** [*it*]*'s certainly true* [*the rout began immediately after the UAL trading halt*]
(2) **Predicative:** [*He*] *is* [*an avid fan of a proposition on next week's ballot*]
(3) **Generic:** [*Program trading*] *is "a racket,"...* [*program trading*] *creates deviant swings*
(4) **Compound modifiers:** *small investors seem to be adapting to greater* [*stock market*] *volatility ... Glenn Britta ... says he is "factoring"* [*the market's*] *volatility "into investment decisions."*
(5) **Metonymy:** *a strict interpretation of a policy requires* [*The U.S.*] *to notify foreign dictators of certain coup plots ...* [*Washington*] *rejected the bid ...*
(6) **Nesting:** *He has in tow* [*his prescient girlfriend, whose sassy retorts mark* [*her*] *...*][3]

It is certainly debatable whether or not the above phenomena should be treated as cases of coreference, or relegated to syntax (cataphora can be described as a purely syntactic phenomenon, i.e. as expletives) or semantics (predicatives may be considered complex predicates, not constituting markables for annotation). There are nevertheless cases

in which we would be interested in each of these, and different corpora and language traditions have handled them differently, with direct consequences for systems trained on such corpora and their evaluation (see Recasens & Hovy 2010). While the above phenomena are not annotated in OntoNotes[4], many coreference resolution systems for English do in fact use, for example, predicative markables internally to facilitate coreference matching, even if the evaluation and output are set to delete them (cf. Lee et al. 2013).

The interest in diverse types of coreference relations has led to projects annotating them (notably ARRAU, Poesio & Artstein 2008), but as of yet, there is no training data source on the scale of OntoNotes that includes all of them. Because of this, the ability to configure a system to include or exclude such relations seems desirable: if we cannot assemble enough data to output these based on training alone, we need to use rules. But the different combinations of rules we might need depending on the target scheme require a flexible, configurable approach. In the next section we will outline our system, which relegates a wide range of coreference criteria to external configuration files, and includes treatments of the above phenomena.

3   A Configurable Framework

3.1   Core System Configuration

The xrenner system is an open source end-to-end entity recognition and coreference resolution system written in Python.[5] The input to the resolution components is dependency syntax data in the tabular CoNLL format, which can be produced by a parser; in experiments below we will use the Stanford Parser (Chen & Manning 2014) with Collapsed Typed Dependencies (CTDs). The decision to use dependencies is related to the configurability that it allows: we can define the desired mention

---

[2] Another phenomenon worth mentioning is bridging, which we will not deal with here, e.g. *Mexico's President Salinas said* [*the country*]*'s recession had ended and* [*the economy*] *was growing again.* (economy = the country's economy).

[3] An anonymous reviewer has noted that for some (non-singleton) mentions, nested pronouns are annotated, e.g. in document a2e_0020: "[*The American administration who planned carefully for this event through experts in media and public relations, and* [*its*] *tools*]". Under singleton mention, however, the nested pronoun is left unresolved, cf. another example: "*an elusive sheep with a star on its back*" (singleton notwithstanding nesting, not annotated in OntoNotes).

[4] A partial exception is metonymy, which is sometimes annotated as regular coreference, e.g. "*Mrs. Hills lauded* [*South Korea*] *...* [*Seoul*] *also has instituted ...*" and sometimes ignored, as in the example above. Often, similar lexemes can appear as non-coreferent, making metonymy detection very challenging: e.g. *Japan ... Tokyo's brat pack* (referring to a group of authors in Tokyo, not Japan in general).

[5] See `https://github.com/amir-zeldes/xrenner` for source code and `https://corpling.uis.georgetown.edu/xrenner/` for a live demo.

borders using dependency function chains in which certain dependencies are set to 'break' the chain. For example, if we include the relative clause CTD label, *rcmod*, (cf. de Marneffe & Manning 2013), we can easily decide to exclude these and 'de-nest' cases like (6). Such settings are configured for each resolution model in text files as regular expressions. The OntoNotes markable definition does not exclude relative clauses and is configured as:

```
non_link_func=/nsubj|cop|dep|punct|ap
pos|mark|discourse|parataxis|neg/
```

This means that mention borders propagate across all dependency functions not matching this expression. The annotation scheme used in the GUM corpus (see Section 4.1) has mentions excluding relative clauses, which can easily be modeled by adding *rcmod* to the setting above. Editing such settings can therefore radically alter the output of the system with very little effort.

The main configuration currently has over 70 settings of this type, including:

- Function labels for subject, coordination, etc., used in subsequent rules (see Section 3.4)
- Functions and tokens signaling modification (to collect a list of modifiers for each head, for coreference matching, see Section 3.4)
- Dependent strings and tags assigning a definiteness status after mention detection (articles, possessives), as well as numerals assigning cardinality (e.g. a modifier *three* maps to cardinality |3| for English)
- Dependent tags or functions required to match in coreference (e.g. possessives, or proper modifiers)
- POS tags which may serve as mention heads, including tags only admissible with certain functions (e.g. numbers, tagged *CD*, only as core arguments, not modifiers)
- Morphological agreement classes to assign to certain POS tags (e.g. map *NNS* to 'plural' agreement), as well as classes to assign by default, or in particular to coordinate markables (e.g. map coordinate mentions to 'plural', recognized via inclusion of the coordination function)

- Language specific settings such as whether person names must be capitalized, whether to attempt acronym matching, how questions and quotation are marked (relevant for direct speech recognition), and more
- Optional stemming for recognizing coreference between definite markables with no antecedent and a verb of the same stem (e.g. [*required*] … [*the requirement*])
- Postprocessing settings such as deleting certain function markables from the output (e.g. noun modifiers or copula predicates, based on CTD labels such as *nn* and *cop*)
- Surrounding appositions with joint markables (OntoNotes style), or deleting coordinations with no distinct mentions

The latter pair of settings, for example, can alter coreference chain output substantially, since according to OntoNotes, (7) would require two separate entity IDs ('apposition wrapping'), whereas in (8) the coordination NP requires no coreference at all (no coordinate markables without aggregate mention):

(7) [[*five other countries*]ᵢ -- [*China, Thailand, India, Brazil and Mexico* --]ᵢ]ⱼ … [*those countries*]ⱼ

(8) [*The U.S.*] and [*Japan*] … [*The U.S.*] and [*Japan*]

3.2   Mention detection and entity resolution

The system performs its own entity type resolution and does not rely on existing NER software. Candidate mentions are recognized via dependency subgraphs as defined by eligible POS heads and linkable dependency functions. Based on the presence of certain modifiers defined in the configuration, properties such as definiteness and cardinality are assigned during mention detection.

Candidate entities are matched against multiple lexical resources, which contain major entity types such as PERSON, LOCATION, TIME, ORGANIZATION, ABSTRACT and more, as well as subclasses, such as POLITICIAN (subclass of PERSON), COUNTRY (subclass of PLACE), COMPANY (subclass of ORGANIZATION) etc. Agreement information can also be provided optionally (e.g. most likely gender for each proper name, or complete grammatical gender information for languages other than English; see below for sources). The model we will evaluate below distinguishes 11 major entity types and 54 subclasses, but the types and number of entity classes and subclasses are not constrained by the system. Instead they are derived directly from the lexicon files, allowing for different scenarios based on the lexical data available for the language and scheme being modeled. The system uses several lexicon files, which it consults in order:

- Entity list – full text of multi-token entities
- Entity heads – single token entity heads
- Entity modifiers – mapping of modifiers which identify the entity type, such as *President X* (PERSON), *X Inc.* (COMPANY), etc.
- Proper name list – first and last names for recognizing persons not in the entity list
- Paraphrase list – for non-identical lexical matching (i.e. 'is-a' relations, such as *company → firm*)
- Antonym list – gives incompatible modifiers that counter-indicate coreference (e.g. *the good news ≠ the bad news*)

The sources of the data for the English model evaluated below are summarized in Table 1.

Data	Sources
Proper names	DBPedia (Auer et al. 2007)
Geo-names	DBPedia (Auer et al. 2007)
Common nouns	GUM, OntoNotes
Is-a list	GUM, OntoNotes, PPDB (Gantikevitch et al. 2013)
Antonyms	OntoNotes, WordNet (Fellbaum 1998)
Named entities	GUM, OntoNotes, Freebase (Bollacker et al. 2008)

Table 1: Lexical resources used for the English model evaluated below.

Beyond explicit lexical resources such as DBPedia (Auer et al. 2007), WordNet (Fellbaum 1998) and Freebase (Bollacker et al. 2008), which provide lists of companies, politicians, animals and more, we use entity type labels from the training sections of OntoNotes and GUM. The system also benefits greatly from the Penn Paraphrase Database data (PPDB, Ganitkevitch et al. 2013), which contains a large amount of entries found to be equivalent translations in parallel corpora. These complement coreference information from GUM and OntoNotes, and help win some of the 'uphill battle' of contextually synonymous lexical NPs (cf. Durrett & Klein 2013). Entity entries from all sources, including entity head lexemes and modifiers (e.g. *Mrs.*), can be specified as 'atomic', in which case the mentions they identify may not contain nested mentions. This will be crucial for ruling out spurious compound modifier coreference below.

The is-a table is also the basis for our handling of metonymy, by including e.g. entries for capitals mapped to their countries (the assumption is that such metonymy usually occurs after the country has been explicitly mentioned, so we do not include the opposite direction). Multiple entries are allowed for each key in the lexicon, so a *bank* can be a PLACE (river bank) and an ORGANIZATION (financial institution). Disambiguation and resolution of unknown entity strings is carried out based on a mapping of dependencies to entity types taken from GUM and OntoNotes training data (e.g. a subject of *barked* is typically of the class ANIMAL).

When this data is missing, the longest suffix match in the lexicon is used (e.g. *vitrification* is classed as EVENT if the longest suffix match with the lexicon is *-ification*, and most items with this suffix are events). As a result, we have a chance of catching metonymy by ruling between alternate entries for an entity as e.g. a country, if it is the dependent of a head that more typically governs a country (for example, a *prep_against* dependent of the word *embargo*). In essence, this means we treat metonymy as a word sense disambiguation problem.

All nominals are assigned an entity type, so that entity type resolution is not restricted to proper name entities, and all pronoun entities are initially guessed via dependency information of the type above, within their respective agreement classes.

3.3 Post-Editing Dependencies

Input dependency trees can be manipulated by a Python module called DepEdit[6], which takes rules identifying relevant tokens via features and graph relationships (token distance or parentage sub-

---

[6] See https://corpling.uis.georgetown.edu/depedit/

graphs), and reassigns new functions or subgraphs based on the configuration. Rules take the form:

$$R = <Tok_{i..j}, Rel_{k..l}, Act_{m..n}>$$
$$Tok = \{f_1..f_k\} \mid f \in \{text,lemma,func,head\}$$
$$Rel = <Tok, op, Tok> \mid op \in \{>, . , .n, .n,m\}$$
$$Act = \{f_i \rightarrow g_i\}$$

Such that a token definition is matched based on the features f_i, designating the token text, lemma, head or dependency function (usually as a regular expression), and relationships are binary constraints on pairs of tokens, via an operator indicating the head-dependency relation (>) or adjacency (.), potentially within n-m tokens. Each action Act_i is a mapping of some feature value to a new value (e.g. changing POS or function), including the 'head' feature, which allows rewiring of dependency trees.

Table 2 shows two such rules, one for handling a certain cataphoric construction, and another for handling age appositions. The first rule specifies 3 nodes: the text 'it/It' and subject function, an adjective (JJ) and a complement clause (ccomp), where node #2 dominates the other two. This catches cataphoric cases like "It is ADJ that …" and assigns a function 'cata' which can be handled later by the system for inclusion/exclusion in coreference resolution. The rule in the second column is useful for the OntoNotes scheme, which considers ages after a comma to be coreferent appositions, i.e. in:

(9) [*Mr. Bromwich*], [*35*]

The age is seen as elliptical for something like 'a 35 year old'. The rule finds a proper noun (NNP), comma and a number in sequence, where node #1 dominates node #3, and sets the function of #3 to 'appos' for an apposition.

	JJ-that-cataphora	*age-appos*
toks	text=/^[Ii]t$/& func=/nsubj/; pos=/JJ/;func=/ccomp/	pos=/^NNP$/; text=/^,$/; text=/^[1-9][0-9]*$/
rels	#2>#1;#2>#3	#1.#2.#3;#1>#3
acts	#3:func=cata	#3:func=appos

Table 2: Some dependency edit rules.

3.4 Coreference Rules

Like all other aspects of the system, coreference matching is done by way of configurable rules of the form:

$$C = <ANA, ANT, DIR, DIST, PROP>$$

Where *ANA* and *ANT* are feature constraints on the anaphor and the antecedent, *DIR* is the search direction (back, or forward for cataphora), *DIST* is the maximum distance in sentences to search for a match and *PROP* is the direction of feature propagation once a match is made, if any. Feature constraints include entity type/subclass, definiteness, NP-form (common/proper/pronoun), cardinality (numerical modifiers or amount of members in a coordination), and features of the head token, as well as existence/non-existence of certain modifiers or parents in a head token's dependency graph.

Rules are consulted in order, similarly to the sieve approach of Lee et al. (2013), so that the most certain rules are applied first. Every mention has only one antecedent (a mention-pair, or mention-synchronous model, like Durrett and Klein but unlike Lee et al.), so that subsequent matching can be skipped, but some aspects of a mention-cluster or 'entity-mention' model (cf. Rahman & Ng 2011) are also implemented, in that antonym modifier checks are applied to the entire chain.

The first rule in Table 3, which illustrates a very 'safe' strategy, searches for proper noun markables with identical text (=$1) in the previous 100 sentences, since these are almost always coreferent.

ANA (1)	*ANT* (2)	*DIR*	*DIST*	*PROP*
form=/proper/	form=/proper/ text=$1	←	100	none
lemma=/one/	form!=/proper/ mod=$1	←	4	→
text=/(his|her|its)/	form!=/pronoun/	→	0	←

Table 3: Coreference matching rules.

The middle rule looks for a mention headed by 'one' with the same modifier as its antecedent within 4 sentences, matching cases like (10). Finally the last rule attempts to match a possessive pronoun (which has not saturated its antecedent yet) to a nominal subject later on in the sentence, matching (11). This is the last rule of currently 27 in the model tested below, which were ordered based on linguistic intuition.

(10) [*the current flag*] ... *the new flag* ... [*the current one*]

(11) *In* [*her*] *speech,* [*the chairwoman*] *said...*

Once two mentions match a rule, they are compared for clashing entity classes, modifiers, agreement and cardinality. Matches from a certain rule are ranked by a weighted score incorporating the dependency based entity identification certainty (e.g. how certain we are that a pronoun refers to a LOCATION), distance in sentences and in tokens, as well as a built-in bias to prefer subject and PERSON antecedents where possible. The one-pass, chain linking nature of the process means that, like Durrett & Klein's (2013) system, resolution is efficient, requires no pruning, and scales linearly with text length. The system is quite fast, taking about 2.5 seconds for an average Wall Street Journal document of about 700 tokens on an Intel Core i7 laptop.

4 Evaluation

4.1 Data

Since our system takes pure dependency parser input, gold syntax information and explicit data about speakers from spoken data are not currently integrated into our evaluation. We therefore focus on newswire material and Wiki data, for which we can also expect reasonable parsing performance. We evaluate our system on two datasets: Wall Street Journal data from OntoNotes (V5), and data from GUM (V2.1), a small corpus with texts from four Wiki based Web genres including not only news data, but also interviews, how-to guides and travel guides. Data from the WSJ corpus test section 23 will represent a proxy for an in-domain but out-of-training-data example for parser input. Good performance on both data sets would indicate that the system is able to adapt to different annotation schemes successfully.

Beyond differences in domain (WSJ reporting/Wiki genres), purpose (news and several other text types in GUM), and time (early 90's vs. 2010-2015), the schemes for the two datasets we use differ substantially, which we also expect to affect

system evaluation (cf. Recasens & Hovy 2010). Table 4 gives an overview of coreference types across the corpora.

	GUM		WSJ	
	train	**test**	**train**	**test**
documents	46	8	540	57
tokens	37758	6321	322335	33306
nominals	11677	1933	104505	13162
coreference	7621	1294	38587	3642
- bridging	488	112	--	--
- predicative	71	14	--	--
- cataphora	52	3	--	--
- compound	506	71	--	--

Table 4: Coreference in GUM and WSJ.

GUM contains substantially more coreference annotation, despite having a very similar amount of nominal heads per token. The GUM training partition is roughly the size of the WSJ test data (section 23), at 37.7K to 33.3K tokens, and they contain similar amounts of nominal heads (11-13K). However, there are almost twice as many coreferring entities in GUM. Several differences in guidelines lead to this:

- All compound modifiers and most predicatives are candidates for coreference
- Cataphora and bridging are annotated (though we ignore bridging in the evaluation below)
- Indefinite or generic markables may have antecedents (cf. the *program trading* case in (3) above)
- Relative clauses are left outside markables, meaning backreference to the head in a clause is annotated ([*a man*] *who lost* [*his*]...)
- Recurring coordinations corefer even if they have no aggregate mention ([[*Jack*]i *and* [*Jill*]ⱼ]ₖ.. [[*Jack*]i *and* [*Jill*]ⱼ]ₖ; even if there is no [*they*]ₖ)
- Singletons are markables for entity type annotation in GUM, encouraging annotators who simultaneously code coreference to consider as many options as possible (although singletons are not counted in the coreference count)

Although inclusion of cataphora, bridging, predicatives and compound modifiers increases the coreference count, these are only responsible for about

1,100 cases in the training data, accounting for about 1/3 of the surplus compared to WSJ. This suggests that the greater portion of the difference is explained by indefinites, coordinate mentions and a general tendency to annotate more 'promiscuously' in GUM as compared to WSJ, as well as possible domain differences (e.g. how-to guides are rich in lists of ingredients that are mentioned repeatedly). Since a single coreferent pair contributes two coreferring entities, the effects of such binary pairs not present in OntoNotes can quickly add up.

4.2 Experimental setup

We compare our configurable rule based approach to two recent systems: Stanford's dcoref component of CoreNLP (Lee et al. 2013), version 3.6.0, and the Berkeley Coreference Resolution System (Durrett & Klein 2013), version 1.1. For both systems we used the recommended settings as of February 2016, and for the Berkeley system we used the 'joint' NER and coreference model (Durrett & Klein 2014) based on Durrett's recommendations (p.c.). In all cases, testing with other settings produced worse results on both datasets.

Since it is not reasonable to expect systems designed around schemes such as OntoNotes to perform well on GUM data, our main goal is to look at the impact of the scheme on performance for our system and less configurable ones. This is especially interesting considering the fact that there is insufficient training data to address the GUM scheme with a machine learning approach. We are also interested in how much of a difference the scheme will make, on the assumptions that high precision in particular should still carry over to settings where more annotation density is expected. None of the systems attempt to resolve bridging, so we will leave the bridging data out of the evaluation: only cases of the GUM coreference labels corresponding to anaphora, lexical coreference and apposition are included.[7]

Although our coreference resolution is rule-based, we nevertheless divide both datasets into training and test data, which means that gazetteer

data, including dependency to entity type mappings, as well as 'is-a' data, may be harvested for our system from the training portions, but not from the test portions. Since we do not have gold dependency data to compare to the gold constituent parses in OntoNotes[8], we evaluate all systems on automatically parsed data using the CoreNLP pipeline for dcoref (including the Stanford Parser) and the Berkeley system's built in pipeline for the joint Entity Resolution System. Dependency parses for our system are generated using the Stanford Parser.

4.3 Results

Table 5 gives precision and recall for mention detection, while Table 6 shows coreference resolution performance according to several measures calculated using the official CoNLL scorer (version 8.01, see Pradhan et al. 2014).

	GUM			WSJ		
	R	P	F1	R	P	F1
xrenner	74.38	63.97	**68.78**	63.86	63.79	**63.83**
dcoref	45.77	68.01	54.72	57.30	60.26	58.74
berkeley	40.14	70.15	51.06	53.45	67.13	59.52

Table 5: Mention detection in GUM and WSJ.

Since dcoref and the Berkeley system only output coreferent mentions (in keeping with the absence of singletons in OntoNotes), mention detection performance is tightly linked to coreference resolution. On both datasets, xrenner has the highest recall, but on GUM it has the lowest precision and on WSJ the second lowest. This is likely related to the fact that under the GUM scheme, virtually all nominals (notably common noun compound modifiers) are candidates for coreference, and many are mentioned multiple times: for each re-mentioned compound, the modifier is likely to be caught as a nested coreferent markable, even if it is non-referential, unless the entire compound is flagged as 'atomic' by lexical resources. Based on 71 cases in the gold data, our precision against compound modifiers judged as referential and co-referring by GUM annotators, is 61%, and recall is

---

[7] More specifically, the OntoNotes 'IDENT' type subsumes GUM's 'ana' and 'coref' types, and GUM's 'appos' label mirrors OntoNotes appositions. We do not distinguish the label type in the evaluation below: only the correct coreference group IDs.

[8] An anonymous reviewer has asked whether constituent trees automatically converted using CoreNLP could be used as gold data: although we initially had the same expectation, it turns out that automatically converted data contains rather many errors, including many dependencies remaining underspecified as 'dep', and some being attached incorrectly as well.

	MUC			B^3			CEAF-e			mean
GUM	**R**	**P**	**F1**	**R**	**P**	**F1**	**R**	**P**	**F1**	**F1**
xrenner	57.12	54.83	55.95	52.01	46.48	49.09	50.27	39.87	44.47	**49.84**
dcoref	35.22	57.25	43.61	25.64	50.53	34.02	33.18	39.03	35.87	37.83
berkeley	40.67	71.77	51.92	27.76	60.65	38.09	29.14	52.17	37.40	42.47
WSJ	**R**	**P**	**F1**	**R**	**P**	**F1**	**R**	**P**	**F1**	**F1**
xrenner	49.47	50.89	50.17	41.13	46.38	43.60	46.17	42.91	44.48	**46.08**
dcoref	46.77	50.50	48.56	36.41	45.81	40.57	39.93	39.48	39.70	42.94
berkeley	45.07	54.25	49.23	37.30	46.81	41.52	35.21	49.46	41.13	43.96

Table 6: Coreference precision and recall on GUM and WSJ plain text data for three systems.

at 66%, which we consider to be a good result. Only very few compound modifiers are found other than by lexical identity, though there are some 'is-a' cases, such as the false negative in (12). Indeed, the most frequent reason for a false positive is identical modifiers not judged by annotators to be referential, as in (13).

(12) [a [Mets]ᵢ fan] … cheer [the team]ᵢ
(13) [[carbon] dioxide] … [[carbon] dioxide]

Human annotators consider 'carbon dioxide' to be atomic, with 'carbon' not being a separate, referential entity; for the system, however, the identical, matching modifier noun is considered a good match under the GUM scheme. The other two systems have no chance of finding these, hence the lower recall and higher precision.

For cataphora and predicatives, we have much fewer cases: our system detects half of the 14 predicatives annotated in the test set, but none of the 3 cataphora in the gold standard. For the predicatives, 3 of the 7 errors are due to parser errors. For example, in the following case, the predicate 'home', annotated as coreferent with 'York', was parsed as an adverbial modifier, with the 'to'-PP parsed as the predicate:

(14) [York] was [home first to the Ninth Legion and later the sixth]

Such examples are likely to throw off the internal predicative recognition used by other systems as well. The remaining mistakes were caused by agreement errors (plural-singular), illustrated here:

(15) [brains] is [the greater producer of wealth]

For cataphora our rules were unlucky in the test set: the one case of fairly normal cataphora was passive (16), which our rules did not account for. The other cases had the form in (17), where within-clause 1st:3rd person mismatch interfered.

(16) [it] being said [that you can see the bottom]
(17) [my] name is [Frank]

Arguably in the latter case, the gold annotation is incorrect, since although the speaker is 'Frank', it's not clear 'Frank' as a name constitutes a mention of the entity. Even if accepted, this case is marginal for consideration under the heading cataphora.

For WSJ data, we excluded non-proper noun compound modifiers from the eligible markable heads, by adding the appropriate POS tags (*NN*, *NNS*) and function labels (CSD's *nn*) to our configuration, and ruled out predicatives and cataphora in the same way. As a result, precision on WSJ data is between the other two systems, while recall is still higher. The higher recall is due to some more aggressive strategies taken by our configuration, including: allowing new modifiers on later mentions (which dcoref avoids, following the tendency for no new modifiers identified in Fox 1993); a large 'is-a' table based on PPDB for non-identical lexical heads; and specific patterns, such as rules for phrases like 'the new one' based on identical modifiers, or verbal coreference based on identical stems (i.e. cases like [required] … [the requirement]).

Performance on coreference resolution for WSJ is also good, despite this being a rather difficult target (note that F-scores for both dcoref and the Berkeley system are well below the 60%+ F-scores reported for the entirety of OntoNotes, based on gold parse data, see Durrett & Klein 2013, Lee et al. 2013). Although our rules for the WSJ configuration prohibit indefinite or generic anaphors, the aggressive matching strategy sees gains over other systems mainly because of a rise in recall, with comparatively smaller hits to precision, depending on the metric (e.g. the Berkeley system has higher precision for CEAF, but xrenner always has the highest recall, and the highest F1 score in total). Some of the hits to precision are mitigated by safeguards not used by other systems, such as the categorical antonym modifier list (preventing [*the good news*] = [*the bad news*]) and cardinality matching ([*five other countries*] ≠ [*17 other countries*]). While the Berkeley system utilizes these cues indirectly via training data, number tokens are varied and sparse, but all number forms have a categorical mismatch effect on our system. By contrast, this information is not used by the dcoref sieves.

In addition, for high coverage classes, including geolocations, financial companies, newspapers and others, fine-grained entity recognition helps catch more is-a cases, such as [*the People's Daily*] … [*the newspaper*]. By appearing in Freebase as a newspaper, such entities are included under the class ORGANIZATION, subclass NEWSPAPER, thereby allowing subclass specific matching for 'newspaper'. This type of information is not captured by more coarse-grained, ORGANIZATION level NER.

5 Discussion

The results above indicate that a rule based approach backed by rich lexical data can perform well on disparate text types and annotation schemes. By relegating the large majority of system behaviors to configuration files, we are able to adjust to rather different annotation guidelines and achieve good performance on different corpora. This is facilitated by the use of dependency input, since many of the rule behaviors, including mention border definitions, can be captured in terms of dependency functions and chains. At the same time, the lack of gold dependency data to test on means that we cannot currently compare performance to gold constituent based results: this is a major goal for our planned future work, which will require careful manual correction of converted constituent data.

Some of the more challenging coreference phenomena we have attempted to model are addressable in the configurable approach: using the direction parameter for coreference rules, configurable dependency re-wiring, and a cascaded, high-precision-rule-first approach, we were able to find predicate markables and compound modifiers with high accuracy and without fatally lowering precision. This is because purely syntactic cases such as 'it is X that Y' are caught by the dependency graph analysis, high certainty cases such as reflexives and appositions are dealt with first, and other less certain cases are only applied as 'last ditch efforts', e.g. matching '*in* [*his*] *speech* [*Mr. X*] *said*' (only used if 'his' remains without an antecedent).

A major caveat for our approach is the need for domain specific lexical data. The fine-grained entity approach is not usable with leading coarse-grained NER software, meaning that high-quality lexical resources, such as the Freebase and PPDB data, are crucial. This means that while we do not require training data to change the coreference matching behavior of the system, we would need a substantial investment in new lexical data to extend to new text types and languages. We have also ordered our rules based on linguistic intuition, which may not be optimal. In future work we intend to test other permutations of our rule orders, following the approach of Lee et al. (2013: 905-906).

We are currently in the process of building models for German, based on the scheme of the largest available corpus (TüBa-D/Z, Telljohann et al. 2015), and for Coptic, an ancient low-resource language with rather limited domain vocabulary (religious texts). We hope to be able to extend our methods to these and other languages successfully by exploiting the configurable approach to change the system's behavior and adapting it to tagging and parsing input for each language as required.

Acknowledgments

We would like to thank Dan Simonson and three anonymous reviewers for valuable comments on previous versions of this paper, as well as Emma Manning for her help in creating the resources used in the evaluation. The usual disclaimers apply.

References

Emilia Apostolova, Noriko Tomuro, Pattanasak Mongkolwat and Dina Demner-Fushman. 2012. Domain Adaptation of Coreference Resolution for Radiology Reports. In *Proceedings of the 2012 Workshop on Biomedical Natural Language Processing (BioNLP 2012)*. Montreal, 118–121.

Sören Auer, Christian Bizer, Georgi Kobilarov, Jens Lehmann and Zachary Ives. 2007. DBpedia: A Nucleus for a Web of Open Data. In *6th International Semantic Web Conference*. Busan, South Korea, 11–15.

BBN Technologies. 2007. *Co-reference Guidelines for English OntoNotes. Version 6.0*. Available online at: `http://www.ldc.upenn.edu/Catalog/docs/LDC200 7T21/coreference/english-coref.pdf`.

Kurt Bollacker, Colin Evans, Praveen Paritosh, Tim Sturge and Jamie Taylor. 2008. Freebase: A Collaboratively Created Graph Database for Structuring Human Knowledge. In *Proceedings of the 2008 ACM SIGMOD International Conference on Management of Data*. Vancouver, 1247–1250.

Danqi Chen and Christopher D. Manning. 2014. A Fast and Accurate Dependency Parser using Neural Networks. In *Proceedings of the 2014 Conference on Empirical Methods in Natural Language Processing (EMNLP)*. Doha, Qatar, 740–750.

Greg Durrett and Dan Klein. 2013. Easy Victories and Uphill Battles in Coreference Resolution. In *Proceedings of the Conference on Empirical Methods in Natural Language Processing (EMNLP 2013)*. Seattle, 1971–1982.

Greg Durrett and Dan Klein. 2014. A Joint Model for Entity Analysis: Coreference, Typing, and Linking. *Transactions of the Association for Computational Linguistics* 2:477–490.

Christiane Fellbaum (ed.). 1998. *WordNet: An Electronic Lexical Database*. MIT Press: Cambridge, MA.

Barbara A. Fox. 1993. *Discourse Structure and Anaphora: Written and Conversational English*. Cambridge: Cambridge University Press.

Juri Ganitkevitch, Benjamin Van Durme and Chris Callison-Burch. 2013. PPDB: The Paraphrase Database. In *Proceedings of NAACL-HLT*. Atlanta, GA, 758–764.

Aria Haghighi and Dan Klein. 2009. Simple Coreference Resolution with Rich Syntactic and Semantic Features. In *Proceedings of Empirical Methods in Natural Language Processing (EMNLP 2009)*. Singapore, 1152–1161.

Eduard Hovy, Mitchell Marcus, Martha Palmer, Lance Ramshaw and Ralph Weischedel. 2006. OntoNotes: The 90% Solution. In *Proceedings of the Human Language Technology Conference of the NAACL, Companion Volume: Short Papers*. New York, 57–60.

Heeyoung Lee, Angel Chang, Yves Peirsman, Nathanael Chambers, Mihai Surdeanu and Dan Jurafsky. 2013. Deterministic Coreference Resolution Based on Entity-Centric, Precision-Ranked Rules. *Computational Linguistics* 39(4):885–916.

Marie-Catherine de Marneffe and Christopher D. Manning. 2013. *Stanford Typed Dependencies Manual*. Stanford University, Technical Report.

Massimo Poesio and Ron Artstein. 2008. Anaphoric Annotation in the ARRAU Corpus. In Nicoletta Calzolari, Khalid Choukri, Bente Maegaard, Joseph Mariani, Jan Odjik, Stelios Piperidis and Daniel Tapias (eds.), *Proceedings of the 6th International Conference on Language Resources and Evaluation (LREC-2008)*. Marrakech, 1170–1174.

Sameer Pradhan, Xiaoqiang Luo, Marta Recasens, Eduard Hovy, Vincent Ng and Michael Strube. 2014. Scoring Coreference Partitions of Predicted Mentions: A Reference Implementation. In *Proceedings of the 52nd Annual Meeting of the Association for Computational Linguistics*. Baltimore, MD, 30–35.

Altaf Rahman and Vincent Ng. 2011. Narrowing the Modeling Gap: A Cluster-Ranking Approach to Coreference Resolution. *Journal of Artificial Intelligence Research* 40(1):469–521.

Marta Recasens and Eduard Hovy. 2010. Coreference Resolution across Corpora: Languages, Coding Schemes, and Preprocessing Information. In *Proceedings of the 48th Annual Meeting of the Association for Computational Linguistics*. Uppsala, 1423–1432.

Utpal Kumar Sikdar, Asif Ekbal, Sriparna Saha, Olga Uryupina and Massimo Poesio. 2013. Anaphora Resolution for Bengali: An Experiment with Domain Adaptation. *Computación y Sistemas* 17(2):137–146.

Heike Telljohann, Erhard W. Hinrichs, Sandra Kübler, Heike Zinsmeister and Kathrin Beck. 2015. *Stylebook for the Tübingen Treebank of Written German (TüBa-D/Z)*. Seminar für Sprachwissenschaft, Universität Tübingen, Technical Report.

Amir Zeldes. 2016. The GUM Corpus: Creating Multilayer Resources in the Classroom. *Language Resources and Evaluation*. Available online at: `http://dx.doi.org/10.1007/s10579-016-9343-x`.

Shanheng Zhao and Hwee Tou Ng. 2014. Domain Adaptation with Active Learning for Coreference Resolution. In *Proceedings of the 5th International Workshop on Health Text Mining and Information Analysis, EACL 2014*. Gothenburg, Sweden, 21–29.

Association for Computational Linguistics
209 N. Eighth Street
Stroudsburg, Pennsylvania 18360

ISBN 978-1-5108-2523-9